Kabbalah

by Rav Michael Laitman, Ph.D.,
with Collin Canright

ALPHA

A member of Penguin Group (USA) Inc.

ALPHA BOOKS

Published by the Penguin Group

Penguin Group (USA) Inc., 375 Hudson Street, New York, New York 10014, USA

Penguin Group (Canada), 90 Eglinton Avenue East, Suite 700, Toronto, Ontario M4P 2Y3, Canada (a division of Pearson Penguin Canada Inc.)

Penguin Books Ltd., 80 Strand, London WC2R 0RL, England

Penguin Ireland, 25 St. Stephen's Green, Dublin 2, Ireland (a division of Penguin Books Ltd.)

Penguin Group (Australia), 250 Camberwell Road, Camberwell, Victoria 3124, Australia (a division of Pearson Australia Group Pty. Ltd.)

Penguin Books India Pvt. Ltd., 11 Community Centre, Panchsheel Park, New Delhi—110 017, India

Penguin Group (NZ), 67 Apollo Drive, Rosedale, North Shore, Auckland 1311, New Zealand (a division of Pearson New Zealand Ltd.)

Penguin Books (South Africa) (Pty.) Ltd., 24 Sturdee Avenue, Rosebank, Johannesburg 2196, South Africa

Penguin Books Ltd., Registered Offices: 80 Strand, London WC2R 0RL, England

International Standard Book Number: 978-1-59257-542-8
Library of Congress Catalog Card Number: 2006940216

09 08 07   8 7 6 5 4 3 2 1

Interpretation of the printing code: The rightmost number of the first series of numbers is the year of the book's printing; the rightmost number of the second series of numbers is the number of the book's printing. For example, a printing code of 07-1 shows that the first printing occurred in 2007.

Printed in the United States of America

Note: This publication contains the opinions and ideas of its authors. It is intended to provide helpful and informative material on the subject matter covered. It is sold with the understanding that the authors and publisher are not engaged in rendering professional services in the book. If the reader requires personal assistance or advice, a competent professional should be consulted.

The authors and publisher specifically disclaim any responsibility for any liability, loss, or risk, personal or otherwise, which is incurred as a consequence, directly or indirectly, of the use and application of any of the contents of this book.

Most Alpha books are available at special quantity discounts for bulk purchases for sales promotions, premiums, fundraising, or educational use. Special books, or book excerpts, can also be created to fit specific needs.

For details, write: Special Markets, Alpha Books, 375 Hudson Street, New York, NY 10014.

Publisher: *Marie Butler-Knight*
Senior Acquisitions Editor: *Randy Ladenheim-Gil*
Managing Editor: *Billy Fields*
Development Editor: *Lynn Northrup*
Senior Production Editor: *Janette Lynn*
Copy Editor: *Krista Hansing*

Cover Designer: *Bill Thomas*
Book Designer: *Trina Wurst*
Cartoonist: *Shannon Wheeler*
Indexer: *Heather McNeill*
Layout: *Ayanna Lacey*
Proofreader: *Aaron Black*

Contents at a Glance

Contents

Appendixes

Introduction

It is hard to find a topic that has been more "banned" than Kabbalah. Here's a (partial) list of the prerequisites you previously had to answer "yes" to in order to become a student: Jewish, male, married, over 40 years old, and proficient in other Jewish studies. So how come Kabbalah is being openly taught and studied everywhere? Because the ban has been lifted.

As Kabbalist Rabbi Yehuda Ashlag, and as the Vilna Gaon (GRA), and as many other prominent Kabbalists have stated, the end of the twentieth century marks a fundamental change in the history of Kabbalah. Now it is open for all.

As we will show inside the book, the bans were there for a reason. But it is for exactly the same reason that now they have lifted. We, humanity in the twenty-first century, have become ready to see Kabbalah for what it really is—a scientific, time-tested, empirical method of achieving spirituality while living here in this world.

Studying Kabbalah is a fascinating journey. It changes your perspective of the world and the people around you, and opens parts in you that you never knew existed. It is a journey of discoveries happening within, and affecting all of life's levels: our relationships with our kin, friends, and co-workers. Kabbalah states very simply that when you know how to connect to the Creator directly, without any go-betweens, you will find an inner compass, a guiding light that shines no matter where you are. And this is the goal of Kabbalah—to help you make, and sustain, direct contact with the Creator. And when you do, you will need no further guidance. So welcome to *The Complete Idiot's Guide to Kabbalah*.

What You'll Find in This Book

The book is set up in four parts with three appendixes. Here's what you'll find inside:

Kabbalah is a science that describes the laws of the spiritual world. In **Part 1, "The Phenomenon, Fallacies, and Facts,"** we'll talk about Kabbalah in general, from an overview of basic principles to some background on how it began. We'll delve into the issue of humanity's natural connection with the root of Kabbalah and the basics of human pleasure and desire.

We'll continue our spiritual journey in **Part 2, "Before the Big Bang,"** by delving into pure and ancient Kabbalah knowledge. It starts with Kabbalah's cycle of reality, which explains how we were created, what we are doing here, and how and at which point we begin our ascent to the Upper World. We'll discuss how the world was created according to Kabbalah and how that ancient knowledge explains what's wrong with our world today and what needs to be done to fix it.

From there, we'll show you how Kabbalah can be applied more specifically to you personally, on a day-to-day basis. This broad nature is what makes Kabbalah so unique. **Part 3, "Kabbalah and Your Life,"** discusses your personal relationship with the Creator, your family, your friends, your co-workers, and the world at large. We'll also discuss how Kabbalah has been used in the past and show you how to practice spiritual development without leaving your "modern life"—through contemporary methods like the web and virtual groups.

The present appearance of Kabbalah is directly connected to the state of the world today. In **Part 4, "Kabbalah in Today's World,"** we will explore the reasons for the global crises we are facing from the Kabbalistic point of view and discuss ways to cure them. Finally, we'll end with a brief tour of how Kabbalah will affect your future.

You'll also find three helpful appendixes to help enhance your journey and point you in the right direction if you'd like to learn more: a glossary, a list of resources, and a list of organizations and associations.

Extras

We've included five kinds of sidebars sprinkled throughout the text for your Kabbalah education and entertainment:

Kab-Trivia

Did you know that few books about Kabbalah were written before 1980? And most were written after 2000? Check out these boxes for little tidbits of Kabbalah knowledge.

Word of Heart

In these boxes, you'll find inspiring quotes and selected poems from great Kabbalists and others reflecting the chapter's topic of discussion.

Red Alert

Check out these boxes for cautions and things to avoid concerning Kabbalah, including misconceptions to be mindful of.

def•i•ni•tion

In these boxes, you'll find definitions of Kabbalah words and terms you may not be familiar with.

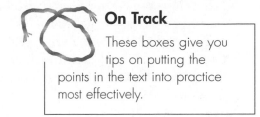

On Track

These boxes give you tips on putting the points in the text into practice most effectively.

Acknowledgments

Thanks to Eli Vinokur, Josia Nakash, Mutlu Meydan, Ron Gilboa, and Rachel Laitman (research); Chaim Ratz (research and reviews); Katrin Weibel (proofreading); Leah Goldberg (assistance); and Avihu Sofer (administration and contracts) at Ashlag Research Institute (ARI). Thanks to the staff at Canright Communications—Chris Schaeffer, Hannah Frank, Libby Munn, and Lindsay Knight—for writing and research support. Thanks to John Woods at CWL Publishing for the opportunity. Thanks to Bob and Judith Wright for their spiritual counsel. Special thanks to Christina Canright for love, support, encouragement, and inspiration. And thanks to the Creator for all.

Trademarks

Part The Phenomenon, Fallacies, and Facts

The list of well-known Kabbalists reads like a who's who in Hollywood. But Kabbalah is more than a pop craze. It's a spiritual way of life.

In this part, we'll explain the general phenomenon and its popularity, and give an overview of what exists today in the world regarding the word *Kabbalah*. We'll discuss what Kabbalah is and what it isn't, and give some background on how it got started.

After reading these chapters, you'll understand why Kabbalah is becoming so trendy. You'll learn that it's more than just a passing fad, but a science detailing the spiritual worlds that Western science can't explain based on empirical evidence.

So read on, and get ready to enter the world of Kabbalah!

Chapter 1

Kabbalah Goes Pop!

In This Chapter

- ◆ Kabbalah comes out of hiding
- ◆ New answers for new questions
- ◆ The current popularity of Kabbalah
- ◆ Mix-and-match spirituality and Kabbalah
- ◆ The future of Kabbalah

It is written in *The Book of Zohar*, the pinnacle of Kabbalah books, that Kabbalah will thrive and become popular at the end of days. With all the publicity—reams of newsprint and great numbers of items in Internet search lists—it appears that the end of days is here.

Kabbalah seeks to illuminate and describe the laws of the spiritual world. It's not religion. It's spiritual science, and for more than 2,000 years, it has been considered one of the highest and most difficult-to-attain levels of spirituality.

Out of the Mist

Kabbalah has traditionally been closed to all but a few select and serious students. No longer. Like never before, Kabbalah has become hot, chic, cool, in …. Moreover, Kabbalists, who were previously so hesitant to open their secrets to the public, have become the key players in doing just that.

Kab-Trivia

Searching for "Kabbalah" on Amazon.com returns over five thousand books, almost none of which were written before 1980. Very few were written before 1990, and only a few more were written before the turn of the century. The vast majority of books on Kabbalah were written after the year 2000. In the last few years, Kabbalah really has gone pop!

The Long Years of Hide and Seek

But Kabbalah wasn't always so popular, and Kabbalists weren't nearly so open. For many centuries, Kabbalah was kept secret, shunning the public's eye for the faintly lit quarters of Kabbalists who meticulously selected each student and taught them in very small groups.

For instance, the Ramchal Group, the students of Rabbi Moshe Chaim Luzzato, who taught in the eighteenth century, made it especially difficult to join its ranks. Membership required agreeing to a rigorous pact of lifestyle and study that had to be met all day, every day, for as long as one remained a member.

Other groups, such as the Kotzk Group (named after a town in Poland), used to dress in worn-out clothes and treat nonmembers with offensive cynicism. They deliberately distanced themselves from others by appearing to disobey the most sacred Jewish customs like The Day of Atonement. Group members would scatter breadcrumbs on their beards to appear as if they'd been eating on this day of fasting. Naturally, most people were repelled.

Nevertheless, the same Kabbalists who hid the wisdom also made tremendous efforts to write the books that remain the pillars of Kabbalah to this day. Rabbi Isaac Luria (the Holy Ari), for example, took only one student, but the publishing of his books made his student, Rabbi Chaim Vital, state that from his time on, the study of *The Book of Zohar* (*The Zohar*, for short) was permitted to all who wished it.

For this reason, in his lifetime, the Ari taught a group of students, but at his deathbed, he ordered all except Rabbi Chaim Vital to stop studying. The Ari said that only Chaim Vital understood the teaching properly, and he was afraid that without a proper teacher, the rest would go astray.

To appreciate the long hide-and-seek of the Kabbalists, understand that it was during the sixteenth century that the Ari (Rabbi Isaac Luria) came to Zefat, the Kabbalah capitol of the time. He begged his only student, Chaim Vital, to refrain from inviting others to study. Chaim Vital, who became a great Kabbalist in his own right, did not heed his teacher's request and invited others to join him in a study group. While teaching that group, the Ari produced some of the most invaluable texts in Kabbalah and in Jewish law to this day. In fact, the Lurianic Kabbalah that the Ari founded makes up most of Kabbalah we see today.

Breaking the Iron Wall

It was not until the last decade of the twentieth century that Kabbalah really began its advent to the center stage of public awareness. The single most dominant figure in the worldwide dissemination of Kabbalah is undoubtedly Rabbi Yehuda Ashlag, who was the first Kabbalist not only to speak in favor of dissemination, but also to do it.

Ashlag published a magazine, *ha-Uma* (*The Nation*), on June 5, 1940. He also tried to convince David Ben-Gurion and other leaders of the Jewish settlement in Palestine, today's Israel, to incorporate Kabbalistic principals in the education system. Then, Rabbi Ashlag also stated that, in the future, people of all religions would study Kabbalah while maintaining their birth religions, with no collision between the two.

Such statements and the act of disseminating Kabbalah seemed so unorthodox and unacceptable at the time that *The Nation* was shut down after the first issue by the British Mandate in Palestine. In justification, the British Mandate stated that it had been told that Ashlag was promoting Communism.

Today Ashlag's "iron wall" has indeed been broken. While this has been helped by the interest of high profile celebrities, the real reasons go deeper than that because the Kabbalah seems to touch the souls of people of all backgrounds, regardless of their religion.

Word of Heart

At the outset of my words, I find a great need to break an iron wall that has been separating us from the wisdom of Kabbalah since the ruin of the Temple to this generation. It lies heavily on us and arouses fear of being forgotten.

—From the introduction to *The Study of the Ten Sefirot* by Rabbi Yehuda Ashlag

Why Kabbalah Now?

To the Kabbalist, the answer to this question is simple. Kabbalah has but a single purpose: it offers an approach that helps answer the question, "What is the meaning of my life?"

Now, more than ever before, people are asking about the meaning and the purpose of their lives. With material needs met—and met even beyond imagining, in some cases—people still feel an emptiness in their lives. Kabbalah is a discipline that invokes insights and new perspectives on life, which provide a spiritual fullness. This is the key to its popularity.

According to Rabbi Yehuda Ashlag in *The Study of the Ten Sefirot*, an extensive commentary on the writings of the great Ari, you are ready for Kabbalah if you sometimes …

- Question the meaning of your life.

- Wonder why you and all life exist.

- Question why life can sometimes be so difficult.

- Speculate why there are difficulties to begin with.

The Purpose in Destructiveness

In the perfect cycle of life, each part has its designated function. No part of creation is free to do as it pleases because the well-being of each part depends on the well-being of all other parts of creation. This interdependency guarantees that no creature will overpower all other creatures because to destroy other creatures would mean destroying oneself.

Human beings, blessed with self-awareness, are no exception to this rule of nature. But many—perhaps most—do not appreciate this idea and in one way or another act in ways that hurt others and thus themselves as well. Why do we do this? Some would say it's part of the path we must travel to learn what doesn't work to bring happiness.

We think by gaining personal control of others, of our environment, we can manipulate and shape the world to our liking. But when we reflect on the results, all we see is unhappiness in those we seek to manipulate. When we reflect deeply, we see unhappiness in ourselves as well. You and I simply cannot do harm to others without it coming back to ourselves in one way or another. That's one of the insights of the Kabbalah.

Any look at the news shows that the forces of destruction in the world are not nature's alone. For many in developed countries, the drive to improve has become a pleasure hunt, with much focus on such questions as "How do I get more money and things?" and "How do I get more/better sex?" and "How do I get more power?"

So if we take a step back, we can see that trying to manipulate others, to destroy that which we think is in our way to gain happiness and contentment, doesn't work and we feel compelled to ask deeper questions about the meaning of our lives.

Moreover, as we will show in Part 4, nothing is created without a reason, not even human destructiveness. Its goal is not only to compel us to ask about the meaning of our lives, although this is certainly the first step. Its ultimate purpose is to make us realize that the very *intention* to gratify ourselves is the reason for our misfortune. The right intention, the one that eventually gives us pleasure, is surprisingly the intention to do good to others, whether other people or the Creator.

In other words, our own egoism, to use the language of Kabbalah explained in this book, is our enemy. In Kabbalah, the egoism is called "Pharaoh." But Pharaoh isn't the bad guy we know of from the Bible stories we grew up with. Kabbalah explains that Pharaoh is actually the "other side" of the Creator, trying to show us the way out of our egoism. Therein lies the key to our success as Kabbalah students. The quicker we come to terms with the fact that it is the ego that we have to correct, and nothing in the outside world, the faster we will progress. Chapter 3 discusses the correction of our inner world in detail, so read on.

A Unique Wisdom for a Unique Time

In this time, it seems our destructive tendencies are creating great unhappiness and displacement of people and threatening our environment. We shouldn't be surprised, therefore, that people are beginning to ask questions about life that the wisdom of the Kabbalah can help us answer, or at least explore more deeply.

More people are beginning to realize that greater wealth, more sex, and additional power do not make them happier. Many have come to the point where they no longer ask "how to" questions; they ask "what for?" questions. Any doctrine that can help us answer "what for?" questions has a good chance at popularity.

Because Kabbalah is a doctrine that specifically explores questions about the meaning of life, it's not surprising that in these troubled times, many people find it appealing. This, coupled with the publicity generated by its celebrity adherents, has brought it to the attention of seekers everywhere.

Kabbalah Goes to Hollywood—and Beyond

Just as Kabbalah was waiting for the time people were ready to discover it, people, some of whom are influential, have been seeking what it has to offer. Here's a quick overview of the who and the how that have made a secretive spiritual discipline of old the spiritual secret of today's stars.

It all started with Madonna, who ignited the interest in Kabbalah in America. A Catholic girl who became one of the most sensational pop performers in the 1980s and beyond, Madonna has become heavily involved in Kabbalah. What first seemed insignificant and a passing fad became a constant and important element in Madonna's life. Despite all the changes in her personal and professional life, her ongoing dedication to Kabbalah studies made many wonder what this Kabbalah business was all about and what it could possibly give someone who seemingly had everything. Her association led other celebrities, including Demi Moore and her husband Ashton Kutcher, as well as (for a while, anyway) Britney Spears, to explore what Kabbalah had to offer them.

Kab-Trivia

Madonna, Britney Spears, Demi Moore, Liz Taylor, Mick Jagger and Jerry Hall, Courtney Love, Sandra Bernhard, and Barbra Streisand are just some of the entertainers who are or have been associated with Kabbalah.

The trend caught on very quickly in celebrity circles. Many stars flocked to the Kabbalah Centers in New York and Los Angeles, as the world looked on in wonder.

There may be controversy over this or that flavor of Kabbalistic teaching. But the controversy and drama surrounding it all has made the entire world familiar with the word *Kabbalah*, taking it quite a long way from that single Kabbalah student of the sixteenth century, Rabbi Isaac Luria!

Indeed, if you search for Kabbalah lessons on the Internet, you'll get, on average, over 200,000 results. For the most part, these lessons are readily available in text, audio, and video formats.

But online lessons are not the only way to learn Kabbalah today. Kabbalah lessons and courses abound in synagogues, Kabbalah and spirituality retreats, and in-person and phone sessions. Almost every Jewish sect offers its own lessons of Kabbalah, Jewish spirituality, or both. Even at Hebrew Union College, a citadel of Reform Judaism, Provost Norman Cohen tells *Newsweek* that "what the Kabbalah can teach us—how to have a relationship with God—has to be treated seriously" (August 29–September 5, 2005).

On Track

Check out www.arionline.info, which provides free video Kabbalah lessons, as well as supporting texts. You will find another highly recommended site at www.kabbalah.info, containing more than 4,300 video and audio lessons, Kabbalah films, and whole books for free download, as well as live and archived Internet and television broadcasts of Kabbalah lessons. (You'll find more sites like these in Appendix B.)

Mix 'n' Match Teachings

In the "anything goes" spirit of today's world, everything's mixed with everything else: science with religion, rock 'n' roll with Beethoven. There is even sushi ice cream (bet you didn't know that). Following the trend, Kabbalah has been associated with more doctrines and teachings than there are toppings for pizza.

But there is another, more serious reason for the sudden emergence of this ancient discipline. Kabbalah has always had a reputation of possessing insight into the highest forces of nature, of the spiritual worlds, and of the nature of God. As a result, people have always wanted to connect Kabbalistic terms with all kinds of teachings, such as yoga, chakras, good-luck charms, meditations of all kinds, chants, tarot cards, power-water and power-drinks, crystals, astrology, numerology, fortune telling, magic, and guardian angels.

The problem with such connections is that they trivialize Kabbalah and undermine its power to help us better understand our human and spiritual natures. This, after all, is at the heart of today's interest in this teaching, and the reason Kabbalah was developed in the first place.

Some of these mixes and matches add flavor to our lives, some are quite bizarre, and some are downright absurd. Following are some of the more common combinations of Kabbalah and other teachings.

Cards and Kabbalah

Without claiming to be experts in this field, there are many kinds of cards used for many purposes, such as fortune telling and coping with day-to-day challenges. Because Kabbalah has long been thought to have mystical and magical powers and because people have always been looking to improve their methods of understanding the unknown, it was only natural for cards to be associated with Kabbalah.

Many followers of the occult believe that the Tarot system has its origins in Kabbalah, though there is no historical evidence supporting this. In the nineteenth century, French occultist Eliphas Levi promoted the link between the Tarot and the Kabbalah, a link that became the main model for the development and interpretation of the Tarot.

Indeed, the most influential decks of the twentieth century were founded on Kabbalistic principles. One of Kabbalah's best-known symbols is the Tree of Life, a diagram of 10 attributes, nine belonging to the Creator and one to the creature (us). The structure, symbolism, and interpretation of Tarot decks follow the structure of the tree of life.

The tree consists of 10 spheres, or *Sefirot*, connected by 22 lines (called paths). The number of *Sefirot* (10) and the number of paths (22) correspond, respectively, to the Minor Arcana and the Major Arcana, which make up the structure of the Tarot. You'll learn more about the tree of life in Chapter 9.

Astrology and Kabbalah

Another common combination is astrology and Kabbalah. Kabbalah-inspired horoscopes are likely to have existed even before ancient Egypt. Since the middle ages, Kabbalistic terminology has been directly associated with astrology. Astrologers added the names of the *Sefirot* to the names of the planets and began to ascribe to planets the powers that Kabbalah presents.

In order to help know what circumstances will unfold in our lives, Kabbalah-inspired astrologers ascribe each of the planets in the solar system a particular function and impact upon the physical and psychological bodies, according to the *Sefer Yetzira* (*The Book of Creation*, one of Kabbalah's original books). They find relationships between astrology and Kabbalah by mapping the 10-*Sefirot* diagram of the Tree of Life against the planets and in this way link the two doctrines.

Meditation and Kabbalah

Meditation is considered by many as part of the spiritual work or practices of a Kabbalist. But not all Kabbalists have practiced meditation, and even those who did meditate did not practice it in the sense we do today.

Today meditation is associated with Eastern teachings, something that Kabbalists in the past did not know. Generally, Eastern meditation is used for relaxation and for uniting with higher levels of existence by "removing" the ego. In Kabbalah, the ego is not removed, but elevated to a higher level of practice. It connects with the divine instead of canceling itself. This embrace of ego and Creator is called *Yihud* (unification).

Numerology and Kabbalah

The term *numerology* did not exist in authentic Kabbalah; contemporary scholars linked the two. Although numerology is not an accurate term to describe Kabbalah's treatment of numbers, there is probably no better word to use if you want to translate the Hebrew term *Gimatria* into English. *Gimatria*, in simple terms, describes a Kabbalist's experience of the divine. In Kabbalah, the ego performs *Yihudim* (unifications) with the Creator. The shape of Hebrew letters depicts such unifications through dots and lines over a white background. The dots and the lines symbolize the states of the Kabbalist, who perceives the Creator. The white background symbolizes the divine light, the Creator.

In Hebrew, each letter of the 22-letter alphabet is assigned a specific number. The first nine letters are assigned the numbers 1–9, respectively, and the next nine are assigned the numbers 10–90, with each letter jumping by 10 in value. The last four letters of the Hebrew alphabet are assigned the numbers 100, 200, 300, and 400, respectively.

The correlation between letters and numbers created a way for Kabbalists to describe to each other what they experienced in a concise and accurate manner. For example, the word *Nega* (affliction) and the word *Oneg* (pleasure) have the exact same letters (in a different order) and, therefore, the same numeric value.

This inversion in the order of letters indicates that when affliction is corrected (from egoism to giving), a person experiences pleasure. Furthermore, this "shorthand" depiction of spiritual experiences is but one aspect of how a Kabbalist describes the divine.

Keep in mind that this is the way Kabbalah helps us get at a deeper understanding of our human nature and stimulates our thinking about the mysteries of life and of spirit.

Magic and Kabbalah

Since ancient times, people have thought that those who practice Kabbalah had the power to perform supernatural acts. They have thought that Kabbalists could change the laws of creation at will. Because of that, Kabbalah is still associated by some with the ability to charm, curse, or bless.

One magical interpretation of Kabbalah perceives the Jewish law as a powerful system of principles to attract supernatural powers to a person. According to this interpretation, if natural magic is connected to natural science, such as agriculture and astronomy, super magic depends on the knowledge of the higher science—Kabbalah.

A Passing Fad or Here to Stay?

Kabbalah has been around for a long, long time and is only now taking its place in the general public consciousness. Those who embrace it as the latest fad will perhaps move on to something else. But those who dig deeply into its principles, which have evolved over the centuries, are likely to find enough to keep them going for a lifetime.

Kabbalah isn't about removing the ego, but about elevating it to a new level. As our egos evolve, we grow more egoistic. As we grow more egoistic, we need new pleasures to satisfy ourselves. The pleasures that society provides today are not only new and more diverse, but they are also much more intense than ever. Computers are faster, cars are more luxurious, gadgets are more sophisticated, sex partners are easier to come by and quicker to leave, salaries are higher, and food is more versatile and quicker to make. But the more we have, the more we discover that all this stuff and all these experiences often don't help us feel more fulfilled. Their true benefit is in the fact that they eventually drive us to search for answers to the hard questions about what life is really all about.

def•i•ni•tion

The root *meta* comes from Greek, and means "beside" or "after." It refers to systems, or discussions about systems themselves. The term serves to differentiate references to the content of a system from the structure of the system itself. In this case, it refers to Kabbalah as a "system of systems."

To the Kabbalist, there are answers to the questions about life's meaning. Kabbalah provides a kind of *meta*system that helps us cope with our growing cravings in positive ways, even before we know we have them. The principles of the Kabbalah help us understand everything else.

The reason Kabbalah has been expanding so rapidly is that more people are asking about the purpose of life and discovering the value of what the Kabbalah has to say about such questions. That, in a nutshell, is why you're reading this book, so continue on to learn more about the extraordinary set of insights the Kabbalah provides human beings.

The Least You Need to Know

- ◆ Kabbalah is a method that answers life's deepest question: "What is life about?"

- ◆ Kabbalah has been waiting in hiding until the questions it answers arose.

- ◆ The current popularity of Kabbalah started with popular music and Hollywood stars.

- ◆ You can find teachers and lessons on Kabbalah on the Internet.

- ◆ Kabbalah has been inappropriately associated with many flavors of spiritual teachings.

- ◆ Kabbalah is not a passing fad, but a time-tested and practical method to understanding human nature, the nature of the Creator, and how to unite the two.

Chapter **2**

What Is Kabbalah, and What Does It Have to Do with You?

In This Chapter

◆ Perceiving reality as it really is

◆ The nature of the five senses and the "sixth sense"

◆ The will to receive delight and pleasure

◆ The essence of Kabbalah and its purpose

◆ Change yourself and change society

You may have heard a lot about Kabbalah in the media and you may have a sense of its spiritual promises, especially given its current popularity. But what's it really all about? This chapter briefly presents the basic concepts of Kabbalah, which we expand upon in upcoming chapters. The terms we present and discuss in this chapter set up the language of Kabbalah that we use throughout the rest of this book.

This chapter also presents how Kabbalah works for you, how to work with it in the best way, and what pitfalls you may encounter along the way. At the same time, you learn how and why your study of Kabbalah is not only good for you, but also for the benefit of society as a whole.

The Reality of Reception

In Hebrew, the word *Kabbalah* means "reception." But Kabbalah isn't just reception. It's a discipline of study, a method that teaches you *how* to receive. Kabbalah ...

◆ Prepares you to be able to receive.

◆ Tells you what you are about to receive.

◆ Explains where it comes from.

◆ Lets you know what you need to have and still have yet to receive.

It's a reception to which everyone is invited. You don't need a special invitation, only the willingness to explore the larger questions of existence: how you and I relate to God, how God created the universe, and what will happen when time ends. Not your typical wedding talk, to be sure, but the kind of talk that can help you, as a citizen of planet Earth in the twenty-first century, understand and receive the wisdom of the ages and have it inform your daily decisions.

def•i•ni•tion

In his essay "The Essence of the Wisdom of Kabbalah," Rabbi Yehuda Ashlag defines **Kabbalah** as follows: "This wisdom is no more and no less than a sequence of roots, which hang down by way of cause and consequence, in fixed, determined rules, interweaving to a single, exalted goal described as 'the revelation of His Godliness to His creatures in this world.'"

What does Kabbalah provide for you to receive? It helps you know where you truly are in relation to where you think you are. It shows the boundaries of the five senses of perception and opens up the spiritual world of actual reality by helping you develop a "sixth sense," a critical concept in Kabbalah introduced shortly and expanded upon in Chapter 3.

This sixth sense not only enriches your present life with a new dimension, but also opens a door to a "brave new world." There is no death in this world, no sorrow, no pain. And best of all, you don't have to give up anything for it: you don't have to die to get there. Neither do you have to fast, avoid any pleasures, or restrain yourself in any way. In short, it is with this sense that you achieve "the revelation of His Godliness to His creatures in this world."

Kabbalah is very different from teachings that promote asceticism and austerity as means to achieve spirituality. It teaches that only one who has developed the desire for pleasures to the maximum can receive what the Creator has to give. Kabbalah doesn't take you away from life; it adds a whole new meaning and strength to everything that happens. If you want to be a Kabbalist, you'll *have to* live life to the fullest.

The Force of Giving

To understand the pleasure and meaning that the Kabbalist receives, it's essential to understand the abstractions used in Kabbalah. The most basic principle in Kabbalah concerns giving. In the whole of reality, there is only a single force, a force of giving. And because that force is giving, it creates "something" to receive what it gives. The giving force in Kabbalah is called "Creator," and what it creates is called "creation," a "creature," or a "created being."

This creature goes through a process of learning and development, and at its end discovers the full grandeur and beauty of its Creator. As Rabbi Ashlag explained, this revelation of the Creator to the creature is the essence and the purpose of Kabbalah. Actually, it is the purpose of the whole creation.

To put it simply: Kabbalah teaches us how to receive the Creator—literally for the creature and the Creator to merge. The result is an experience of tremendous beauty and joy in every moment of every day.

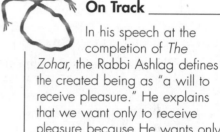

On Track

In his speech at the completion of *The Zohar*, the Rabbi Ashlag defines the created being as "a will to receive pleasure." He explains that we want only to receive pleasure because He wants only to give us pleasure. Therefore, our whole purpose in life is to learn how to enjoy the pleasures that the Creator wants to give to us.

Revealing the Creator

Now let's talk a little more about receiving the Creator. When Ashlag describes the purpose of Kabbalah as "the revelation of His Godliness to His creatures in this world," he means that the essence of Kabbalah ("reception") is to reveal, or discover, the Creator.

Understanding the tight link between reception and revelation is a key element required to understand Kabbalah. Given the abstract nature of Kabbalah—that your five senses cannot perceive the forces it describes—Kabbalah often uses metaphors to describe its concepts. Rabbi Ashlag describes the wisdom of Kabbalah as a "sequence of roots." He uses a reference to nature (roots) to show that what happens in our world doesn't begin here, but in the spiritual world.

In Kabbalah, the metaphor of nature extends even farther: discovering the Creator means discovering nature. The Creator *is* nature. Because you perceive only a tiny fraction of nature, the goal of the wisdom of Kabbalah is to disclose reality in its entirety, the whole gamut.

Discovering the whole of reality isn't just about expanding your view of life and your understanding of it. If you can understand all sides of nature, you can reach far beyond your present physical life, far beyond the boundaries of your five senses, as if someone has removed a blindfold from your eyes and allowed you to see the true vastness and beauty of the world. The wisdom of Kabbalah is designed to lift you up to another world view while opening up a whole new mental and emotional level of existence.

Promises, Promises

You may have read about charms and amulets used to ward off evil spirits. Not here. You may want to learn how you can meditate on a number or a letter and hit the jackpot next time you're in Vegas. Sorry. You may have heard a lot of big promises about how the wisdom of Kabbalah can and will change you forever. It will—but this change has nothing to do with luck or superstition of any sort.

Kab-Trivia

So it may not work in Vegas, but it's a pretty nifty number notion nonetheless. Here's how the Kabbalist knows that the Creator is nature: in Kabbalah, each Hebrew letter has a unique numeric value, symbolizing a certain spiritual state. It is no coincidence that the numeric value of the words "the nature" and "God" are the same. If you add the numeric value of all the Hebrew letters in each word, the result in both cases is 86.

How? How does Kabbalah work, and what do you actually receive?

Imagine having no senses. You cannot see. You cannot hear. You cannot smell, taste, or even touch anything. How would you know that the world exists? How would you be aware that there are objects and people to communicate with? How would you even know that you exist? Would there be any fundamental difference between the senseless you and one who has died?

Kabbalah teaches that everything you experience comes from your contact with the human and natural environment. Your communication and interaction with the outside world activates your sensations, emotions, views, actions, and experiences. So whatever exists within you remains passive and unfelt unless it comes into contact with something on the outside. This does not mean that nothing exists inside you if there is nothing on the outside. It means that until you come into contact with the environment, everything is *potential*, not *actual fact*.

At the same time, the actual fact of a person's experience to the same environment is, of course, different. No two people react the same way in a given situation, even when all the external conditions are the same. For example, most people would be very happy if they suddenly won the lottery and received a million dollars. If you were already a multimillionaire, however, you may not even notice it. It turns out that if the external circumstances are the same, the reason we react differently must be that our *internal* circumstances differ.

Here is the heart of the matter for the Kabbalah way of thinking: the reason people act differently is *not* because the outside circumstances are different, but because we *perceive* the outside circumstances differently. Different people are sensitive to different things. Although our senses of perception work the same way—they see, hear, and taste—we *interpret* the sensations differently. Some interpretations are so different that what is tragic to one healthy, normal person may go completely unnoticed by another, or even be a source of joy.

So you do not perceive or feel, really, a certain external phenomenon unless, so to speak, your receptor is pretuned, your antennae are aligned, and your internal computer is programmed to recognize that phenomenon. Otherwise, it is as if the phenomenon doesn't exist. Think about how many times you have talked to someone, even someone you know well, and they mention something they saw or felt, and you didn't even notice it. For whatever reason, this person was pretuned to or programmed for that experience, and you weren't.

On Track

The beauty in Kabbalah is that it is simply about who we are as human beings and how to live in a way that brings us happiness. At some level, we already know this stuff, we just haven't articulated it in any organized way. Kabbalah is a way to help us do that. When you read some of these baffling concepts for the first time, you often can't remember the beginning of the sentence when you reach its end. But as you reread the text, it slowly begins to make sense. When that happens, it's a sure sign of progress because it is coming alive within you.

The Sixth Sense

The "how" of reception in Kabbalah is all about perceiving the spiritual world, a world invisible to the five senses, but one we certainly experience in some way. If everything you perceive depends on your senses, it stands to reason that all we need to sense the spiritual world is a special sense that perceives it. In other words, we don't need to look for anything outside of ourselves, but we need to cultivate a perception that already exists within us that lies dormant. In Kabbalah, this perception is called "the sixth sense."

Actually, the label is misleading; it is not a "sense" in the everyday, physiological meaning of the word. But because it enables us to perceive something that we otherwise wouldn't perceive, Kabbalists have just decided to call this different means of perception "the sixth sense."

Here's the Kabbalah crux of it all: our five senses are presently "programmed" to serve personal interests. For this reason, all we perceive is what seems to serve our best interests. If somehow your senses were programmed to serve the interest of the whole world, then that's what you would perceive. In this way, each of us would be able to perceive what every other person, animal, plant, or mineral in the universe perceives. We would become creatures of unlimited perception—omniscient, literally Godlike people.

> **On Track**
>
> Another way to explain how *Kavana* or intention expands our perception is to think of it as the "goal" for which we act. If we want to benefit ourselves, then all we see is ourselves. But if we want to benefit the world and its Creator, then all we'll see will be the world and its Creator.

In such an unbounded state, even the five senses would be used in a very different way. Instead of focusing so much on personal interests, the senses would serve more fully as a means of communication with others. The fact is that in Kabbalistic terms, the sixth sense, which enables perception of the spiritual worlds, is not a sense in the usual meaning of the word, but the intention with which we use our senses. In Kabbalah, this intention is called *Kavana*. Intention is a critical Kabbalah concept that we explore more fully in Chapters 4 and 15.

The Right Stuff

Kabbalah, like everything else, is very simple once you know it. It explains that the Creator is benevolent and that He wants to give us endless, infinite pleasure. Because the Creator is benevolent, He created us with an endless, infinite desire to receive the pleasure He wants to give. In Kabbalah, this is called "the will to receive delight and pleasure," or, in short, "the will to receive."

The words of Kabbalist Yehuda Ashlag, in his introduction to *The Book of Zohar*, show how Kabbalah sages explain the Creator's necessity to create the will to receive (creatures):

The Creator created the world for no other reason but to delight His creatures .... Here we must set our minds and hearts, for this is the final aim and the act of the creation of the world. Since the Thought of Creation was to delight His creatures, He had necessarily created the souls with a great amount of desire to receive what He had thought to give .... Therefore, the Thought of Creation itself dictates the creation of an exaggerated will to receive, to fit the immense pleasure that His Almightiness thought to bestow upon the souls.

In other words, we have the capability and potential and even unconscious desire to connect with the Creator and, in receiving His pleasures, enhance our joy in living.

Give Me More

The picture is, however, neither as simple nor as idyllic in practice as it may seem. Ashlag himself depicts one part of the complexity of human condition in his essay "Peace in the World":

Each and every individual feels as a sole ruler in the world of the Creator, that everyone that is created besides him was created only to ease and improve his own life to such an extent that he feels no obligation whatsoever to give anything in return. And in simple words we shall say that the nature of each and every individual is to exploit the lives of all other people in the world for one's own benefit, and all that one gives to another, is only out of necessity.

Of course, this is a stark characterization of traits you don't feel all the time and maybe don't feel at all. But when you dig deep into your soul, you find things that you did not know were there. At first they may seem quite similar to this extreme description, and in Kabbalah, this stark self-interest is critical in the process of self-awareness that leads to correction.

Indeed, there is a reason for traits that your mom and dad probably criticized as just plain selfishness. In Kabbalah, that reason is so important that Kabbalists have an oft-used term for it: egoism. This extreme egoism, when corrected, becomes the highest level of altruism and benevolence.

I Want to Give More

So how *can* the most extreme egoism be turned into its opposite? Remember that the Creator is benevolent; He has nothing on His mind but giving. As a result, He creates creatures that want only to receive. These creatures begin to receive what He gives, more, and more, and more. Endlessly.

As the will to receive evolves in creatures, an almost magical transformation takes place. They not only want what the Creator gives, but they also want to actually *be* Creators. Think of how every child wants to become like his or her parents. Think, too, how the very basis of learning is the little one's desire to grow. Kabbalists say the child's will to be a grown up stems from the creature's desire to be like its Creator.

If your parents are your role models, you would study their actions and do your best to emulate them and become a grown-up, too. Similarly, if the Creator is your role model, you would study the Creator in order to become like Him. If the Creator you study is all about giving, about benevolence, you can see how the extreme egoism of wanting to become "Creatorlike" can be turned into altruism (which we explore more fully in upcoming chapters), because that's what He is. In Kabbalah, the ability to be like the Creator is called "acheiving the attribute of bestowal."

On Track

Another way to think about this idea of altruism is to remember that the Kabbalah reminds us that we are not separate from but part of our world. Altruism is about being one with others, united with them. Because we know ourselves only by our connection to everything else, altruism from this perspective is an intelligent way to look out for our own welfare, as well. So if we are all united, being kind and generous to others is being kind and generous to ourselves. Neat, huh?

The implication, though it may sound like an oxymoron, is that every person's *most egoistic desire* is to be like the Creator: a total altruist.

The Wisdom of the Hidden

In Kabbalah, then, the desire to be like the Creator is the innermost wish of every person and stands beneath every move you make, every breath you take, and every thought you think. This desire, however, initially eludes our consciousness, hidden under mountains of misconceptions about life and about ourselves. These misconceptions are not there by chance; they are placed there by the very same power that gradually removes them. They are hidden to keep us from seeing the truth prematurely. The wisdom of Kabbalah, then, is the method and means to reveal that hidden truth, hence its name: "the wisdom of the hidden."

The Purpose of Kabbalah

When you begin to study Kabbalah, you begin to connect to that innermost part of yourself. The powers that shape your life become increasingly clearer and more familiar. In Kabbalah, the power that illuminates the deepest point within you is called "Surrounding Light." When you study with the aim to draw as much of that power as you can, your spiritual progress accelerates hundreds of times more than your progress would have without it.

The Essence (in a Nutshell)

When all is said and done, Kabbalah is a teaching about something that exists beyond our present perception. It not only teaches you that it exists, but it also accompanies you on the journey. Eventually, it allows you to perceive the spiritual world, the Creator, in your very senses. But when you perceive the Creator, the same sensations your senses receive acquire a completely new meaning, deeper and more intense. With the Creator in your sight, your routine life acquires a whole new meaning. Think of it this way: if you take a cucumber, a tomato, a green pepper, lettuce, and an onion, they all have their distinct flavors. But put together, they create a completely new flavor: a salad.

On an everyday level, we're living in the material world, not the spiritual world. The steps that Kabbalah teaches are designed to bring you closer and closer to the spiritual world. Kabbalah takes you on a magical tour, until you enter a higher level of reality than the one you know today. When that happens, you become knowledgeable not only about the spiritual world, but also about your own everyday material world. You learn the "secret" rules that govern our world, the rules scientists are still discovering or perhaps better stated, affirming and the rules they have yet to discover. Most of all, students of Kabbalah are said to gain the ability to roam freely among all worlds, physical and spiritual.

Word of Heart

There is a wonderful, invaluable remedy to those who engage in the wisdom of Kabbalah .... [T]hey awaken upon themselves the Lights that surround their souls .... [T]he illumination received time-after-time during the engagement draws upon one grace from above, imparting abundance of sanctity and purity, which bring one much closer to perfection.

—From the introduction to *The Study of the Ten Sefirot* by Rabbi Yehuda Ashlag

The Right Place

Why do we exist? What's the point? Kabbalah is gaining popularity today because it provides insight into questions that people are asking in this troubled time. Kabbalah is a means to an end. If you want to know the deepest, truest answers humans can formulate to the reason we exist—and what those answers suggest for our lives—you're in the right place. But if you want to use Kabbalah to make more money, find a good mate, or improve your health, you've come to the wrong place. It's not in this store.

Red Alert

In the introduction to *The Study of the Ten Sefirot,* Kabbalist Yehuda Ashlag cautions that you must study Kabbalah with the right aim in mind (which he refers to as "quality"). If you study with the wrong aim, meaning not with a desire to become like the Creator—benevolent—you will not benefit from what Kabbalah has to offer. You would be misleading yourself into thinking that you are actually learning something meaningful. Why is that? Because Kabbalah is not about rewards, but about becoming like the Creator. This is the (only) right aim when learning Kabbalah.

If you want what Kabbalah offers—to grow into being like the Creator—you'll find that the personal transformation you undergo will extend from you to your society as a whole. Even though the growth, the insights, and the transformations are internal, they will also transform how you view your connection with your world and the ways in which you interact with your world.

Think about it like this: if the Creator is benevolent, He wants to give. If He wants to give, He must have someone to give to. Similarly, if you want to be like the Creator, you, too, must want to give. So you, too, must have someone to give to, and that someone comes through a new and deeper connection you learn to have toward all other beings in the universe.

There is a direct link between the change within you and the change in your attitude toward your surroundings. Kabbalah is, first and foremost, about your relationship with the world around you, for the benefit of the world around you. Through that transformation, you begin to become aware of your God-like nature.

The Least You Need to Know

- The word Kabbalah means "reception," and Kabbalah provides a method by which you learn to receive.

- The Creator's primary desire is to give pleasure to His creations, who are imbued with a desire to receive.

- In Kabbalah, the five senses provide your internal experience of the external world. The "sixth sense" of Kabbalah allows you to perceive higher spiritual worlds.

- The purpose of Kabbalah is the revelation of the Creator while we are living here in this world.

- When you learn to receive from the Creator, you will naturally want to give like the Creator.

- Kabbalah isn't just about transforming the individual but transforming society one person at a time.

Is Anybody Out There?

In This Chapter

- ◆ Our perception of reality: more than meets the eye
- ◆ The limitations of "reality"
- ◆ Is free choice really free?
- ◆ The four factors of transformation
- ◆ The power of thought

Armed with a basic understanding of how Kabbalah developed and what it is, it's time to take a deeper look at how Kabbalah works and what it does for you. This chapter expands upon the concepts introduced in Chapter 2, in order to show how Kabbalists understand the Creator and what the Creator wishes for you.

This chapter also explores more fully the nature of reality and what you perceive and don't perceive about reality. You also learn more about the ultimate purpose of Kabbalah and how it leads to both personal and social transformation.

How We Perceive Reality

Look around you. What do you see? What do you hear? What was the first thing you tasted this morning or the last thing you remember touching before drifting off to sleep last night? Are there any sights or sounds or flavors that you've never encountered in all your days? Have you ever wondered if there's anything out there that your five senses can't reveal?

Perhaps other worlds and creatures exist within the space that you perceive and sense in a limited way—worlds that are transparent and unrecognizable from our point of view?

Sounds deep? Well, it is, and it's at the core of Kabbalah. The methodology is complex, but here's the good news: anyone can learn it and attain the insights offered by Kabbalah. Why else would thousands of books in many of the world's languages have been published on the subject? If you're ready to learn more, let's begin by turning inward.

Illuminating the Darkness

One way to think about conventional understanding is that we are living in darkness and not able to see the greater reality, although it is still there. This conventional understanding comes to us through our five senses. Without knowing any better we take this view of the world as the way it is. It is a metaphorical darkness. Think of Kabbalah as a way of illuminating that reality so that it is plain to see. Once that happens and we take it all in, our perceptions of reality are changed. We can no longer act like we did when we were in the dark, and this is to the mutual benefit of ourselves and others.

All metaphors aside, neither science nor philosophy may be able to help us see the deeper reality. But perhaps if we arm ourselves with the wisdom of Kabbalah, we can more fully understand our own limitations and begin to test the boundaries of conventional reality and how we can transcend them.

def•i•ni•tion

The *Kli* is the sixth sense, the "will to receive" introduced in Chapter 2. *Kli* is also referred to as a "spiritual vessel," waiting to be filled.

One of the most important elements of Kabbalah is the *Kli* (vessel, receptacle), the desire to receive. It is the reason that Kabbalist Yehuda Ashlag stresses the importance of containing yourself to your level of understanding. But that's easy to interpret the wrong way. That doesn't mean that you should avoid knowledge or depth of spirituality. Rather, Ashlag suggests that learning what we can and can't perceive helps avoid confusion and creates a clearer path to reach greater understanding.

Five Senses, Going on Six

Human perception is limited. You and I really cannot feel or truly imagine anything outside of it. Through honest self-examination, and with the help of Kabbalah books, you can begin to discover that you are enclosed within yourself. Because you perceive only with your five senses, you comprehend only things that exist on the inside. Moreover, what you sense is only a fragment of what actually exists in the world—the fragment known as our world. Recognizing this limitation is the first step toward understanding true perception.

Do you ever think that your hand feels odd because you have only five fingers? Probably not. Although you can widen the boundaries of your five senses, you cannot really imagine what perceptions you lack. It's impossible to recognize true reality because it isn't something you feel the absence of any more than you would feel the lack of a sixth finger.

Because imagination is the product of the five senses, Kabbalists suggest that you can never envision an object or creature that is not in some way familiar. Think of the most creative children's book illustrator or the most abstract artist you know. Do their designs in some way resemble the physical world? Try to imagine the wildest thing, something no one else knows. Does it still happen that you create something that everyone knows or at least can puzzle out from their experience of everyday reality?

> **Word of Heart**
>
> Our five senses and our imagination do not offer us anything more than the disclosure of the actions of the Essence, but not of the Essence itself. For example, the sense of sight offers us only shadows of the visible Essence, according to how they are formed opposite the light.
>
> —From the preface to *The Book of Zohar* by Rabbi Yehuda Ashlag

No matter how much you and I progress technologically, we will never be free of the boundaries of the five senses. However, some individuals have acquired an additional sense that enables them to perceive a wider reality. They still exist within our world, but they have extended the boundaries of their perception to include the entire picture of creation. Such people are called *Kabbalists*.

Going beyond the five senses doesn't happen literally. It's more of a way to describe a higher level of perception where we understand the interconnectedness of everything and our place in this interconnected reality. We know we are a part of the dance of reality and the implications of that. Calling this ability a "sixth sense" is just a convenient way, within the context of Kabbalah, of expressing this ability to go beyond conventional perception.

Like Kabbalists, you and I receive sensations from external objects. But because your internal senses do not have the same qualities as those objects, you do not really perceive the object itself. You perceive only that part of the object that resonates to qualities you already have within. For a complete perception of anything, you need to first be complete within. In other words, you have to be aware of all the forms of reality that can and do exist in you, and then your picture of reality will be complete.

Different experiences lead people to interpret the same perceptions in very different ways. We all do this and may be unaware that others don't share our interpretations at all. What we think of as "objective" is in fact completely "subjective" based on what we've learned and what we've experienced.

So how do we attain the sixth sense that enhances and broadens our ability to perceive and interpret the world beyond conventional reality? In fact, it exists in everyone but is hidden. But we have the ability to search and find this sense within ourselves and gain its benefits.

As the retina matches its range of perception to the wavelength of visible light, you must learn to match your spiritual perception to the Creator's wavelength, known in Kabbalah as His Form. Through study, you can learn how to be like the Creator and build your sixth sense. You begin to know His thoughts toward you and His plan with respect to you.

def•i•ni•tion

The **Upper World** is the world of the spirit, the unknown world, the world of becoming Godlike. The lower world, conversely, is the physical world, the world of everyday reality. By slowly gaining access to the Upper World, we become aware of what was hidden before and the nature of the spirit begins to reveal itself. Kabbalah assists in achieving this awareness.

Even before beginning to cultivate the sixth sense—even while still blind to the Creator—you can search for a way out of the darkness with the help of three elements: a teacher, a book, and a group of friends. (More on that in Chapter 16.) Eventually, through persistence and study, you will perceive a tiny ray of light, a weak perception of the world of the Creator. In Kabbalah, that world is called the *Upper World*. By study and development of the sixth sense, you gradually begin to feel and to understand the Upper World.

Beyond Self

Your perception of the Upper World, or world to come, varies depending on your present spiritual state. To the Kabbalist, the Upper World is the next degree a person can attain. Initially, our perception of the Upper World is dormant. Because our qualities are opposite from the Creator's, we can only perceive the material world we presently live in. In such a state, everything we believe the spiritual world to be is strictly a figment of our imagination.

But once we acquire the first spiritual quality, the first bit of altruism, we also gain the ability to see the spiritual as it truly is. Kabbalists call this "crossing the barrier." Once we cross the barrier we no longer need a teacher to lead us because in that state we are under the conscious guidance of the Creator.

In most cases, Kabbalists continue to study with a teacher even after they cross the barrier, but their relationship with their teacher changes drastically. The teacher no longer needs to lead a blind person by the hand, but the two walk together on an enchanted route of discovery.

Beyond the barrier, one learns through observation, using the new observation tools that the student now refines and improves. This modus operandi is called "One's soul shall teach one." Yehuda Ashlag describes it in a letter to a student as a process of seeing one's friend approach from afar. Imagine seeing a person a long way from you. First, you're not even sure it's a person, it's more like a black dot. Next appear the basic features—head, hands, torso, and legs. When the person comes a bit closer you can see if it's a man or a woman, and after a bit longer you can tell features in the person's face, you can recognize your friend.

In learning to transcend our egoism, it's important to understand how perception is measured. Every sense has an internal measurement tool that operates in a simple manner.

Think of the eardrum. The hearing mechanism reacts to something on the outside, working in the same way as the exterior force, but in the opposite direction, pressing back from within. It therefore keeps itself in balance, enabling you to measure, in this case, the volume and pitch of a sound.

On Track

Bina means "understanding." In Kabbalah, it generally refers to the contemplation of the ways of cause and effect and to benevolence. *Bina* is also the example of the Creator's quality of altruism within us. Therefore, *Bina* is our inner spiritual teacher. This is why she is also called *Ima* (mother).

Here's the hitch: for this type of perception to occur, there must be some uniting force between the perceiver and the object of perception. In the case of our eardrum, the common bond might be the wavelength of sound necessary for us to hear.

But what's the uniting force that can tie our perception to the Creator? Perhaps what we need is an "eardrum" to place over our sixth sense, which would have the same quality as what's given out by the Creator? Well, such an "eardrum" exists; it is the intention, or *Kavana*, introduced in Chapter 2. Whatever you do with an honest *intention* to give is considered "giving" in spirituality. The spiritual problem is to see where your intention is to receive and turn it into an intention to give. This is where the teacher, the group of friends, and the books help.

On Track

During our spiritual ascent, we might come to recognize that the Creator made the condition of darkness to help us develop a need for His help and bring us closer to Him. The spiritual principle is simple: if we consider our state of being as dark and unpleasant, and the Creator's state of being as bright and pleasant, then we will want to be in it. This is why below the barrier the process we experience is called "recognition of evil," where we define our state of being as evil (to us). If we consider our state as totally evil, and His state as utterly desirable, we will cross the barrier. This is the condition for entering the spiritual world of the Creator.

Through the five senses we perceive an external stimulus not as it is, but as we have learned to interpret that stimulus. But if we attain spiritual qualities, we can start perceiving new worlds around us and gain a clearer picture of the Creator's true form, until, at the last stage of elevation, we perceive the whole Him in His entirety.

The (Nonexistent) Objective Reality

Our understanding of what we sense is based on the genes we inherit, our experiences, our socialization, and what we have learned. It's all very subjective. Regardless of what our senses take in, what we eventually understand of it and how we act as a result are very personal.

For example, if we were deaf, wouldn't there still be sounds around us? Wouldn't there still be music and the sound of jet planes roaring over our heads? Would birds stop singing because we wouldn't be able to hear them? To us, they would. There is no way to explain to a deaf person what a nightingale sounds like. Moreover, no two people experience the same emotions when they hear the song of the nightingale. Everything we perceive is totally subjective. This is why Kabbalists can only show us the way to the spiritual world, but we have to march it ourselves.

Knowing this, doesn't it seem obvious that there are alternatives to our version of reality? These alternatives may help us make better judgments about what we're perceiving and our subsequent behavior may lead to more positive results for ourselves and our world. Kabbalah recognizes this and provides a way to make it happen.

Everything you and I believe to exist outside of us actually exists within us. When we refer, then, to objective reality, we are referring to what *we* view as objective through the lens of our own perception. We refer to a viewpoint, that is, by its very nature, subjective.

On Track

Here's a fact of human nature: because of our subjective perception, we can never apprehend or explain nature objectively. It comes to us through our senses. Further, we do not explain nature, we explain our *understanding* of nature. The apprehension and explanations we offer, in the end, are a manifestation of our brains at work. One of our gifts, as human beings, is our ability to know this about ourselves and learn to deal with it intelligently.

Freedom of Choice

It has long been said that people are only truly happy if they are truly free—free from bondage, free from oppression, and free to make their own decisions. Likewise, people of faith have long wondered how to reconcile the concept of free will with the existence of a greater power, and in the case of Kabbalists—the Creator. The Creator's singular desire is for you and me to be fulfilled and made joyful. This state can occur only when we reach His state, His degree or awareness. This can happen only when our desire to enjoy is equal to the Creator's desire to bestow enjoyment. If it sounds circular, it is: it's the reciprocity that brings us ever closer to perfection and the Creator's desire for us. So how do we reconcile this idea of free will with what the Creator wishes for us?

Here's the Kabbalist's logic, step by step:

1. The Creator is absolutely benevolent.

2. As a result, He wants to bring us to the absolute good state.

3. The absolute good state is His own state.

4. That means that we have to become like Him: benevolent.

5. Therefore, we have to come to feel that His state—benevolence—is the absolute good state. In other words, we have to *choose* it of our own free will.

6. Free choice can only be made on condition that the Creator does not apply force upon us, so that we are independent from Him.

7. Therefore, He is hidden and gave us existence in this world.

8. Without feeling Him as either fearsome or good, but from a completely "neutral" state, we could decide freely that being like Him is the absolute good.

Rabbi Yehuda Ashlag once wrote an allegory in a letter to a student:

> Once there was a king who wanted to know which of his subjects were trustworthy. He announced that anyone who wanted to come and work for the king would be handsomely rewarded by a festive meal, fit for kings. When the people arrived, there was no one at the gate, just a sign indicating where to go and what to do, but no guards to watch over the arrivals. Those who worked in the designated place were unknowingly exposed to a magic powder, and those who went elsewhere were not. In the evening, when everyone sat at the table, those who worked in the designated place enjoyed the meal tremendously, but to those who didn't, the food was the worst they'd ever tasted. Thus, only those who freely chose to follow the king were rewarded with enjoying what the king enjoys.

How Do We Choose?

Kabbalah teaches that even though the Creator wants to enter into a relationship with His creation, He has concealed Himself from us to give the impression of free will. Under these conditions, we seem to be able to act, think, and choose, completely independent of the Creator's presence. Our choices appear to be made of our own volition and free will; we do not detect an unseen hand guiding our actions and, as far as we can tell, our choices are truly free.

Think of it this way: the Creator has your entire life planned out for you, down to what you will have for lunch today. So you're at the deli and you're having trouble deciding between turkey and roast beef. After a brief internal struggle, you decide to get the roast beef on rye with extra mayo—just as the Creator knew you would. But at the moment of your decision, did you just resign yourself to predestination, throw up your hands, and allow the Creator to choose for you? Not exactly, but He had that moment mapped out all along. And that doesn't make your roast beef sandwich any less delicious, does it?

But if the Creator has all of our decisions and moves mapped out in advance, is free choice truly free? The answer is that our choices are free when looking from our perspective. The fact that the Creator knows what we will decide is meaningless to us, as long as *we* don't know what we will choose.

The Pleasure and Pain Principle

The Creator's only wish is for you and I to be filled with joy. Recognizing this truth is central to our path to perfection. It should be clear to any observer of the human scene that most people, whether seekers of the Kabbalah or good old-fashioned hedonists, desire pleasure and often go to great lengths to find it. If the Creator's intent was for us to seek and experience endless pleasure, how does pain fit into the equation?

You and I do not commit to any action unless we believe that it will, in some way, bring us happiness. Additionally, we do not make lateral moves in our search for joy. Each action is committed with the calculation that our happiness will increase. In this way, you and I consciously put ourselves through painful situations to gain greater pleasure.

> **On Track**
>
> Happiness does not always mean some event that puts a big smile on our faces. It means moving toward goals that help us live the kind of life we think is in our best interest at the time. So that is the sense in which our actions are always aimed at making ourselves "happy."

Certain painful situations make us reevaluate what we believe are the causes of our happiness and rank them according to importance. Say you have a Rolex watch, the ownership of which brings you great pleasure—what it represents in the way of achievement, what it says about your values and status, your admiration for how it works and who knows what else. One day, a mugger puts a gun to your chest and demands your beloved watch … or else. Most sane people would agree to a painful act (in this case, giving up a cherished item) in order to avoid a more painful act (injury of some sort or worse).

Think of it as a sort of pleasure-ranking system. Which items or experiences are of the greatest value? What items or experiences are less important? Are you willing to endure temporary pain for increased joy and happiness?

People can change their awareness of future pleasure—everyone has an imagination—and calculate that any discomfort in the present is worth the future pleasure. In other words, suffering may be worthwhile in order to obtain pleasure, even if the pleasure is not immediately apparent and may not be known to you for years and years.

Rabbi Ashlag defines it as a state where the future pleasure "shines" on the present and illuminates it. He explains that we cannot really sense the future. Rather, we sense the future pleasure while we are in the present state. In this manner, the present unpleasantness becomes bearable, and even desirable, if we focus our minds on the rewarding goal in the future.

Four Factors (Elements)

You and I are always in a new state, or mood, or frame of mind. Who designs and determines that state? Better yet, what elements design it? Kabbalah states that four factors determine a person's state in each and every moment:

1. **Origin.** This is the starting point for transformation, but it is not the same thing as a blank canvas. Think of it more as a wall that has been painted and repainted many times. The layers of previous coats of paint are there beneath the surface. Perhaps they cannot be seen or distinguished, but they are a part of the composition of that wall, always the starting point for the next layer of transformation, as a wall's current paint is always the undercoat for the next coat.

2. **Paths of development that stem from human nature and are unchanging.** This factor deals with the unchanging and unchangeable parts of a person's nature. These include such things as hereditary traits, such as skin color, eye color, and predilection toward heart or other disease, as well as one's nature, such as being good tempered or irritable.

3. **Paths of development that change under the influence of external factors.** This is our attitude toward the external environment. Say you get a bad performance review from your boss at work. You may be upset and angry, and feel that the feedback is unfair, or you may decide your boss has your best interest at heart and told you what you need to do in order to succeed. Either way, your attitude to the event will inevitably change you.

4. **Paths of development of the external factors themselves.** The fourth factor is the external environment and its continued evolution. To continue the previous example, your boss will be affected by your choice of action, which, in turn, will change her attitude toward you. It turns out that your attitude changes the environment.

As the four factors show, the confluence of a person's origin, inner nature, and unchangeable outside forces all contribute to our inner makeup. However, of all four elements, the only element we can modify is the fourth one, our environment. But because the elements affect each other, by changing our environment, we can ultimately shape all other elements within us.

The same principle of "change one, affect all" pops up in science as well. You may have heard of the so-called Butterfly Effect, a theory that suggests that the flapping of a butterfly's wings in Brazil could set in motion a tornado in Texas. Put simply, the smallest, seemingly insignificant occurrences can have massive consequences down the line. Thus, to control our lives and determine our future, we need only to know which element to change, which "button" to push.

On Track

Why does your attitude, whatever it is, change the environment? The answer is that you are not separate from but another part of the environment. Therefore, your actions, like the actions of everything else, affect that environment. Given this, an important question to ask is "How can I act so as to make the environment better?"

Kabbalists assert that the origin (the first factor), the actions of the origin (the second factor), and the evolution of society (the fourth factor) are not dependent upon us at all. What could be dependent upon you is the third factor—namely, your attitude toward external factors. If you think about it in broader social terms, you can see that your attitude and decisions can affect society as a whole (including yourself). You choose your society according to its goals.

You can influence those aims as well, but if society's aims don't go along with yours, change your society. In the end, according to Kabbalah, you are the product of your society, which is why it is so important that you carefully select it, and constantly shape and improve it.

Why did the Creator set up existence this way? In the coming chapters, we will see how Kabbalists explain that it stems from the structure of The First Man (*Adam ha Rishon*), the collective soul of which we are all parts.

This quote from writer John Woods captures this idea about thought and its affect on reality: "The world is exactly like we think it is, and that's why." This is true because our thoughts affect our actions, which affect the world as we perceive it. This leaves only one question open: "Where do our thoughts come from?"

Just Think!

Kabbalah is a study of how you and I sense the Creator. Think back to our discussion in this chapter about senses and perception. When the sun begins to shine and your skin heats up, you do not, in a cognitive way, *know* that you are hot. You sense the sun's heat in a way that bypasses thought and reason. Kabbalists have learned to merge the disparate realms of thought and sense, and, in doing so, can achieve new levels of perception. They have learned that thoughts create reality, not actions, and center their efforts on evoking the kind of thoughts that create a positive reality.

What Did We Say About Reality?

Recall this chapter's section on reality, how human perception is limited. People know only the reality that they perceive through their five senses, and what they experience is an internal copy of what's on the outside. The Kabbalists' sixth sense, however, allows you to feel a whole new reality and make different decisions concerning the external environment—to open up different possibilities in your attitude toward the world of which you are a part.

The wisdom of Kabbalah allows us to shift our attitude to the outside more readily. It allows us, for instance, to shift from being affected by the negative force that pushes us from behind into achieving rapid progress from the positive force that propels us forward. After all, Kabbalah reminds us that the Creator is benevolent and wants to give us pleasure, and that this is His *only* thought. It turns out that all we need to do is change our own perception of reality, and the world will be united and unified under the Creator's one thought to do good to His creations.

The Strongest of All Powers

Kabbalists assert that "one is where one's thoughts are." This means that if you think in a diminished world, you will remain in that world. If, however, your thoughts aspire to the Upper World, this kind of thinking will bring you closer to the Creator and will allow you to perceive higher levels.

Broader thinking has great everyday applications. If you view your life and your surroundings as products of the Creator, you begin to perceive seemingly negative situations as part of this plan for you. This type of thinking doesn't stop things from happening, but it teaches you to deal with events in positive ways that bring you closer to perfection and more in line with the Creator.

Have you ever seen a magnet propel another magnet across a table? It's kind of amazing when you consider that magnetic waves can't be seen or touched. The same goes for radio waves and electric fields, even gravity. The only way you know these forces exist is through their effects in the world. Thoughts work the same way. They cannot be seen or heard, but their effects resonate more than our words or actions. According to Kabbalah, thoughts are the strongest of all powers, and your thoughts lead to speech and action.

Once you have recognized the power of your thoughts, you can begin to affect positive change in the world through learning how the Creator thinks and adopting it as your own. You might say that the whole method of Kabbalah is focused on teaching you how to control your innermost thoughts and the innermost desires, the ones you usually aren't conscious of but feel and know only by their results.

Word of Heart

We must understand His thought in creating the worlds and the reality before us: His operations did not come to be by many thoughts as is our way. That is He is One, Unique and Unified, and as He is Simple, so His Lights extend from Him—Simple and Unified …

You must therefore understand and perceive that all the names and appellations, and all the worlds, Upper and lower, are all one Simple Light, Unique and Unified. In the Creator, the Light that extends, the thought, the operation and the Operator and anything the heart can think and contemplate, are in Him one and the same thing.

Thus you can judge and perceive that this entire reality, Upper and lower as one, in the final state of the end of correction, was emanated and created by a single thought. That single thought performs all the operations; it is the essence of all the operations, the purpose, and the essence of the labor. It is by itself the entire perfection and the sought-after reward, as the Ramban explained, "One, Unique and Unified."

—From *The Study of the Ten Sefirot* by Rabbi Yehuda Ashlag

The Least You Need to Know

- Our senses give us an incomplete picture of reality. What we perceive as our world is a fragment of what the Creator has given to us.

- The Creator wants only to give to you, and as you receive, you will want to be like the Creator and give to others.

◆ There are four factors that determine your state in any moment: origin, factors resulting from and determined by origin, the attitude toward the external environment, and the evolution of the environment.

◆ If you want to change your thoughts and desires, you must take control over the third factor, the environment you live in.

◆ By changing your environment, you will change your thoughts in a direction of your choice, and your thoughts will change society.

4

The Desire for Spirituality

In This Chapter

◆ Our desire and drive for more

◆ The purpose of "evil"

◆ A point in the heart

◆ Intention as a driving force

You could tell the story of humankind as the story of human desire and how it has evolved and developed over thousands of years. The search for ways of fulfilling these emerging desires determines the level of a civilization's evolution and defines how it measures progress.

This chapter explores the development of human desires, from basic needs all the way up to the highest level: the need for spirituality. You can begin a serious study of Kabbalah only after reaching this level; it is the gateway to understanding the Creator and the role of humans in the world.

Our Desire for More, More, More

The list of humankind's achievements is parallel to a list of its desires. The Pilgrims' desire for freedom from religious persecution, for instance, led them to migrate to what became Massachusetts. The Colonies' desire for sovereignty led to the Revolutionary War.

Given that desires generally move from smaller to larger, simple to complex, a civilization advances. As collective desires grow, civilizations advance.

Kabbalah divides the entire complex of human desires into five levels:

> Level 1: Meeting basic natural desires, such as food, shelter, and sex
>
> Level 2: Striving for wealth
>
> Level 3: Craving power and fame
>
> Level 4: Thirsting for knowledge
>
> Level 5: Desiring spirituality and the Creator

Once the immediate craving is fulfilled, however, what can be best described as a feeling of "emptiness" returns, leading to, you know, the same old thing. Until a person wonders if there is something more. When a person reaches that point, where the desire for the things in the first four levels is exhausted, that person often ends up with a strong desire to attain Kabbalah's fifth level, spirituality.

On Track

Perhaps you have heard of Abraham Maslow's "Hierarchy of Needs," a tool to help explain human motivation. He explained that initially we have basic physiological needs for food, protection from the elements, and so on. When these are fulfilled, our needs proceed to safety and security needs then to love and a sense of belonging, then status needs, and finally, at the top of the hierarchy, the need for self-actualization and transcendence. This hierarchy roughly parallels the Kabbalah's progression of desires and demonstrates something universal in these concepts.

The "Good" Purpose of "Evil"

It may come as no surprise that several of these levels of desire, while not intrinsically evil, lead people to acts of what Kabbalists refer to as "egoism," where people work for themselves instead of trying to be more like the Creator. There is nothing inherently wrong with that. In fact, you might say that it's the Creator's way of leading you to Him.

Systems of holiness and impurity, or evil, exist only to serve the purpose of creation. The Creator started creation. To be more precise, He created the will to receive pleasure—creation—and we turned it into a world of evil or corruption by turning the will to receive into egoism.

In the previous chapter, we talked about the recognition of evil. We said that if we consider our state as totally evil, and His state as utterly desirable, we will cross the barrier and enter the spiritual world. The question that remains open is which is the best way to recognize our evil and do it more quickly, and painlessly. This is where Kabbalah comes into play. The advantage in Kabbalah is that it teaches you about human nature without having to physically experience the evil. This is why Kabbalists say we don't have to suffer; we can study instead.

In that sense, humans finish the Creator's creation, meaning that they *correct* it. Because humans have the ability to be like the Creator, the Creator passes on to them the leadership of creation, once they are corrected. So the good purpose of evil is realized only if egoism becomes a driving force to the Creator, which we know is not often the case. Otherwise, evil is evil is evil. And it produces evil, as egoistic acts throughout history show.

def•i•ni•tion

In Kabbalah, **correct** refers to correction. No one will tell you that who you are or what you do is correct or incorrect. But if you've satisfied a desire to become more Creator-like, then you've done the correct thing. Kabbalists refer to correction to mean turning the intention with which we approach a desire from "for me" to "for the Creator."

The Creator increases the pressure on us to make us take leadership upon ourselves. That is why the world seems to become increasingly hostile; the Creator made it that way so you and I would begin to correct the world and ourselves. If He hadn't done it this way, you and I would sit under a tree and work on our tan. Although that may sound great, it doesn't bring you any closer to becoming like the Creator, which is why He created us in the first place.

The Creator's goal is that humans correct His creation. If you remember that, all your calculations stop being passive. Instead, they become vessels, or aims, with which you contact the Creator and experience Him. Every negative, or evil, attribute in you becomes a means to an end.

In Kabbalah, there is no other way to make contact with the Creator—only through our negative attributes, through the evil. The recognition of evil is the beginning of the revelation of good.

This explanation of the Creator's goal leaves one question open: if he wants to give us pleasure, as Kabbalists say, what's wrong with a good tan, if we enjoy it? Well, according to Kabbalists there is nothing wrong with it, if that's what you really want. But if you have a question nagging in the back of your mind (while you're lying on the beach), and you can't enjoy sunbathing anymore, then maybe you need something more, and maybe that something is Kabbalah. As Kabbalist Yehuda Ashlag puts it: Kabbalah is for those who ask (even unconsciously), "What is the meaning of my life?"

I Feel Good—or Do I?

Kabbalah explains that life is based on only one desire: to feel good, regardless of whether that good feeling comes through obtaining a better job, a new car, a mate, or successful children. Behind all those desires is the search for satisfaction. You try to attain what appears to bring you that sensation of pleasure.

When you begin to feel spirituality, it changes your scale of desire. You may begin to see that some desires have become more important and others have become less so. You begin to weigh your life not just according to what you see and know in this world, things that your physical body sees right now, but also to consider your past and future lives. You begin to see what favors you and what does not for generations to come. As a result, you naturally change your evaluation of your environment.

When you begin to realize that you are a part of a single soul and that all of humanity are parts of that soul, too, you begin to think that it may be in your (still egoistic) interest to help them. In short, Kabbalah reminds you to look at the big picture.

Ironically, however, the more you want spirituality, the more you want mundane pleasures, too. A Kabbalist is not a person without desires for food, sex, money, power, and knowledge. On the contrary, a Kabbalist is one with stronger mundane desires than most people experience, but also with a greater desire for spirituality than all his or her mundane desires put together. In other words, having a greater sense of your spirituality doesn't exempt you from being human and all that carries with it.

This process of intensifying is designed to make you develop such a strong desire for spirituality that you will be willing to do anything to attain it, including giving up all desires for anything that is not spirituality. And to give up those desires, you must experience them. This is why Kabbalists explain that the higher your spiritual degree, the greater your mundane desires, too. This is how Kabbalists progress, by experiencing the greatest worldly pleasures, and then being given the awareness that there is something that's even better and greater than all those pleasures combined.

In the view of Kabbalah, you change in accordance with your ascent in the spiritual world and begin to understand a greater good more thoroughly. It is the same as your development in this world. As a child, you wanted a toy car. When you grew up, you wanted a real car.

So, too, your desires change as you grow in spirituality. The earlier objects of your desire seem like toys now compared to the real things that you begin to seek. That search finally leads to the absolute good—direct contact with the Creator, achieved through equivalence of form with Him, through being like Him.

The Height of Giving Is Receiving

But if the Creator made the world in order to bestow His abundance to the created beings, then what's wrong with wanting to receive everything "for oneself"? Why is it perceived as evil or egoism? Why was it necessary to create a world so imperfect and a creation so corrupted that it must be corrected?

Kabbalists have worked out the answers to such questions over the centuries. They explain that the Creator receives pleasure by giving pleasure to people. If those people delight in the fact that receiving pleasure gives the Creator a possibility to delight them, then both the Creator and the people coincide in qualities and in desires. All are happy with the process of giving. The Creator gives pleasure, whereas the people create the conditions to receive it. Everyone thinks of the other, not of him or herself, and everyone still receives pleasure; it's a win, win situation.

Because humans are egoists, however, they are, in their initial state, incapable of thinking about others and think only of themselves. Humans can give only in situations in which they see personal benefit—and a greater benefit than the one they give. In that sense, a human being is utterly distant from the Creator and, therefore, does not perceive Him.

We can compare it to a salesperson at a store: the salesperson smiles to the clients and tries to make them feel good while they are in the store. Both the clients and the salesperson know that the goal of the salesperson isn't really to make them feel good, but to encourage them to spend their money at the store. Therefore, just because the salesperson is nice, we don't necessarily think that he or she is a good-hearted person, but we may indeed think that he or she is a pro.

In other words, the "price" the salesperson "pays" for your money is a smile and a welcoming appearance. But this is an egoistic giving. Without the prospect of earning money, the salesperson wouldn't smile because he or she wouldn't have the incentive.

This is our natural behavior, and this is why Kabbalists say that we are all initially ego-istic.

An individual's goal is to transcend egoism and move toward the Creator by emulat-ing the Creator's qualities of giving. Only then can an individual receive the same pleasure from altruistic acts as from self-serving or egoistic acts. (But don't forget that because we're not separate from but a part of the world, altruism is how we look out for the whole that includes us. Self-serving actions that don't take this into account will come back in one way or another to haunt us.) If an individual learns to enjoy giv-ing because it makes him or her more similar to the Creator, then the individual has reached a state known in Kabbalah as "giving for the sake of giving." The gratification of the person comes only from having the ability to do something for the Creator.

The desire for this spiritual level is present in everyone, though in most people it is unconscious. When it first appears, Kabbalists say that it is felt in the heart as a point in the heart, at the center of all desires. What that point means is something we must all discover for ourselves.

The Point in the Heart

When the last degree in the evolution of human desire, the desire for spirituality, is evoked, it is called *a point in the heart*. When desires for worldly pleasures—food, sex, family, wealth, power, and knowledge—are satisfied, the point in the heart begins to develop. It's a desire for something higher.

def•i•ni•tion

Kabbalah distinguishes the desire for the Creator from all other desires. Desires for worldly plea-sures are called "man's heart," while the desire for the Creator is called **a point in the heart.**

The point in our heart is like a drop of desire, a yearning for supreme attainment, for the Creator. The point is sensed as Light. It is the sensation of the Source. From that point, a person's spiritual evolution begins.

A Tiny Black Speck

The point in the heart is referred to in Kabbalah as "a black point." The point in the heart, the desire for Light, awakens from within the egoistic desires, which an individ-ual cannot fulfill. Faced with the inability to satisfy the desire for the Creator through worldly means, a person comes to the end of the evolution of the will to receive. A person may feel depressed by the absence of fulfillment, the inability to satisfy desires.

By feeling the point in the heart, an individual is drawn to the Light. When that happens, that person often feels dark inside. But this is not because he or she has grown worse. On the contrary, it is because that person has become more corrected, drawn more Light, and the new Light shines on new places in the soul. But because these places are not yet corrected, they often give off a "dark" feeling. When darkness appears, it's a sure sign that you have made progress and that Light is sure to follow.

A Light at the End of the Tunnel

An individual whose point has awakened feels in the dark, standing over a chasm, without a future, a past, or a present. All of the person's egoistic desires are represented by the dark tunnel because the worldly desires simply no longer satisfy the individual.

But there can appear, as it were, a light at the end of the tunnel, a point that awakens and draws the individual forward, as if to an important but unknown destination. The individual senses that a solution exists, in some direction. The sensation of a solution provides a point of meaning, something to want, a quest to live for. The Creator has appeared in the person's dark, egoistic desires.

One way to think about how this happens is as a deep insight we suddenly experience. It's a profound "a ha!" where we recognize that it is with our spiritual self that true happiness lies.

In the introduction to *The Study of the Ten Sefirot*, Baal HaSulam writes that it's as if the Creator appears to a person from among the cracks in the wall and offers hope for future peace. In Kabbalah, this is called "putting one's hand on the good fortune."

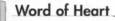

Word of Heart

For man looks on the outward appearance, but the Lord looks on the heart.

—Samuel 1, 16:7

Beyond Thoughts: Intentions

Once the point in the heart is experienced and opened up, however, the real work begins. In Kabbalah, the activating principle of change is *intention*. Intentions create our thoughts, which, in turn, create our actions and ultimately our whole reality. Using the study of Kabbalah, you can concentrate on developing intentions so they affect reality in a way that will elevate you to experience the Upper World, the Creator.

In the science of Kabbalah, the thought is the intention, because it is its progenitor. In a regular life, thought is the considerations made by the desire to receive. The desire to receive in and of itself isn't bad—that's how you and I were created, and when used correctly it is beneficial to us and to the Creator. The intention in which we use our desire is where we must focus our attention. In simple words, we have to become aware of *why* we do what we do, what we want to get out of it, and whom we want to please by experiencing pleasure, ourselves or the Creator. This intention will then create a work-plan, a thought, and the thoughts will determine our whole reality. So the only part that needs mending in reality is our intentions. That's why Kabbalists say that what you do doesn't matter, only what you aim to achieve by it.

The hardest part in working to develop your spiritual essence is to maintain an intention to focus on the Creator. Intention is often hidden and not felt. It doesn't express itself in any way except in the result of your thoughts and actions.

You have to constantly awaken awareness of intention over all the other activities and inner processes. To be on a spiritual path means to identify with and connect to the intention, not just the action. The recognition of evil relates to focusing your intention, as expressed in the Psalms as "get away from evil and do good." (Psalms, 34:15) All is in relation to the intention.

Life's Secret Driving Force

Intention is the driving force of life. All thoughts are generated by desires, but they are directed by intentions. The intent can be "for me" or "for the Creator." The desire finds the intent "for me" if it does not feel the Creator, and the intent "for the Creator" if it does feel Him. Good intentions are those that aim to be like the Creator, and bad intentions aim to enjoy regardless of the Creator.

On one hand, it is possible to feel the Creator only after you are equipped with an intent for the Creator, but on the other hand, you can get such an intent only through the revelation of the Creator, through the sensation of the Light. The miracle of the attainment of the intent for the Creator hides within that very contradiction. In other words, if we weren't egoistic, we would not have the ability to experience the futility of egoism. However, when we do truly understand that egoism cannot bring happiness, it is at that point the light of the Creator is revealed and our lives take a new direction.

The spiritual desire is to delight in the Light, in the Creator. If that desire is self-oriented in its intent, it is considered impure and is called a "shell." If it is a Creator-oriented desire, it is considered pure and is called *holiness*.

def•i•ni•tion

The word **holy** is derived from and means being whole. It is also related to the word health, which, in terms of its derivation, means "a state of being whole." To be holy is to be aware of the whole, to have a correct sense of who you are, who the Creator is, and to work for the welfare of the whole. Curiously, in Hebrew, the word "holy" is *Kadosh*, which actually means separated. But there is no contradiction here because *Kadosh* actually refers to separation from egoism, and dedication (unification) with the Creator.

Therefore, in the beginning, through the influence of proper study and labor, a desire to enjoy spirituality for self develops. A person begins to want the Upper World, the Creator, more than the everyday world. Even when desires are worldly, they are still spiritual because the overriding purpose of the desires, the intent, is to delight in the Creator.

The Creator made humans with a desire to receive pleasure and with nothing else. However, we can experience real lasting pleasure only in the one pleasurable state that exists: the Creator's state, meaning unity and benevolence. To fully enjoy life means learning to enjoy being like the Creator.

In a nutshell, to improve the world, it takes good thoughts, and to have good thoughts means having good intentions.

Kab-Trivia

Many people believe that an evil thought can kill. Science also has learned that if a person with bad intentions approaches a plant, even though he may only water the plant, the plant reacts to the negative energy. Science now recognizes that a person's thoughts, not actions, have the most powerful influence on the world.

Change Your Aim, Not Your Act

The intent of the Creator from the start was to make the desire complete. However, this happens only when your intent resembles the Creator's attribute of bestowal by your free choice. This requires transforming your will for self-enjoyment into the will to please the Creator. And the Creator is pleased when you acquire His qualities.

When you acquire this intent, the desire to enjoy becomes equal to the Creator's desire to give. You bring yourself to perfection by the correct use of your only attribute: the reception of pleasure. This is a change in intent, a change in the aim of your actions and not your actions themselves. Changing the intent of one's desire involves three phases:

1. Avoiding the use of desire in its original form.

2. Isolating from your desire to enjoy only those desires worthy, in quantity and quality, to be used to please the Creator.

3. Spiritually coupling with, and discovering, the Creator. This is possible only through the isolation of the desire and correcting its aim if it is not focused on the Creator.

In short, Kabbalah asks you to change your normal attitudes about perception. It asks you to look through matter and into the forces behind it.

In spirituality, you turn away from looking at the picture of reality you are born with. Instead, you get to know the forces that paint the picture. You get to know the artist. You acquire the ability to connect to the forces that create the picture, and ultimately to govern those forces. You begin to understand how reality is made.

On Track

Kabbalah is like embroidery. When you look on the surface you see a coherent picture. But when you look behind the picture, at the threads that make up the picture, you find a mess of strings and cords that you can't decide where they begin, where they end, and which part of the picture they belong to. Kabbalah helps you understand the threads behind the picture, and teaches you how to become an embroiderer yourself, so you can build a picture that suits *your* liking.

This goes for society as a whole as well as individuals. As a society, at least in the West or developed world, we have completed Levels 1–4 and are now embarking on Level 5, the spiritual level. This is a time when people will want to know what they are living for. Before exploring the evolution of Kabbalah to this point, however, it helps to understand some of the myths and misunderstandings of Kabbalah that have sprung up over the centuries.

The Least You Need to Know

◆ The history of humankind is a history of ever-increasing desire for more.

◆ Knowing your negative attributes, or evil, eventually leads you to know the Creator.

◆ The desire for more worldly things can lead to greater emptiness, which leads to a desire for spirituality.

◆ The inability to achieve complete satisfaction through worldly desires opens the desire for spirituality, the Kabbalist's "point in the heart."

◆ Intention is the force that drives the outcome of actions, the aim behind the act.

Chapter 5

Debunking the Myths

In This Chapter

- ◆ Kabbalah is not a religion
- ◆ Kabbalah is not restricted to a few
- ◆ Kabbalah is not magic
- ◆ Kabbalah is not a cult
- ◆ Kabbalah is not a New Age thing

There are many myths and beliefs, some quite old, about Kabbalah. Now that you have a better understanding of what Kabbalah is, what it provides, and how it works, let's look at some common misunderstandings. This chapter clarifies Kabbalah by addressing some of the incorrect ideas that people have about Kabbalah and showing what Kabbalah is *not*.

Myth: Kabbalah Is a Religion

This is a common misunderstanding, and one worth addressing from the start. The wisdom of Kabbalah is related to no other religion or belief. It does not deal with meditations, prophecies, questions of religion, or even one's mental state. Religions, however, are combinations of rituals designed by humans to support them in their earthly existence. While religions such as Judaism and Christianity have similar concepts of the Upper World (heaven, the afterlife, etc.), much of religion teaches how humans should exist in this temporal world.

Kabbalah, however, is better thought of as a science, not a religion. As such, Kabbalah studies and provides a way of understanding of the essential core of humanity, the Higher World, the entire universe, and the Creator. The outcome of that study is the discovery that humankind wishes to become like the Creator. The wisdom of Kabbalah is the science of the system of creation and its management.

Kabbalah teaches how anyone can attain the revelation of the system of creation. Every soul, every person must ultimately attain the complete sensation of all creation, and not just the small part you perceive with your five senses. Kabbalah isn't so much about worshipping a deity or adhering to a belief system, as religions tend to be, but rather moving toward bonding with the rest of creation in the fullest sense of the word.

One of the key differences between Kabbalah and religion is that a Kabbalist takes an active approach, and a religious individual takes a passive one. In other words, a religious person prays to ask of the Creator for benefits. For instance, if I am sick, I will pray for the Creator to grant me health. A Kabbalist, however, prays to the Creator asking for correction, in most cases totally ignoring one's personal health. Such a person says to Him, "Change me," rather than "Change how you are treating me."

Another misconception is that Kabbalah is a "Jewish thing." In fact, the roots of Kabbalah are not in Judaism, they reach far back into the days of Babylon, before the birth of Judaism. Kabbalah began some 5,000 years ago in Mesopotamia (today's Iraq) in the town of Babylon. Judaism as we know it started only after the ruin of the second temple, about 2,000 years ago. Kabbalists maintain that Moses was given the 613 laws of the Kabbalah, a set of spiritual actions that one performs internally. When all 613 actions are performed, one reaches the complete bonding we've just mentioned.

Judaism, on the other hand, is a collection of religious rules that dictate how to conduct oneself in this temporal, physical world. Kabbalah teaches something entirely different from what you must know in this world, such as how to provide for your livelihood,

> ### On Track
>
> A religious person believes that a superior force that governs him or her determines all the laws that an individual must follow. Kabbalah is different, in that it adds the opportunity to feel the Creator directly. It is indifferent to whether one keeps religious laws because its only concern is our internal contact with the Creator.

how to behave, how to dress, or how to raise a family. As previously mentioned, Kabbalah is concerned with the Upper World; this world and our physical bodies serve merely as a stepping stone to attainment of the Upper World. So we see that Kabbalah really is not Judaism and does not even share the same concerns.

In fact, Kabbalah can be seen as *opposed* to religious practices. The wisdom of Kabbalah naturally directs you toward inner reflection and transformation, which alienates you from performing rituals and following any religious injunctions. That is why religions tend to oppose Kabbalah.

Myth: You Have to Be 40, Male, and Married

It's true that in the past you had to be at least 40, male, and married to study Kabbalah. But that was in the distant past. The Ari, Rabbi Isaac Luria, opened Kabbalah study to everyone beginning in the sixteenth century.

As we'll explain more fully in the next chapter, the Ari determined that from his generation onward, the Kabbalah would be permitted to all: men, women, and children. All that is required is a desire and passion for spirituality and a search for the meaning of life. Those are now the only testimonies to your readiness to study the wisdom of Kabbalah. Although the Ari instructed his loyal student, Chaim Vital, to keep the knowledge to himself, he did refer to his generation as the last generation, meaning the last generation of corruption and the first in the correction period.

Kab-Trivia

A famous story about the Ari's students demonstrates just how ripe the Ari believed the time was. One day he said to his students, "If we all go to Jerusalem [they were in a different city then], we will bring end of correction, and reach the highest degree. We need only do it together." Alas, most people couldn't come: one had a sick child, another couldn't come to terms with his wife and she wouldn't let him go, and another just didn't have the energy for such a long walk. They stayed in their town, and the end of correction stayed away from us. But the Ari believed that it was possible.

Myth: Kabbalah Is All About Magic

It is a common mistake for people to think that Kabbalah deals with fortune telling, revelations of the past, and the study of the present. The definition of Kabbalah, as we have written in chapter two, is the revelation of the Creator to people in this world today, not after death. Perhaps some draw this parallel as a result of the perception of secrecy that surrounds Kabbalah.

Either way, Kabbalah has no connection to magic. In fact, Kabbalah forbids fortune telling or any attempt to find out about the destiny of the physical body. The body is temporary, negligible, and, thus, insignificant. It is not worthy of attention beyond the question of how it serves the soul.

Karma in Kabbalah?

Karma, a concept from Hinduism, is based on the principle of cosmic retribution, that good deeds will be rewarded and bad deeds will be punished. In simple terms, karma is the sum total of a person's actions and deeds that determines a person's destiny. Because this belief deals with life in this world and ignores the Upper World, it has no use for Kabbalists.

The Evil Eye

Kabbalists may not believe in karma, *per se*, but they do recognize that humans can have direct influences on one another's well-being. They use the term "evil eye" to convey this idea of psychological harm transferred between people. Kabbalists believe that every person affects others with one's internal force. It is a psychological phenomenon that exists as an influence of every body, whether still, vegetative, animate, or human, on one another, and it is called (by people) "spiritual influence." However, it is not a spiritual influence, but an energetic influence. In people, it is a very powerful influence because the desire of one person affects others.

Myth: Kabbalah Is a Cult

Cult, according to American Heritage Dictionary, is from the Latin *cultus*, which means "worship" and derives from the past participle of *colere*, "to cultivate." In our times, however, *cult* has taken on the negative connotation of, again according to American Heritage Dictionary, "a religion or religious sect generally considered to be extremist or false, with its followers often living in an unconventional manner under the guidance of an authoritarian, charismatic leader."

There may be many spiritual groups in the world that practice various ceremonies that are seemingly related to Kabbalah. They are not, however, related to Kabbalah whatsoever. Kabbalah does not engage in ceremonies or rituals, nor does it have the element of worship present in the Latin meaning of the word *cult*. Therefore, Kabbalah is not a cult. It is, rather, a way of understanding our human and spiritual natures.

Keep in mind that in the quest for spiritual fulfillment, some people have cherry-picked elements of Kabbalah and incorporated them into their evolving belief system. One person may believe that he or she is closer to the truth, to the Source, and to eternity, but it is all an illusion from the Kabbalah point of view. These systems of belief tend to rely on the guidance of an individual or a close-knit group.

Red Alert

It is still often believed that in order to unite with the Creator, one must annul or cancel one's physical self. Kabbalah states very clearly that all you need to change is the intention of your actions, not the actions themselves. The more obsessed you become about physical actions that "cleanse" your soul, the more off track you are. You need not live like an ascetic to practice Kabbalah; just get your intentions right.

Indeed, every religion relies on a certain prophet, a person who was connected with spirituality and circulated his knowledge among people. Everything, whether Judaism or any other religion, begins with a person who reveals the sublime truth, the Creator appears before the prophet, the founder. Kabbalistic books, on the other hand, describe what a person who feels this world and the upper-spiritual world at the same time experiences. The author describes his feelings of a world that others do not feel, thus opening that world for others to understand and follow on their own.

This is why a Kabbalist teacher does not attach the students to him or herself. Instead, a Kabbalist shows you the book, the group, and tells you to study. You will discover the Creator within you. In Kabbalah, a prophet is not a person, it's a degree that exists within each of us, and all the teacher does is to help us find it in ourselves.

Kabbalah understands that we are human, with all the attendant frailties and strengths that suggests. However, it also reminds us that we have the ability to transcend every-day reality and get in touch with our spiritual nature as well. In other words, it helps us take full advantage of our humanity to the benefit of all.

The wisdom of Kabbalah, therefore, is a method to attain the Creator that is open to all, much like today's "open source software" is open for all to use and modify to meet their needs. Kabbalah allows any person to come by him or herself, without any mediators, to a spiritual contact with the Creator.

> **On Track**
>
> Here's a good question to ask yourself: what would you think of a person who came up to you and said, "You can't use, find, talk to or otherwise communicate with the Creator. The Creator is a trademark, and I have the copyright"?

In the books of Kabbalah, people who have attained spiritual perception describe the process they went through, step by step, so that readers may follow them and reach their attainments by themselves. Indeed, there is a special force in the books of Kabbalah: any person who studies those books under the right guidance can attain the spiritual degree of the author. Your spiritual connection with the Creator is based on your own discovery of Him, not on the leadership of the charismatic cultist.

Myth: Kabbalah Is a New Age Thing

These days, many people rush to use so-called "New Age" techniques, trying to change themselves, their lives, and their destinies. Popularized by the media beginning in the 1980s, the term *New Age* came to mean anything spiritual and out of the realm of traditional Western religion. Everything from prayer, meditation, ancient healing practices, the energetic power of crystals, Eastern religious concepts, and miracles and phenomena Western science cannot explain fall under the term.

Kabbalah as a New Age phenomenon was a natural. Like New Age practices, Kabbalah deals with spiritual concerns. New Age thinking, however, stresses taking an individual path in searching for spirituality, encouraging a kind of mix-and-match belief system.

Although Kabbalah is based on the individual, the study of Kabbalah is a rigorous, prescribed method that leaves little room for flexibility. Kabbalah is not a do-your-own-thing affair. Nor is there anything "new" about it, as Kabbalah has been around for more than 5,000 years.

No Protection from Harm

Kabbalah has nothing to do with any New Age or Old Age spirituality, sorcery, or self-help psychology. Kabbalah is not stones, or fortune telling, or holy water, or cards, or astrology. It provides no protection from outside forces, seen or unseen. Moreover, Kabbalah states that there are no outside forces at all, only the world we feel and build within.

New Age spirituality is only a collection of psychological phenomena from the vantage point of Kabbalah. As long as one does not think that this is the real spirituality and stops one's search right there and then, there is no harm in any of these practices nor from their teachers. There is no harm in one person seeing or experiencing more than others. For example, the Bedouin tribesmen, who live in the desert, can see much farther than ordinary people can, and gain far more knowledge from what they see. They can look at a cloud and know of something that is going on many miles away from them, just as an animal can feel the death of its mate a few days ahead of time. But this is not spirituality, simply because this is not altruism. It isn't egoism either, it's just a characteristic that certain people possess.

> **Word of Heart** _____
>
> Since people did not possess the right key to the secret, the thirst for knowledge here eventually led to vanities and superstition of all kinds, from which ultimately developed a kind of Vulgar Cabbala, which lies far away from the true one, as well as diverse fantastic theories under the false name of magic; the books are teeming with those.
>
> —From *Hauptschriften zur Grundlegung der Philosophie* by Gottfried Wilhelm Leibnitz (1646–1716), German philosopher, mathematician, and political adviser

There is also no protection from harm, including the much-heralded Kabbalistic evil eye. The red string, as with other ornaments (such as *Hamsa*, a palm necklace, and a horse's shoe) that people wear or hang on their walls to ward off the evil eye or negative energy really have no relation to the spirituality of the Upper World described by Kabbalah. These techniques help only because they can awaken in you some inner confidence. They may activate in you a psychological force that provides comfort, even healing. But it is more of a psychological sensation, not the true spiritual attainment of Kabbalah.

These lucky charms are more like a placebo medicine, and placebo medicines can cure patients simply because the patient believes in their power. People who believe in the healing and protection of all the psychological and mystical elements of the New Age ascribe great powers to them and consequently affect themselves. To the Kabbalist, however, there is a difference between influence that is purely psychological and a true influence on life.

The Real Protection in Kabbalah

People have always searched for any possible way to end the misery of mankind and society. They look to the gods and religion. They look to science and technology.

They have also gained experience and become convinced that the progress of science and technology, including medical technology, does not deliver us from pain and torment, and ultimately does not make us happy human beings.

Along with the explosion in technology, courses in astrology and the supernatural are opening everywhere around us, even in universities. Books about mysticism abound on the shelves of bookstores; horoscopes, prophecies, and clairvoyants are found in every form of the media.

If you look back to the "merry" days of Babylon, where mysticism, charms, cards, and fortune telling thrived, you will find surprising similarities to our society in the twenty-first century. If we remember that Kabbalah started with this atmosphere in the background, it will not surprise you to see that now the time has come for Kabbalah to emerge again. After all, Abraham's father was an idol builder and worshiper, and so was young Abraham himself, until he began to ask, "Who put the stars up in the sky?"

The Zohar, one of the primary books of Kabbalah, predicted this time as a necessary phase in the collective development of humanity. Kabbalah is a completely pure, clear, and internal attainment of the Upper Worlds, nothing else. This attainment does not manifest externally, nor can it be sensed. No external tools or means are needed for it. What one needs are the books that simply describe, in real terms understandable for ordinary people …

- The structure of these worlds.

- How they interrelate.

- How they interact with our world.

- How a person affects these worlds and is affected by them.

Therein lies the unique "protection" of the books of Kabbalah. They describe things an ordinary person cannot feel, though they are attainable. A Kabbalist is not just a person who feels the Upper World; he or she is someone who can describe his or her emotions to him or herself in a clear language. A Kabbalist teacher, however, must also be able to clearly describe these emotions to others, so they, too, can understand them. Studying books written by Kabbalist teachers, such as Yehuda Ashlag and the Ari, allows you to nurture the latent senses inside you, the ones with which you can feel the Upper World.

This is Kabbalah.

The Least You Need to Know

◆ Kabbalah is a science, not a religion. There is no central figure, as in most religions, and no ceremonies or rituals.

◆ The study of Kabbalah is open to all who seek their purpose and the meaning of life, regardless of age, sex, or religion. There are no prerequisites.

◆ Elements of Kabbalah have been adopted by many movements over the years, but these movements tend to be concerned with psychological phenomena, not with spiritual attainment, which is the essence of Kabbalah.

◆ Kabbalah is solely concerned with describing the Upper Worlds of the Creator and provides a method for individual sensation and attainment of the Upper World.

Chapter 6

The Condensed History of Kabbalah

In This Chapter

- The creation of life, the universe, and everything
- Adam and *The Angel of God's Secret*
- Abraham and *The Book of Creation*
- Moses and *The Torah*
- Shimon Bar Yochai and *The Book of Zohar*
- The Ari and *The Tree of Life* bring Kabbalah to the masses

The real stuff in Kabbalah lies beyond the physical existence of the universe, but it all has a corresponding part in the physical universe. In this chapter, you learn about the entire history of Kabbalah, from its first appearance nearly 6,000 years ago to the foundation of modern study.

From the Beginning of Creation to Adam

The history of Kabbalah corresponds to the history of creation. The Thought of Creation caused creation to happen. The Thought of Creation is called the

Root Phase or Phase Zero. Phase Zero generated four more phases, which then generated a Root World, which is still a spiritual world, not a physical one. The Root World, called *Adam Kadmon* (The Primeval Man), generated four more worlds, called *Atzilut, Beria, Yetzira,* and *Assiya.* Those, too, are spiritual worlds, not physical ones.

At the bottom of *Assiya* was a black point, called "the point of This World," which materialized into what you and I know as "the universe." Within our universe there is a galaxy, called the Milky Way, and in that galaxy there is a tiny planet called Earth.

Earth's evolution from fiery lava to cool seas to the upheaval of mountains and the break-up of landmass into the continents continued for many millions of years. It is the physical parallel of the spiritual Root Phase. When Earth cooled, vegetative life began and reigned the globe for several millions years. This period was not nearly as long as Earth's inanimate period, though it did stretch over many millions of years.

Life on Earth continued to evolve until, at some point, the first animals appeared. Just like the vegetative and the mineral phases, the animals' reign of the planet was much shorter than that of their vegetative predecessors.

The last significant animal to evolve was, you guessed it, man. Humans first appeared several tens of thousands of years ago. They first lived like animals, finding whatever food was available.

Gradually, humans evolved and became the first animal to ask about the origin of their own existence. The name of the first person to ask where he came from was Adam. Yes, *that* Adam. This is why Adam is considered by Kabbalists as the first person to reach spirituality, to discover the source of his own existence—and yours, too.

If you look back at this short history of evolution, you will notice that it consists of five phases before a major change occurs. Kabbalists describe five phases, five spiritual worlds, and five stages in the physical world: inanimate, vegetative, animate, human, and spiritual.

On Track

When we talk about moving from inanimate to vegetative, to animate, and to human, we automatically think of Darwin, or of the explanation of creation that suits our belief system. But you should know that according to Kabbalah, the only reason for the appearance of the next step of creation—or of anything else, for that matter—is the completion of the previous step. When a phase is completed, the very end of the phase is the incentive for the appearance of the next stage in line.

Adam

Adam, partner of Eve and temporary resident of the Garden of Eden, stands for yet another phase in evolution: the spiritual phase. In Kabbalah, Adam is considered the Root Phase of human spirituality. This is why he is called *Adam ha Rishon*, The First Man.

Adam was also the first person to write a Kabbalah book, *The Angel of God's Secret* (*Hamalaach Raziel*), a small book that included a few drawings and tables. (It should be noted that even though Kabbalists ascribe this work to Adam, there is no written proof that he is indeed the author.) The name *Hamalaach Raziel* comes from the Hebrew words *Malaach* (angel), *Raz* (secret), and *El* (God). Thus, *Hamalaach Raziel* reveals to us the secrets of the Creator.

It's important to remember that Kabbalah doesn't stem from ancient texts or rituals; it comes from humankind's natural curiosity and desire to know more about this world and the world beyond. It acknowledges that a desire to understand our nature is part of our nature. Something's going on, and we seek to know what it is.

The Angel of God's Secret

The Kabbalistic tradition has it that Adam wrote *The Angel of God's Secret* more than 5,767 years ago in a language that is difficult for us to understand. Adam presented it allegorically, using metaphors. He tells us how he sensed that he lived in two worlds, the earthly and the spiritual. He felt the entire Upper Existence, but he could not describe it in a manner we can relate to today. He attained it in his feelings and thus pictured it the best way he could.

Red Alert _____

Kabbalah books are packed with vivid descriptions of anything from two people walking and talking to their donkey driver to flying towers. As you would expect in such a setting, angels play a major role. However, we can be easily misled into thinking that there are worlds where these things happen on a physical level. They do not. All the stories in Kabbalah describe one's connection to the Creator, one's level of altruism, and one's efforts to become whole. This is why it is so important to study with a teacher who can provide the correct explanations, which bring you "down to Earth."

Adam describes the general forces called "angels" that govern the universe and consist of particular lower-level forces, "subangels," if you will. He explains the structure of these forces, their mutual interaction, and the way they act upon and influence our world.

Adam, who was also the first soul, tells about the evolution and descent of all souls. He writes about the procreation of souls that come from him: the souls of his children, grandchildren, and great-grandchildren. He says that the entirety of humanity would stem from him (talk about a big dinner table!).

If you open the book, it is evident that the author is not an uncivilized, uneducated mammoth hunter. He was a Kabbalist of a very high degree who discovered the fundamental secrets of creation in his spiritual journey. He studied the Upper World, where our soul roams prior to its descent to Earth when we are born and where the soul returns after one's death. Adam tells us how these souls will regroup into one soul, in a much higher degree than our own, and build what we call "man," of which we are but fragments. More on how that works in Chapter 9.

You can buy a version of *The Angel of God's Secret* today. Search for "Raziel" on Amazon.com for some choices.

The First Point in the Heart

Humans have existed for tens of thousands of years. Some 5,700 years ago, a point of aspiration to reach the Divine, to come to its original state, emerged in humans. It is called a point in the heart. A heart is all our desires, and a point in the heart is an aspiration to a higher state. That is why Adam, who lived at that time, wrote *The Angel of God's Secret.* Then these aspirations began to develop.

Abraham

Abraham was the second Kabbalist, 20 generations after Adam. Kabbalists consider the patriarch Abraham to be the first known Kabbalist and the first to conduct organized Kabbalah studies. He saw the wonders of human existence and asked questions of the Creator, and the Upper Worlds were revealed to him.

Abraham passed the knowledge and the method he used to acquire the Upper Worlds to the generations following him. In this way, Kabbalah was transferred from teacher to student for many centuries. Each Kabbalist added his unique experience and personality to this body of accumulated knowledge.

Abraham lived in Mesopotamia and, as all inhabitants there did, he worshiped the sun, the moon, the stones, and the trees, until one day he began to wonder: How is the world created? Why does everything "spin" around us? Why is there a flow of life? What does life mean? Indeed, there must be some pattern in this flow, he thought, a beginning, end, cause, and effect. There must be a force that sets everything in motion! Abraham asked himself those questions and, eventually, through the picture of our world, felt and saw the same as Adam did, that he lived in two worlds at once, the spiritual and the material.

And, yes, these are all the very same questions that have begun to bring Kabbalah to the fore in today's society.

Like Kabbalists after him, Abraham wrote about his discoveries. His book, *The Book of Creation (Sefer Yetzira)*, is the next important text after *The Angel of God's Secret*. Unlike longer Kabbalah books, *The Book of Creation* has only several dozen pages.

Abraham's purpose in writing his book was not to teach attainment of the Upper World, but only to mark out a few principal laws that he discovered about the spiritual world, like an outline. Kabbalists consider it a difficult book to study correctly, because it was written for people who lived thousands of years ago. In those days, souls of people were not as coarse as they are today, and they could understand the text, even though it is written very succinctly. Today we need a much more detailed text to be able to relate to it. This is why Kabbalist Yehuda Ashlag wrote his commentaries on the ancient texts of *The Book of Zohar* and *The Tree of Life*. The language is ancient and esoteric, and invites arguments over what it means.

The Book of Creation explains how each person receives a special force from above. The force determines what will happen to it in this world and what will finally become of it. The short answer, so you don't have to worry about whether you'll ever be able to read it, is that all of humanity will come under the influence of the Upper Forces. If you do want to give reading it a try, you'll find a copy for sale at mysefer.com or Amazon.com.

 Kab-Trivia

Abraham is known as "the father of three faiths" for his centrality in the histories of Islam, Judaism, and Christianity.

When Abraham discovered spirituality, he immediately started disseminating his knowledge. This is why it is written that he would sit at his tent door and invite people in. He taught them what he had learned of the spiritual. These students that Abraham would invite into his tent became the first study group in the history of Kabbalah.

Moses

The name *Moshe* (Moses) comes from the Hebrew word *Moshech* (pulling), as in pulling out of this world. Moses was different than other Kabbalists, in that alongside his revelations, he was ordered to publicize it to humankind in writing and establish learning centers.

Moses had 70 disciples, and Yehoshua Ben Nun (Joshua, the son of Nun) was the one who inherited from him. Moses did more than research the Upper World. He dealt with the practical realization of his spiritual attainment in our world, such as the exodus from Egypt. With the wisdom he acquired and the Upper Forces he received from above, he brought the people of Israel out of exile.

His next task built on the movement of the people out of Egypt. This task was to write a book with which any person could "conquer" the Upper World. They could exit Egypt in the spirit and stop worshiping idols, objects, the sun, and other false gods. It would enable them to obtain entrance to the *spiritual* Israel—*Atzilut*, a world of eternity and wholeness. It is a situation that one attains inwardly, beyond the boundaries of time and space.

Moses created a method in his book, *The Torah* (Pentateuch), from the word *Ohr* (Light). It contains instructions on how to use the Light as a means to enter the spiritual world. All people can uncover the entire picture of creation, though they may experience just a tiny fraction of it. They can reach the desired outcome and reach the final goal that Moses wanted to attain. That is what a person who studies by the method that Moses developed gradually comes to.

Moses' method from *The Torah*, adapted to today's souls, allows anyone to attain Moses' degree of spirituality. One learns to exit this world and enter the Upper World and the entire creation.

Shimon Bar Yochai

The Book of Zohar, the next major work in Kabbalah and perhaps the most famous, was written by Rabbi Shimon Bar Yochai, "the Rashbi," around the year 150 C.E. He was a pupil of Rabbi Akiva (40 C.E.–135 C.E.), famed first and foremost for his maxim: love thy friend as thyself.

Rabbi Akiva did not, however, live a similar fate. He and several of his disciples were tortured and killed by the Romans, who felt threatened by his teaching of the Kabbalah. They flayed his skin and stripped his bones with an iron scraper (like today's currycomb) used for cleaning their horses.

Before that, a plague killed almost all of Rabbi Akiva's 24,000 students except a handful, among which was Rabbi Shimon Bar-Yochai. Kabbalists saw this plague as a result of their growing egoism, which led them to unfounded hatred. This was the opposite of their teacher's rule of "love thy friend as thyself."

Following the death of Rabbi Akiva's 24,000 disciples, the Rashbi was authorized by Rabbi Akiva and Rabbi Yehuda Ben Baba to teach future generations the Kabbalah as it had been taught to him. It was felt that only those who hadn't fallen into this unfounded hatred survived and they wrote the next great chapter in Kabbalah, *The Book of Zohar.*

Kab-Trivia

Academics and Kabbalists differ on the question of where and when *The Book of Zohar* was written. Kabbalists trace *The Zohar* back to Rabbi Shimon and the academia to Rabbi Moshe de Leon of thirteenth-century Spain. Yehuda Ashlag, a.k.a. Baal HaSulam, clearly states that *The Zohar* was written from the highest possible spiritual degree. According to Ashlag, only one as high as Rabbi Shimon could have written it, and not a Kabbalist at the degree of Moshe De Leon, even though he is a respected Kabbalist. Baal HaSulam even said that *The Zohar* is written from such a high degree that it wouldn't surprise him to discover that Moses himself wrote it.

In the Cave

What would you bring with you if you were stuck in a cave for 13 years? If you said a good book, you have something in common with Rabbi Shimon Bar Yochai and his son Elazar.

Rashbi and four others were the only ones to survive the plague and the wrath of the Romans, who killed their teacher. Following the capture and imprisonment of Rabbi Akiva, Rashbi escaped with his son to a cave for 13 years. They emerged with *The Book of Zohar,* a crystallized method for studying Kabbalah and achieving spirituality.

In the cave, Rashbi reached the highest level a person can achieve during one's life in this world. *The Zohar* tells us that Eliyahu the Prophet himself came to teach him, which is a Kabbalist's way of saying that Rashbi reached the highest possible spiritual level in Kabbalah.

Kab-Trivia

The Zohar disappeared for hundreds of years until it was discovered by Arabs, who used its pages as paper to prepare fish for the market. It was then discovered by a hungry Kabbalist.

Kab-Trivia

The Zohar states that it is written for a time when *chutzpah* (impudence) mounts and the face of the generation is as the face of a dog. When prominent Kabbalists such as the Vilna Gaon, Baal HaSulam, and others looked into the future, they declared the present generation as the one that *The Zohar* referred to. Clearly, they didn't mean it as a compliment.

Rashbi did not write *The Zohar* himself; he dictated the book to Rabbi Aba. Aba rewrote *The Zohar* in such a way that only those who are worthy of understanding would be able to do so. Rashbi was the greatest Kabbalist of his generation. He wrote and interpreted many Kabbalistic subjects that were published and are well known to this day.

The story of the creation of *The Zohar*, which roughly means "splendor," is colorful and interesting, if somewhat "fishy." After its writing, when Rabbi Shimon and his pupils saw that their generation wasn't ready for its content, they hid it until the time was ripe and the people were ready. Many prominent Kabbalists say that this time is our time, and indeed *The Zohar* is more in demand today than ever before.

The Zohar Reemerges

The book was discovered earlier, however, purely by accident. It fell into the hands of a Kabbalist, Moshe De Leon, who kept it and studied it in secret. When he died, his wife sold the book because she had to make ends meet with her husband gone, and he probably didn't tell her about its importance. This is why the writing of *The Zohar* is often ascribed to Moshe De Leon.

Moshe De Leon lived in thirteenth-century Spain, and he's known today primarily because many scholars believe that he actually wrote *The Zohar*. There are, in fact, many views on how *The Zohar* was written, including one that argues that the book was written by a group of Kabbalists at different times. Moshe De Leon himself, by the way, never claimed to have written it, but said its author was Rashbi. Whatever the case may be, all agree that Moshe De Leon possessed the book.

The Zohar was written on the eve of a spiritual exile and predicts a new dawn of spiritual attainment, beginning at the end of the twentieth century (starting from 1995). Even though some mystery surrounds the actual origins of the text, you can now see why *The Zohar* remains one of the most important writings in Kabbalah.

Rabbi Yitzhak Luria ("The Ari")

The second period of the development of Kabbalah is extremely important to the Kabbalah of our generation. This is the period of the Ari, Rabbi Isaac Luria, who created the transition between the two methods of Kabbalah study. The Ari proclaimed the start of a period of open mass study of Kabbalah.

Until the arrival of the Ari, the predominant study method was that of the Ramak (Rabbi Moshe Cordovero) of Safed. It was a more emotional method, where a Kabbalist simply experienced the Upper World, almost intuitively.

When the Ari came to Safed, however, it was clear that times had changed. It was the middle of the 1500s, and the world was moving toward the age of science and industry. The Ari realized that Kabbalah study required a new and more systematic method to meet the terms of a new and more scientific era. Not all agreed so enthusiastically, but the Ramak himself, by then an old and revered Kabbalist, abandoned his own method and sat down to learn the new way from the new teacher, the Ari. Many brows were raised at this step, but the 36-year-old Ari knew what the generation needed, and the Ramak acknowledged it.

Lurianic Kabbalah: A Systematic Order

Rabbi Luria was born in Jerusalem in 1534. A child when his father died, his mother took him to Egypt, where he grew up in his uncle's home. During his life in Egypt, he made his living in commerce but devoted most of his time to studying Kabbalah. Legend has it that he spent 7 years in isolation on the island of Roda, on the Nile, where he studied *The Zohar*, books by the first Kabbalists, and writings by the Ramak.

The Ari arrived in Safed, Israel, in 1570. Despite his youth, he immediately started teaching Kabbalah. His greatness was soon recognized; wise men came to study with him, and he became famous. For a year and a half, his disciple, Rabbi Chaim Vital, committed to paper the answers to many of the questions that arose during his studies.

The Ari's important works include *The Tree of Life*, *Mavo She'arim* (*The Entrance to the Gates*), *Sha'ar HaKavanot* (*The Gateway of Intentions*), and *Sha'ar HaGilgulim* (*The Gateway of Reincarnation*), all of which explain the creation of the world. The unique part of the Ari's method is its systematic order, which was suitable for the approaching era of the scientific and industrial revolution.

Today, his method, called Lurianic Kabbalah, is the leading study method of Kabbalah, because it is adapted to the souls of today's humanity.

The Ari died in 1572, still a young man. His writings were buried along with him, according to his last wish, in order not to reveal his doctrine before the time was ripe.

Baal Shem Tov Continues to Spread the Word

The spread of Kabbalah that began with its emergence from the cave through the discovery of *The Zohar* and the arrival of the Ari, continued with the Baal Shem Tov. Born in 1698, Yisrael Ben Eliezer, who became known as the Baal Shem Tov (The Master of the Good Name), was central in the spread of Kabbalah to a wider audience.

With that in mind, he founded *admorut*, an institution of the Jewish society in which each community had its own Kabbalist leader. Those leaders chose "the worthy ones" to study Kabbalah, as a way to groom the future generations of Kabbalists who would at once study the mechanisms and laws of the Upper Worlds and become spiritual leaders in their communities.

The writings of Kabbalah shed a unique light on history and can be said to comprise a history of the Light of the Creator. During most of this time, however, Kabbalah was hidden, studied in the dark, away from the public eye. It was a private affair and, for the most part, even secretive.

With the prophecies of *The Zohar* and the work of the Ari, Kabbalah was meant to shed its light on all. The journey of how Kabbalah sheds its light publicly continues with the work of Rabbi Yehuda Ashlag, who, as the next chapter shows, opened the study of Kabbalah to more people than ever.

The Least You Need to Know

- The Creation according to Kabbalah consists of five phases.
- Adam, the first Kabbalist, authored the book *The Angel of God's Secret*.
- Abraham started the first "Kabbalah groups" through his teaching.
- Moses is the force that pulls us out of egoism and into spirituality.
- *The Zohar*, one of the seminal books in Kabbalah, predicted that the desire for spirituality would dawn in our generation.
- The Ari, Rabbi Isaac Luria, created the scientific method of teaching Kabbalah that is the predominant teaching method today.

Chapter 7

Kabbalah Revealed

In This Chapter

◆ The spiritual roots of Kabbalah

◆ Yehuda Ashlag: a man with a mission

◆ The development of Kabbalah wisdom over the ages

◆ The legacy of Kabbalah from the past to the present

When Kabbalah first started, it was in demand by only a few, who searched for the meaning of their lives. These first Kabbalists continued to develop it through the generations, adapted it to the changing times and made it more scientific, as our generation demands. This chapter introduces the way Kabbalistic texts work and how they have developed over the centuries so that their wisdom is more available and accessible to everyone.

In particular, this chapter discusses the work of the most "universal" of all Kabbalists: Yehuda Ashlag. It was Ashlag who clearly stated that Kabbalah study is open for all: that Kabbalah can be disclosed, distributed, and taught to everyone, without any consideration of age, sex, or religion.

It could be argued that this chapter is biased and does not present the Kabbalists evenly. That would be right! This is done to bypass "learning for the sake of learning," and to tell you just what Kabbalah lessons can do for you. In that way, Yehuda Ashlag is the ultimate "What's in it for me?" Kabbalist.

The Essence of the Wisdom of Kabbalah

The task of Kabbalah is to create a method for individuals to become spiritually fulfilled. As you know by now, *Kabbalah* handily means "reception." The meaning of life in this world is for a person to completely fill his or her spiritual desire.

According to Kabbalah, souls repeatedly come back to this world in people until their goal is reached. The spiritual goal is different from creative and intellectual aspirations, which are part of understandable but less evolved desires. As described in Chapter 4, the quest for spirituality is the final stage of human development. Kabbalah guides and offers a path to spiritual fulfillment.

Spiritual Ice Cream

The method of Kabbalah provides never-ending enjoyment. Once fulfilled, mundane desires compel you to seek fulfillment again. So the first step in Kabbalah is to desire something on the spiritual level that can be fulfilled on the spiritual level because it is at the spiritual level where you can be continuously fulfilled.

Think of it like this. Earthly desires can be thought of as a need for ice cream: it tastes good and keeps you wanting more. Desire in the spiritual realm, on the other hand, is as if your enjoyment of the ice cream could produce more ice cream. By giving and receiving from the source of the Creator, the gap between desire and fulfillment is filled, allowing for continuous enjoyment.

> **On Track**
>
> The screen is the most important tool for a Kabbalist. With it, one avoids receiving the Light selfishly, and then chooses if and how much of it to receive for the Creator, because that's the only reception that produces real and lasting pleasure.

This state of the soul is achieved in Kabbalah and called a *Masach* (screen). The *Masach* separates possible continuous spiritual pleasure of the soul from the fleeting, earthly pleasures. The process of acquiring a *Masach* is, in simple terms, the subject of Kabbalah studies.

Kabbalah Communication

Kabbalist writers describe their experiences and offer recommendations so others can follow in their path. Kabbalistic books are accounts of their journeys into the Upper World, as suggested in Chapter 6.

Kabbalah books are also filled with drawings that illustrate spiritual concepts and events. It is important to remember that the shapes in the drawings are not real objects, but images used to explain *spiritual* states concerning your relationship with the Creator.

The languages of narrative and prophecy are often used. It is acknowledged that earthly words are problematic in dealing with spiritual issues, which is why the Language of the Branches, described in Chapter 10, is used in Kabbalah.

But Kabbalah books don't show you the whole picture. To really know what the spiritual worlds look and feel like, you have to experience them for yourself. Kabbalists think of themselves as tour guides whose job is to get you to a place and let you admire it for yourself. This is why, in texts that were written to teach, the descriptions you'll find are partial, displaying only what you need to know to get to spirituality yourself. Such "didactic" texts include *The Book of Zohar*, *The Tree of Life*, and *The Study of the Ten Sefirot*.

> **Red Alert** _____
>
> The use of mundane words in Kabbalah, like drinking, sitting, mating, and animal names, leads to false conceptions and erroneous conclusions because it makes us think of physical objects as having any spiritual merit. And they don't. They only *symbolize* spiritual states. Hence, Kabbalah forbids imagining a connection between the names used in our world and their spiritual roots. This is considered the grossest error in Kabbalah. (This is discussed in detail in Chapter 10.)

It makes no difference to a Kabbalist in which language a book about the Creator is written. Like a musician who hears music while reading the notes, a Kabbalist feels what the author describes while reading the words and illustrations.

The Life of the Party

The wisdom of Kabbalah is about spiritual roots coming down from above. When you think of roots, you might think of things that are underground, but not here. Roots in Kabbalah come from the source, which is outside this realm.

Picture roots growing in from the outside of a bubble. Because you are in the bubble, the area of creation, the roots come down to you. They can be thought of as colorful party streamers hanging from above.

The main goal of this wisdom is that the Creator will reveal his Godliness to his creatures (that's us). You should note that the roots appear by specific causes and fixed rules; they are not random. Their presence makes the party of life more interesting and developed. Actually, they *are* the life of the party, and the party itself. The people or sages who most understand this concept may be connected to the "life of the party," but everyone can enjoy it.

Kabbalah Commentaries

The spiritual topics of the Kabbalah do not occupy time or space. They are beyond this realm. The beginning of time was not a void, but everything was filled with a simple, boundless light. This is the setting for *The Tree of Life*, which is a Kabbalah creation story for the universe written by the Ari.

In this story, the Ari seeks to illuminate the nature of the Supreme Light, also called the Endless Light or, simply, the Creator. This light has always been shining, and the Creator had a desire to create the world and "emanate emanations" so that his deeds, names, and appellations would be known. He wanted to create something that could experience his perfection.

Because Kabbalists describe their internal experiences and understanding using metaphor and a language suitable for the souls of their time, succeeding Kabbalists have written interpretations to make the spiritual journey clearer and more accessible for us. This is why Rabbi Ashlag wrote a commentary on *The Tree of Life*, published in his major work *The Study of the Ten Sefirot*.

Rabbi Ashlag's commentary on *The Tree of Life* provides details on the stages, events, and forms of life's creation, originally written about by the Ari. Ashlag did a similar thing with Rashbi's *The Book of Zohar*, where he took Rashbi's abstruse text and clarified it in a commentary he called *HaSulam* (*The Ladder*). This is why Rabbi Yehuda Ashlag is also known as Baal HaSulam (Owner of the Ladder).

A Man with a Mission

Yehuda Ashlag spent much of his life studying and writing about important Kabbalah texts. Born in 1884 in Lodz, Poland, he absorbed written and oral law, and later became a judge and teacher in Warsaw. In 1921, he immigrated to Israel (then called

Palestine) with his family (including his first-born son, Baruch) and became the rabbi of *Givat Shaul* in Jerusalem. While writing many other important works, such as *The Study of the Ten Sefirot*, he also began *The Sulam Commentary on The Zohar* in 1943. He finished just 10 years later, in 1953. He died the following year and is buried in Jerusalem at the *Givat Shaul* cemetery.

He is the only writer in this time period who tackled a fully comprehensive and updated commentary of *The Zohar* and the writings of the Ari. These books, with the addition of Baruch's (Ashlag's son) essays, allow Kabbalists to study ancient texts in modern language and are thought of as indispensable tools for those who aspire to spirituality.

Kab-Trivia

Baal HaSulam didn't plan on becoming a famous rabbi and Kabbalist. He came to Palestine with a small group of students and planned to start a leather processing shop. He knew the smell of the chemicals for processing the leather would deter uninvited guests. They planned to work during the day and study at night. But when he arrived, the word of the arrival of the great orthodox judge from Warsaw quickly spread, the plans for a leather factory faded, and Ashlag became Baal HaSulam.

Kabbalah explains that one gains the knowledge of the Upper Worlds when the time is right. Having a solid interpretation of older, often very difficult-to-read texts makes studying Kabbalah and achieving its enlightenment easier and more direct. Rabbi Ashlag is a highly respected figure in Kabbalah because he is the medium who provides this service to others at what to Kabbalists is a special time in history.

Time to Act

The wisdom of Kabbalah seems to disappear and reappear at different times in history. Kabbalists explain that the wisdom waited until humankind ripened and became able to process its concepts and assist in their completion. Because this knowledge is coming to light, Rabbi Ashlag writes that we are living in a special time.

In his article "Time to Act," Rabbi Ashlag explains that before the printing press, when scribes were in vogue, no one would bother bending their back to copy a book with wild claims—it wouldn't be worth the time, expense, and candle wax. As bookmaking advanced, theories and connections to Kabbalah were enhanced by authors, which were easily published.

With many people trying to define it, an atmosphere of frivolity developed around Kabbalah. Therefore, Ashlag's goal in his writing was to reveal what he could of its true essence. He also urgently wanted to make people understand that their leisure time is *not* sufficient to study the subject. To get a full understanding of Kabbalah, therefore, read *The Complete Idiot's Guide to Kabbalah* twice.

In his introduction to *The Book of Zohar*, Ashlag says that he must write Kabbalah books because every generation has its own needs, and therefore its own books. Our generation, too, requires books that we can all understand. Since the books of the Ari were written hundreds of years ago, and *The Book of Zohar* was written almost 2,000 years ago, he has taken it on himself to interpret them for us. This way, we can come to know what these ancient Kabbalists knew, and experience the spiritual worlds for ourselves.

> **Red Alert** _____
>
> These days, Kabbalah has attained a kind of popularity and notoriety often ascribed to the latest fads. In an era when people are always looking for easy answers to hard questions, Kabbalah seems like the latest in a long line of such fads. And if that is the reason for your study, you will likely be disappointed for two reasons. It does not provide easy answers, and to approach it as the latest fad is to completely misunderstand what it's about. On the other hand, if you study it with an honest desire to learn how to access your spiritual nature, you're likely to be thoroughly satisfied by this study. However, even if you're looking for easy answers and something resonates here, that's all for the good as well.

Take Your Time or Make Time

But the spreading of Kabbalah is happening today not only as a result of the appearance of incorrect and inaccurate books. Ashlag explains, in his introduction to *The Book of Zohar* and in many of his essays, that the spreading of Kabbalah is a must today. He explains that now is the time that Prophet Jeremiah referred to when he said, "for they shall all know Me, from the least of them unto the greatest of them."

We can take our time and let it happen naturally, but Ashlag says that such a decision will cost us heavily, because we would be compelled to evolve into spirituality by nature itself. He says that the other option is to study what nature wants of us and do it. This, according to Ashlag, will not only prevent the suffering he was talking about, but will show us how to receive the pleasures that the Creator wants to give us. Ancient Kabbalists called these two choices "in due time or accelerating time," or "taking our time or making our time." (There's more on the urgency of our time in Part 4.)

The Creator Has Even Less

There is a beautiful story that Ashlag's wife once complained to him that all the other rabbis had thousands of students, and he had only six. "So how does Kabbalah help you if you have only six students?" his wife asked. Ashlag raised his eyes from the essay he was writing, took a sip from his teacup, looked at his wife, and quietly replied, "The Creator has even less."

Ashlag wanted to share his knowledge and experiences in Kabbalah with others, even if it was not commonly accepted or sought-after. He wasn't choosy in his means of dissemination, and wherever he could spread the word, he did. Today, study groups or individual online study, or both, are legitimate ways to develop a relationship with Kabbalah.

Ashlag himself might even say that today Kabbalah is the only way to develop a relationship with the Creator and achieve the goals of Kabbalah. The goals of Kabbalah are meant to manifest the goals of the Creator.

There is a reason why Kabbalah is thought of as a salmon swimming upstream rather than a fish going along with a school. Because we are pleasure-seeking creatures, the idea of giving isn't naturally appealing to us. It's hard to convince us that the real pleasures lie in the intention to give. It gets even more confusing that after we have managed to explain that to enjoy we need to want to give, we then say that to give to the Creator, you must receive from Him. However, time is on Kabbalah's side. The more people become frustrated with receiving satisfaction from mundane desires, the more open they will become to the ideas of Kabbalah.

Because Kabbalah finds answers in the Upper Worlds and knows that pleasure can't be found in the things on Earth, Kabbalists may be less likely to pursue material goals. They do participate in life but may have a different outlook on activities because the focus is on spiritual ascent and other worlds, and they use what happens there to positively affect our world.

Kabbalah has not always been as "in fashion" as it is these days. It can be thought of, however, like an old outfit that has been tucked away, coming back as needed. Unlike that stuffy outfit in your closet, each time it comes back, it is specially designed to fit the present time and place, and is ready to hit the green.

Kabbalists believe now is a great time for tee-off. People's lifestyles and dissatisfaction with the answers society offers them on spiritual matters is making it attractive.

Two Monumental Works

To fully appreciate the influence and legacy of Rabbi Ashlag, it's worth reviewing the history of Kabbalistic writing and study described in Chapter 6, particularly *The Zohar* and the teachings of the Ari. Rabbi Yehuda Ashlag is the recognized spiritual leader for this era because of his comprehensive and updated commentary on those major Kabbalistic works.

His two master works are *The Sulam Commentary on The Book of Zohar* (a book that needs a commentary because it was written 2,000 years ago, with symbols we cannot understand today) and *The Study of the Ten Sefirot*. Don't let it fool you that there are only *10 Sefirot*—there are six volumes and 2,000 pages of details included. Moses is a figure in Kabbalah but perhaps never held a conference with Kabbalists on how to keep text as short as his commandment project.

The Sulam Commentary on The Book of Zohar

The Sulam Commentary on The Book of Zohar is a 21-volume commentary on *The Zohar*. It's a modern interpretation of *The Zohar* and provides a method for applying the book's knowledge to contemporary people's understanding.

Rabbi Ashlag first translated each item from Aramaic, the language in which *The Zohar* is written, to Hebrew; even fewer people speak Aramaic than those who speak Hebrew. Below the translation he added his commentary on the text, taking each phrase in *The Zohar* and explaining its spiritual meaning.

Rabbi Ashlag's commentary shows that the picturesque descriptions of people crying, hugging, eating, and walking actually speak of spiritual processes that *all* of us will experience. To make sure we understand *The Zohar* in the spiritual sense, and not as a narrative of physical events, Rabbi Ashlag added five introductions to *The Zohar*: introduction to *The Book of Zohar*, preface to *The Book of Zohar*, preamble to *the Wisdom of Kabbalah*, preamble to *The Sulam Commentary*, and a general preamble. All but the last are available on the Internet at www.kabbalah.info.

The method he outlines lays the foundation to correct understanding of the structure and workings of the Upper Worlds. From here, you learn how to relate to Kabbalist texts, and how to work with your desire in the most efficient manner to bring you to spirituality. These introductions empower you to improve and fulfill yourself.

Rabbi Ashlag's method is universal. The "ladder" (or *Sulam*) he built in his writings offers a path that can be followed for achieving spirituality. He says that no one should be intimidated by studying Kabbalah. Many Kabbalists feel that studying according to the writings of Rabbi Ashlag allow for true correction and progress.

The Study of the Ten Sefirot

The Study of the Ten Sefirot, all six volumes of it, is available in limited translation also at www.kabbalah.info. It defines Kabbalah terms and provides details about the structure of the Upper Worlds. The information involves a mere 2,000 pages (in small print). The path to attaining spiritual fulfillment is described in other writings of Yehuda Ashlag, such as the book *Shamati* (*I Heard*).

Kabbalists who want a practical approach to mastering their methods study books such as this one. It is compiled like a school textbook: in each of its 16 parts, it explains the structure of the Upper World in modern language. Studying it is a large undertaking but is an endeavor Kabbalists embark on to understand and identify stages in their journey to be more like the Creator.

Each part is divided into sections such as "Inner Reflection," "The Meanings of Words," and "Questions and Answers." These sections elaborate and comment on the dynamics of the spiritual processes and the evolution of the Upper Worlds. They are also used to explain terms and vocabulary for Kabbalah, and general answers to often-asked questions.

> **Red Alert**
>
> Kabbalah satisfies an aspiration to the Upper World, but take care not to confuse it with the earthly "aspiration to loftiness," which normally stands for creativity, poetry, music, and art.

The Legacy

Here's a summary to help you understand the literature of Kabbalah and its legacy, as laid out in Chapter 6 and earlier.

The history of Kabbalah has a long line of writers and teachers, beginning with Adam, the first man. Adam existed in both the earthly and spiritual realms, and wrote the first Kabbalah book, the *Hamalaach Raziel* (*The Angel of God's Secret*).

The legacy continues with Abraham, who wrote *The Book of Creation* (*Sefer Yetzira*) and taught others in what amounted to the first Kabbalah study groups. Then came Moses (from the *Torah* and the Bible), through the foundational writings of *The Book of Zohar* and the Ari's *The Tree of Life*. Those works lead to Rabbi Yehuda Ashlag and his modern explanations of the ancient texts.

Kabbalists believe information is discovered when the time is right for the generation or individual. Hiding and finding of books is an accepted aspect of Kabbalah.

Kabbalah knowledge was originally kept away from the religious masses because Kabbalists felt that the knowledge was waiting for the time when humankind matured sufficiently to accept this wisdom and use it correctly.

It was Rabbi Yehuda Ashlag who advocated universal study of Kabbalah, knowing that its time of critical importance would soon arrive.

His oldest son, Rabbi Baruch Shalom Ashlag, ensured that his father's legacy of Kabbalah study continued. As the son of an important Kabbalah figure, Baruch Ashlag, also known as "the Rabash," took it upon himself to follow in his father's footsteps and make his own contributions to Kabbalah. He was born in Warsaw, Poland, in 1907 and moved with the family to Israel in 1921.

His father taught groups on spiritual matters, but, following traditional Kabbalah practices, Baruch was allowed to be included only after he was married. After some time he was allowed to teach his father's new students. He also wrote books according to his father's instructions.

Following his father's death in 1954, the Rabash continued teaching with his father's method. He wrote numerous essays on aspects of Kabbalah. Like his father, he kept a modest way of life. He worked as a cobbler, construction worker, and clerk. He lived like an ordinary person but devoted every spare moment to studying and teaching Kabbalah before his death in 1991.

All these great Kabbalists left behind them methods for reaching the spiritual world that were clear and understandable to people of their time. Their writings enabled other people to reach what they had attained and experience the same spiritual delights. Their legacy is one of sharing knowledge with all who wish to know.

Today, according to Rabbi Ashlag, it is no longer a mere "good idea" to share the knowledge; it is the call of the hour.

The Least You Need to Know

◆ Kabbalah provides a method for attaining spiritual fulfillment.

◆ Rabbi Yehuda Ashlag is credited with making older, difficult-to-read Kabbalah texts easier to interpret.

- Kabbalah study has evolved from emotional descriptions of an individual's experience, to a systematic and scientific method of study.

- The wisdom of Kabbalah has been made more concrete and has opened up over the generations.

- The wisdom of Kabbalah disappears and reappears when the time for its insights is ripe, and now the time is ripe.

Part 2

Before the Big Bang

Curious about the meaning of life? About why we were created and why we're here?

Those questions have been asked since the beginning of time, so join the rest of the world in your queries. But the answers may be more easily understood than you thought.

Kabbalists seek to understand the questions of the purpose of life, and all it takes to begin your own understanding is to ask. In this part, you'll reach an understanding about pure Kabbalah knowledge and find some of the answers to those age-old mysteries.

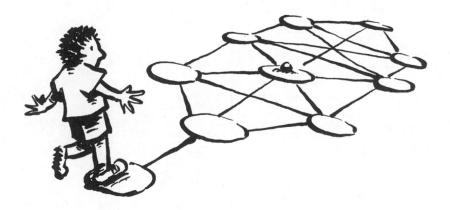

Chapter 8

The Reality Cycle

In This Chapter

- ◆ A ladder for every spiritual lad and lass
- ◆ 5 × 5 × 5 = 125 spiritual degrees
- ◆ Create a relationship with the Creator
- ◆ Set the stage for a better future

In his introduction to *The Book of Zohar*, Rabbi Yehuda Ashlag depicts three states that souls experience. The first state is the beginning of creation, which contains everything that will later evolve in the soul, like a seed contains the plant that will grow. The second state is the birth of the soul, somewhat like the seed's stages of growth. The third state is when the soul realizes its potential to the fullest, reaches the level of the Creator, and bonds with Him. In the third state, the soul returns to the first state, but this time it is a conscious and mature act.

Another way to think of these stages is like a baby's growth: in the first stage the child is at his mother's height because she's holding him next to her chest. In stage two, the child stands on his own two feet and begins to grow from below. In the third and last stage, the child has become fully grown, once more reaching the level of his mother, but this time as a conscious and mature adult.

In other words, the first state is a potential existence of the soul, the second state is the awakening of the soul, and the third state marks the soul's return to its original state. This chapter explains the cycle of spiritual reality as explained by Kabbalah.

Down the Rungs

The cycle of spiritual reality is like a ladder, as we discussed in Chapter 7. This ladder is probably not available at your local hardware store. The Spiritual Light is at the top of the ladder. It is the starting point, the zero, or Root point, in Kabbalistic language. The starting point is Phase Zero, which we introduced in Chapter 6, but here we are referring to it as the beginning of the circle, hence the different name. Kabbalists often use different names for the same spiritual states, to emphasize a different function of the same spiritual entity or degree.

The Light came down in four steps: 1, 2, 3, 4. Because the cycle starts at the Root or zero, Kabbalah's ladder has five stages and four steps. A barrier at the end of Phase 4 stops the spiritual Light, except for a fraction of Light, which develops and evolves into our universe.

Note the similarity to the five levels of human desire presented in Chapter 4. Kabbalah is a system in which cycles in one aspect of existence match cycles in another. The five levels of desire in our world correspond to the five cycles in the spiritual reality of the Upper Worlds. As you will see throughout this chapter, the number 5 reappears in Kabbalah in different ways, describing different aspects of an overall Kabbalistic journey to spiritual attainment.

The fraction of Light that penetrated through the barrier continued to evolve, and Earth was formed. The planet cooled and vegetative life appeared, then animals, humans, and finally humans who are reaching the last degree of evolution, a desire for spirituality. So the Creator came "down" the ladder to Earth, as described in Chapter 6.

Kabbalah follows the same path "up" the ladder to the Creator, which the Creator took to get "down" to us.

Five Spiritual Phases

The Creator gave humans a desire to become identical to Him. Because the Creator started out by giving, this is the foundation for the relationship with the Creator, marked by five phases of spiritual development. The starting point for you and I, right from the meaning of the word *Kabbalah*, involves receiving. The Creator gives, and you receive.

So Phase Zero is the Creator, the desire to give, and happily receiving is Phase 1 in the cycle of spirituality. But the Creator gave humans more than a mere desire to enjoy. He gave us the desire to become like Him because what could be better than being like Him? Because being like the Creator is even more pleasant than mere receiving, Phase 2 is wanting to give, and in this case, it means wanting to give back to the Creator.

In Phase 3, we (the created beings) understand that the only way to give to the Creator is to do what He wants, because there is nothing else we can give Him. Because He wants us to receive, that's what we do in Phase 3. But note the difference: this isn't like the receiving in Phase 1. Here, in Phase 3 we receive because He wants to give, not because we wish to receive. Our *intention* has changed from receiving for ourselves to receiving for the Creator. This, in Kabbalah, is called giving.

Phase 3 could have been the end of the process if it hadn't been for this tiny issue called "the third stage." We previously said that our goal is not merely to be attached to the Creator, but to become like Him. This can only happen when we have His Thoughts, when we know and actually participate in the Thought of Creation.

Therefore, Phase 4 introduces a new thrill: the desire to understand the actual Thought of Creation. Here you want to understand what the giving is for, what makes it pleasurable, why giving creates everything, and what wisdom it provides.

The four phases and their Root each have a second name. Phase Zero is also called *Keter*, Phase 1—*Hochma*, Phase 2—*Bina*, Phase 3—*Tifferet* or *Zeir Anpin* (*ZA*), and Phase 4—*Malchut*. These additional names are called *Sefirot* (Sapphires), because they shine like sapphires.

On Track

The whole business with the *Sefirot* may sound confusing, but it is less so if we remember that they stand for desires. *Keter* is the Creator's desire to give Light (pleasure); *Hochma* is our reception of the pleasure; *Bina* stands for our desire to give back to the Creator; *ZA* is our desire to receive in order to give to the Creator; and *Malchut* is our pure desire to receive, the actual Root of the creatures—us.

Screens and Faces

The Creator did not instill this new wish, however. It is a hallmark of this phase of independence, much like a 2-year-old or teenager wants to be independent of his or her parents. In Phase 4, you decide that you will receive only if you understand *why* the Creator wants to give—until you understand what's in it for Him.

For example, imagine that you offer to take your children to the mall to buy them whatever they want. Unlikely, granted. Now imagine that they say to you, "Why are you suggesting that? What does that do for you? If we don't understand why you are giving, we're not interested in the gifts." Much more unlikely. This conditioning of not receiving for yourself is called *Tzimtzum* (restriction). It is the first thing we do to become nonegoistic, and the mechanism that enables the *Tzimtzum* is called a *Masach* (screen).

Once we have acquired a *Masach* we can begin to calculate if and how much we can receive while focusing on our parents' pleasure instead of our own. When we acquire this ability, it is considered that we have a complete *Partzuf* (face).

Five Spiritual Worlds

The five phases of spiritual development correspond to five spiritual worlds, and each spiritual world, as you might have guessed, contains five *Partzufim* (faces). To continue the ladder metaphor, the worlds begin at the top of the ladder, closest to the Creator, and continue on down. The worlds, from the top of the ladder to the bottom, are *Adam Kadmon*, *Atzilut*, *Beria*, *Yetzira*, and *Assiya*. The world closest to the Light and the Creator, *Adam Kadmon* is also the most spiritual. The other worlds move downward to Earth, becoming more "earthly" and less "spiritual" as they descend.

> **On Track** _____
>
> It is important to try to understand the five worlds because the effort itself brings you closer to them, just as we feel naturally close to a person who wants to be like us. Besides, even if you don't understand them as you study, you will understand them when you climb the spiritual ladder yourself because you will discover that these worlds already exist within you. They are part of your spiritual makeup, just as they are part of creation's makeup.

A person's task is to attain the highest degree in his or her advancement toward the Creator. There are 125 degrees in the spiritual ladder that move you up through these five worlds. Why the number 125? Because there are 5 worlds, and 5 *Partzufim* in each world, and 5 *Sefirot* (*Keter–Malchut*) in each *Partzuf*. Therefore, 5×5×5 equals 125. (You may have noticed that Kabbalists have a thing with numbers.)

Note that our world does not count as a *spiritual degree*. The degrees begin above our world and move up. *Assiya* is the closest spiritual world to our own and the starting point of spiritual attainment.

def•i•ni•tion

Two elements make up a **spiritual degree**: a *desire* for something and the *intention* to use it for the Creator.

The advancement from one degree to the next happens only when a person has experienced the full measure of desire in the present degree, with the pure intention to give to the Creator. A higher degree is characterized by a greater desire for pleasure and a stronger intention to give that pleasure to the Creator.

As Rabbi Ashlag explained in *The Study of the Ten Sefirot*, the smallest element in spirituality is called *Sefira* because it shines like a sapphire. We already said that there are five basic *Sefirot*: *Keter, Hochma, Bina, Zeir Anpin,* and *Malchut*. However, *Zeir Anpin* (*ZA*) is made of six internal *Sefirot*: *Hesed, Gevura, Tifferet, Netzah, Hod,* and *Yesod*. So whether we talk about the five *Sefirot*—*Keter, Hochma, Bina, ZA,* and *Malchut*—or about the 10 *Sefirot*—*Keter, Hochma, Bina, Hesed, Gevura, Tifferet, Netzah, Hod, Yesod,* and *Malchut*—we're refering to the same basic structure of 10 *Sefirot*. Kabbalists like it confusing.

Each five *Sefirot* make up one *Partzuf* (face), and five *Partzufim* make up one *Olam* (world). Interestingly, the word *Olam* comes from the Hebrew word *Ha'alama*, which means "concealment." So when Kabbalists explain what you find in a certain world, they also tell you what you won't find there because it's hidden. The higher the *Olam*, the less there is *Ha'alama* (of the Creator). So when you get to the Higher Worlds, too, you'll know where you are by seeing what's around you and comparing it with the "tour guide," the Kabbalah books.

Kab-Trivia

The evolution of the five worlds was affected by a little snack: Adam eating from the Tree of Knowledge of Good and Evil, which caused the worlds to shatter.

Each of the five worlds is marked by a certain ability to receive pleasure (Light) with the intention to give to the Creator. As we've said, our spiritual task, from the Kabbalistic point of view, is to move up through each of the 125 degrees, from the Creator's total concealment to the state of His complete revelation.

One of the mechanisms of this progression and development is the concept of the *Tzimtzum* (restriction), which we mentioned earlier. It works like this: if you have a desire for object A, but a much stronger desire for object B, then your desire for object A gets *Tzimtzumed* (restricted). For example, say you're very tired and want to go to sleep. You tuck yourself in and cuddle under the warm blanket. Suddenly, someone knocks on your door and shouts that there is a fire and that you have to get out to save yourself. Naturally, your desire to save your life is stronger than your desire to sleep. At that moment that fatigue vanishes as if it never existed. In truth, it does exist, and you will feel it again when the danger has passed, but the desire to live restricts it and covers it completely.

Turning back to our topic, to move from degree x to degree $x + 1$, we need to want degree $x + 1$ more than our present x degree.

In *The Study of the Ten Sefirot*, Rabbi Ashlag says that even though *Malchut*, the *Sefira* that corresponds to the future us, wanted to receive the Creator's Light very much, she couldn't. *Malchut* didn't know how to receive the Light with the intention to give (remember the mall example from earlier in this chapter). Without the intention to give, she would become different than the Creator and, therefore, separated from Him. Because she did not want to become separated from the Creator, she *Tzimtzumed*, or restricted, her desire to receive so she could stay close to the Creator.

This is why the first thing you must learn when entering the spiritual world is how to restrict your egoistic desires. If you can't do that, the doors to spirituality remain closed, which brings us to the barrier.

A Barrier Between Worlds

Kabbalah teaches that the sole purpose of everything that happens in our world is to take you across the barrier between our world and the spiritual world. Once you cross it, you can start advancing in spirituality.

On Track

Think of the barrier as an electric gate with a numeric password that you have to click. That code exists within the spiritual system, and if you click the same code from outside the gate, it opens.

Where did this barrier come from? You may recall that contact with the Creator can exist only if you, like Him, have the intention to give. Because He created you without the intention to give, you are separated from Him. This separation is called the barrier because it bars you from direct contact with Him. The good news is that you can cross the barrier and meet the Creator "face to face" simply by wanting the intention to give.

High Five, Low Five

Kabbalah has many divisions. One division is into *Sefirot*, another is into worlds, and another is into levels of vitality. So spiritual as well as corporal life are divided into five levels of vitality:

1. Still (inanimate)

2. Vegetative

3. Animate (alive)

4. Speaking (human)

5. Spiritual (point in the heart)

Every being has all five levels, but the predominant level determines its category. Animals, for example, have some characteristics that are typically human, such as the ability to communicate messages but this is not their predominant trait. Humans, as we well know, have animalistic characteristics, too, but we are still fundamentally different from animals.

What makes people human in the spiritual sense is their ability to experience a uniquely human state: the desire to be spiritual (like the Creator), the point in the heart. This is the highest state, where you can cross the barrier into the spiritual realm.

Achieving this stage involves different factors than the first four levels of vitality, which are based on biological factors. Levels 1–4 evolve through pressures from nature that push evolution along unconsciously. Level 5 evolves with a pulling force (the word *Messiah* is rooted in the Hebrew word *Moshech*, which means "pulling"). This evolution to the fifth level is voluntary and conscious, made out of one's own *free choice*. A desire for it is the first step to crossing the barrier. It's the desire mentioned in the beginning of this book, the desire to ask what life is about, the desire upon which Kabbalah itself is based.

def•i•ni•tion

The voluntary and conscious evolution at the human level is what we call **free choice**. Free choice makes us similar to the Creator because we choose to be like Him.

At the Bottom of the Ladder

All these discussions of worlds, degrees, and levels come down to this: Kabbalah is a process and a journey. It starts with a desire for spiritual understanding.

At the bottom rung on the spiritual ladder, where you and I start, you are disconnected from the Creator. Here, the human task is to refurbish your desire for spirituality and make it a working vehicle to drive you up the spiritual ladder once more.

All souls started out at one with the Creator. In a sense, then, you and I have been developing and refurbishing ourselves for many thousands of years. In the framework of Kabbalah, the last 6,000 years have been the culmination of this process. Now the process is nearing its end, a time when all humanity is becoming spiritual. So let's look at the process and see how Kabbalah shows a way to go about this spiritual process.

A 6,000-Year Journey

Kabbalah is a journey for all souls to become corrected, and not in the way a grammar teacher would hope for. Kabbalah provides a method for spiritual correction and specifies a 6,000-phase route, referred to in the literature since the beginning as "6,000 years."

After their complete correction, all souls reunite into one common soul and start working as a unified system. The construction of this common soul binds the individual souls together so that each of them feels what all the others feel. This is the achievement of absolute attainment, called the "end of correction."

To Kabbalists, the soul is so much more important than anything else that they don't write anything about this world, only about the Upper or spiritual worlds. What seems to describe or relate to corporal matters is only metaphor. Kabbalists use earthly life to symbolize spiritual processes. They call this symbolic language "the language of roots and branches," or simply "the language of the branches."

All souls will achieve the end of correction no later than 6,000 years from the beginning of the count. The year 2007 aligns with 5,767 years from the starting point. There is little more than 200 years left, but efforts by Kabbalah practitioners may speed things along.

Picking Up the Pace

The only thing necessary to embark on this spiritual journey is the desire to do so. No spiritual progress can possibly occur in you if you do not want it beforehand. At the spiritual degree, evolution should be conscious and voluntary. You must want it *first*, and when you do, *Bina*, the Creator's quality of giving, comes and develops you. More on that in Part 4 of this book.

Questions such as "Why am I suffering?" "Where does pain come from and what does it want of me?" "Is there a purpose to suffering?" and "Do I want to live this way, and is it really worthwhile?" are useful if the predicaments preceeding them give you the sense to ask for directions on how to evolve. They are even more useful if you can use them to increase your desire for spirituality. When you begin to ask yourself these questions, it is a sure sign that you've begun your way up the spiritual ladder.

On Track

Don't worry if you want to be a "speed demon." On the route of your spiritual journey, the faster you progress, the better.

Moving Up the Ladder Again

The desire to be spiritual is the first step up the ladder. You start by wanting to fulfill this desire, and you will obtain it by simply asking (in your heart). Asking to be more spiritual is called "raising *MAN*" (Aramaic: *Mayin Nukvin*—Female Water). It is like raising your ladder to climb upward. Raising *MAN* is also called a prayer. *MAN* comes from two sources: One is your own spiritual structure, *Reshimot*, which are the soul's unconscious recollections of its past states. The second is the environment (friends, books, films, and all other media), which enhances and speeds up the *MAN* that the *Reshimot* evoke.

Your Own Ladder

There is a seeming contradiction to the ladder. If you remember at the beginning of the chapter, we stated that the Root was the beginning, at the top of the ladder. You and I contain the seeds of the Root within us—the seeds of the Creator, if you will.

So the Root is both the beginning of the cycle of spirituality and our ultimate goal. Having "fallen," you and I seek to regain the top, or correct ourselves. That requires climbing the spiritual ladder, from the earthly world back up to the Root. To understand how to return to your Root, you need to know your Root and how you came down from there (the *Reshimot*). How else could you know where to return if you hadn't already been there in some way? The emergence of new desires, new *Reshimot* indicate that you are making progress, how fast you are progressing, and if you're on the best and fastest route. In the end, we will all reach the end of correction, but a correct use of the *Reshimot* can save us much trouble, time, and effort.

Kabbalah provides a method and works with you so that you move up the ladder back toward your Root. Remember, this Root is above you, not below you. The Root is also called the Source, the Creator, and the Light.

You move up the ladder each time you increase your desire to be spiritual. As you become more spiritual, you build on the last degree of spirituality to achieve the next. Every time you increase your need, your future spiritual degree, responds by elevating you to it. The cycle repeats itself and moves you to become more like the Creator. Here you attain eternity, perfection, and an altogether new dimension of life.

Back to the Future

Roughly speaking, *Reshimot* are "recollections of past states." Your soul has been on other journeys before entering your body at your birth. Every *Reshimo* (singular for *Reshimot*), or state, that a soul experienced down its evolutionary path is collected in a special "data bank." As you climb up the spiritual ladder, these *Reshimot* comprise your trail; you reexperience them. The faster you reexperience each *Reshimo*, the faster you advance in spirituality.

def•i•ni•tion

Reshimot are the soul's unconscious recollections of its past states.

Word of Heart

Although our senses tell us that everything is transient, this is only how it seems. In fact, there are only incarnations here, and souls do not rest for a moment, but incarnate on the wheel of transformation of the form losing nothing of their essence on their way.

—From "The Peace" by Rabbi Yehuda Ashlag

By cultivating desires to be more like the Creator (altruistic) and less like your birth nature (egoistic), you attach yourself to a higher, more spiritual state. It is very similar to the way children learn by imitation. They mimic others, and the mimicry increases their desire to learn. The desire sets off the *Reshimo*, which brings the state of knowing to the surface.

Spiritual progress is desire driven. You awaken a higher state of spiritual perception, if you want to. If you haven't realized that you want it, you remain in your current *Reshimo*, unable to climb above it. The more you want to change, become altruistic, and be like the Creator, the more quickly the *Reshimot* surface. This reawakens the hidden states in your mind. These attributes already exist; your desire only brings them to the surface faster.

Once you have examined all your egoistic desires on the egoistic level, called "this world," a new *Reshimo* appears. This new desire is special. It is your first nonegoistic intention. This event in a Kabbalist's life, though it is a natural evolution of the surfacing of the *Reshimot*, is so radical that it is known as "The Crossing of the Barrier," or "the admittance to the spiritual world."

Reshimot assure you that everything you have done has already been determined. Whether your day is planned or unplanned, you are within a picture of reality created by the *Reshimo* within you. This *Reshimo* situates you in this picture and creates all the decisions in it. In addition, your conscious efforts to "choose" what will happen are a product of the unfolding *Reshimo*, and nothing more.

Red Alert

The environment can speed you up, but it can also slow you down. If you surround yourself with people, books, and media that do not appreciate spirituality, (that is, altruism), you, too, will not want it. According to Kabbalah, once you've placed yourself in a certain society, you cannot choose your thoughts, you subconsciously absorb them from the environment. The free choice we *do* have, however, is in the environment itself. Choosing the right environment will lead to or from spirituality, and determine our speed.

If you realize that you are only a puppet and that at the same time you *can* change your future, you could then make a choice. You could choose an environment that would influence you positively and assist in your spiritual development (see the "Red Alert" above). Here you could sense your *Reshimo* and move in the same direction that your spiritual ladder already leads. Now, though, you would do it willingly instead of mysteriously.

In any state that your soul is in, the *Reshimo* is predetermined. If you have an urge to realize the *Reshimo*, this urge stems from within. But if you use the environment to strengthen your desire and accelerate the unfolding of the *Reshimo*, that would not only shorten the unfolding period, but also elevate the experience to the spiritual level and make it adventurous and exciting.

Doing It Alone

Reality shows us that an individual cannot exist without a sufficient number of people around to serve and help provide for their needs. A person is born to live a social life. Every individual in society is like a wheel that is linked to other wheels on the same

On Track _____

In Kabbalah, the collective group and the individual are treated as one and the same. What is good for the whole is good for the individual, and vice versa. Therefore, a negative society harms the individual, and a positive society benefits the individual.

machine. This single wheel cannot move by itself. However, it joins the motion of all the other wheels and helps the machine perform its purpose. If the wheel breaks, the problem is not the wheel's problem, but the problem of the whole machine because the broken wheel stops the machine from running. A person is also judged not alone, but according to his or her service to society. A "bad" person is only as bad as he or she harms the public, not because he or she didn't perform up to the level of some abstract value of good.

Good and bad attributes and deeds are good or bad according to whether they benefit the public. If a part of the group does not contribute its share, those individuals not only harm the collective, but they, too, are harmed. This is why a negative society harms the individual.

Likewise, a good society benefits the individual. Individuals are part of the whole, and the whole is not worth more than the sum of its individuals. In Kabbalah, the collective and the individual are one and the same.

One of the key ideas to understand about Kabbalah is that people will come to see that their own benefit and the benefit of the collective are the same. As people realize that, the world will be much closer to its full correction.

Alone Together

Kabbalah explains that our experiences are personal, but they are described in general terms that apply to everyone. For example, we all agree that blood is red when we look at it, but we each experience it very differently. Some people faint at the sight of blood, some say "Cool!", and some say "Ugh!"

Existence is the same way. People perceive it differently because they are in different stages of it. Even Kabbalists at different levels of ascent realize that they may not know the same things about Kabbalah as a fellow Kabbalist. It is similar to a high school student knowing more than a grade school student, even if they may be studying the same subject. Both may be studying about the Civil War, for example. But to get an A, a high school student is required to know many more details and have a much more extensive understanding of the topic.

Who Was I?

In Kabbalah, a soul is continually reborn into this world until it reaches the highest state of spirituality—this, again, is why reality is a cycle. Your soul may have memories of these other states, but they are not available to your conscious mind until you cross the barrier, when they gradually become known to you.

In other lives, your soul was in various stages of correction. Now that Kabbalah is more accessible, your soul has the opportunity to advance more readily.

But let's be clear about one thing. You are "you" and you only. Past lives involve your soul, not your person, so you don't have to worry about past identities. The important thing in Kabbalah is to achieve your life's purpose, which is to become more like the Creator. (Learn more about Kabbalah reincarnation in Chapter 12.)

Doing It Together

The meaning of existence is a global question, and it is a personal question that everyone faces. People have pondered the question for centuries and show no sign of stopping. This shows that we still have not found satisfactory answers.

Kabbalah is not about researching an ancient mystical body of knowledge. It is a modern science close to today's needs. It researches forces that we do not see but that govern this world nonetheless. It can change the future of individuals and of humankind. Once the process has arrived at the point of spiritual ascension, the entire world will gradually rise to a higher state of being.

The Time Has Come for All

Kabbalah states that now there is a window of opportunity for those seeking answers to the meaning of life. A different level of being awaits, a level of being that promises to be more pleasant than our current situation.

People have to do their part to make it happen. So citizens of the world have a choice: they can either continue watching escalating affairs around the globe, or they can spend their time discovering how to eliminate global troubles.

Red Alert

Kabbalah believes that the spiritual path is predetermined, but this does not mean that you do not have free will and choices. You will be on the same path, but you can progress faster or slower, pleasantly or painfully, *depending on your participation*.

Kabbalists say that the future will be better. Instead of continuing to advance as people have since the beginning of time, this infinite source of knowledge can control our destiny. You can actively embrace this ultimate source of fulfillment to reduce suffering in the world for all and help bring about a better future that much sooner.

Kabbalah is a living science. Just as results of experiments change earthly theories, a Kabbalist deepens his or her understanding of the spiritual worlds until, at the end of correction, the absolute understanding is attained. The Kabbalistic viewpoint answers all questions. All that's required to understand these answers is to reduce our level of egoism.

The More, the Merrier

All souls—and, of course, all people—have the potential to reach the enlightened states of Kabbalah. Reaching this state causes no harm to others. So the more, the merrier.

Our world is a world of results. It is rooted in the spiritual worlds and displays the spiritual processes in a physical robe. In much the same way, the heat from a heater is a robe of the electric force that generates it.

Because Kabbalists attain the spiritual realm, they are expertly aware of the processes influencing this world. They potentially hold the key to safeguarding the future of the entire human race. Until recently, only a relatively small number of people were studying the construction of the universe. In a sense, they were doing the work for the rest of humanity. But today a growing awareness of this knowledge is necessary to reach a critical mass for a major breakthrough.

Kabbalah allows you to elevate your spirit and achieve absolute satisfaction. With the study of Kabbalah, you gradually become free of your egoism and free of suffering.

The Least You Need to Know

◆ First, our souls were like the Creator. They have gone down the ladder, and now we must travel up it and become like Him again.

◆ Crossing the barrier into the spiritual realm is done only through a conscious desire to be like the Creator.

◆ Kabbalah allots 6,000 years for all souls to achieve correction, which can be experienced as a joyous and exciting journey or as an ordeal.

◆ If we want to reach spirituality, we have to choose a spiritually supportive environment made up of friends, books, and all kinds of media.

◆ Free choice exists only in choosing our environment. Everything else is determined by the *Reshimot*.

Chapter 9

How the Creator Set Things Up

In This Chapter

◆ What a world … what worlds within a world

◆ The Thought of Creation

◆ Four for your understanding

◆ Meet Adam and learn his story

◆ Many people, one soul, one correction

This chapter explains the story of creation according to Kabbalah. When you learn it, you will grasp the essence of the Kabbalistic journey toward spirituality, and how Kabbalah provides a way for humanity to correct itself for the good of all.

This chapter is the heart of the book, the core of Kabbalah. We discussed its general structure in the previous chapter. Here, we focus more on the individual in the process and less on degrees, worlds, and *Partzufim*. (Just so you know: the material here is explained in more than 2,000 dense pages in *The Study of the Ten Sefirot*, but we'll make it shorter than the original version!)

A World Within a World Within a World Within a World ...

As we've mentioned in Chapter 8, there are five worlds of spirituality: *Adam Kadmon*, *Atzilut*, *Beria*, *Yetzira*, and *Assiya*. The only thing that is real is the world of *Ein Sof* (No End). Recall that we explained that the word *Ha'alama* (World) means concealment. Therefore, the worlds are incomplete appearances of the Creator. The only place where He is completely revealed is therefore the world *Ein Sof*, where there are no limitations, hence the name *Ein Sof*, no end to our perception of the Creator. (In our world, we're totally opposite in our qualities from the Creator, and this is why we can't see Him in this world. This is also why our world is considered by Kabbalists "an imaginary world."

Word of Heart

All the worlds, upper and lower, are contained within.

—From preamble to *The Wisdom of Kabbalah* by Yehuda Ashlag

Each of the spiritual worlds is experienced differently, just as different grades of sandpaper are experienced. Each grade of sandpaper has increasingly larger grains of "sand" on the paper. Accordingly, the coarser grades feel rougher to the touch. The finer the paper, the higher the world, and the coarser the paper, the lower the world is considered.

Our world is like the coarsest grades of sandpaper. It's the "coarsest" of the worlds.

The Upper Worlds affect objects in the worlds below, as all the worlds are essentially the same reality—that of *Ein Sof*. For example, if you thought about doing something, and knew for certain that that thought would come true, than your plan would be experienced as existing in you, even before the thought was actually carried out. Our body knows this process very well, this is why the stomach produces digestive juices before the food actually gets there. In that sense, the thought of eating is a higher world, which creates the lower world where the eating occurs. But in both worlds the event (substance) is the same—eating. Because our thought is not limited, you could say that it is in the world *Ein Sof*, and our body is in one of the lower worlds.

Keep in mind that although Kabbalah speaks only about the spiritual worlds, it uses physical examples, such as eating, to explain them. Although the examples are used to understand *how* things work in spirituality, don't be misled into thinking that there is physical eating (as in the last example) in spirituality.

Something from Nothing

We previously defined Kabbalah as a sequence of causes and consequences that hang down from Root to branch, whose purpose is the revelation of the Creator to the creatures. But how do Kabbalists know that? As they reach the top of the spiritual ladder, they discover two things: that creation is made of pure, unadulterated desire to receive pleasure, and that the Creator is made of pure, unadulterated desire to give it to creation.

This brings up another question: if the Creator's only wish is to give, where did creation's pure desire to receive come from? Kabbalists explain that the Creator *had* to create us; otherwise, He wouldn't have anyone to give to. This is the beginning of the root and branch sequence.

> **Red Alert** _____
>
> Discussing what the Creator wants is dangerous because it can lead us to thinking about the Creator instead of our own correction, which is what is needed if we want to become like Him. Whatever other desires He may or may not have is irrelevant for us because what created us is His desire to give. Hence, to us, this is all that matters. What Kabbalists discover once they reach the Creator's level isn't written anywhere, but we, too, can get there and find out for ourselves.

I Have a Thought Today!

Continuing the line of thought we started in the previous section, we can see why Kabbalists determined that all He thinks about is giving. Therefore, they called the desire "to do good to the creatures," to us, the Thought of Creation. If we keep this in mind, the whole wisdom of Kabbalah will begin to make sense.

If I want to give, like the Creator, there is nothing that can limit me, because you can't "lock" a desire in a certain place or time. Of course, we, people, are also unlimited—we want only to receive, and that desire is just as unlimited as the desire to give. In that sense, we are equal but opposite to the Creator: our orientation is toward receiving, and His is toward giving.

Another element that becomes clearer when we understand the Thought of Creation is why it takes giving to create. When you want to give, you're looking outwardly, to see where you can do good. But when you want to receive, you are concentrated on yourself, and want only to take from what already exists. Now let's look at the stages of creation.

One, Two, Three, Four 'n' More

One of the most frequently used terms in Kabbalah is the Tree of Life. The Tree of Life is really the whole story of creation, from the Root Phase, mentioned in the previous chapter, down to our world and back to the Root, at the end of correction. Kabbalists often picture it as ten *Sefirot*, but these ten *Sefirot* contain within them the whole story of creation, so for them the tree symbolizes the whole creation. This is why the Ari's primary composition is called *The Tree of Life*.

Creation started with a root (His desire to do good to His creations), and expanded in four more phases. This is the origin of the Tree of Life, its first root, if you will. In Phase 4 creation restricted itself, performed a *Tzimtzum*, and rejected all the Light (pleasure) that the Creator wanted to give. Such an act seems to contradict the very Thought of Creation, but it is a necessary step in determining creation as a separate and independent entity from the Creator.

Shame on You

The power by which creation stops receiving the Light is a very special kind of shame, the root of all disgraces, called the bread of shame. Kabbalists explain that shame, and its offspring—the desire for honor and respect—is the most powerful force that drives us. Now hold tight, because we're about to plunge deep into the heart of man: the bread of shame is the mother and father of all shames. It is an experience unlike anything in this world. It is a burning sensation that has only one name fitting for it: Hell. But don't worry, in Kabbalah no bad comes without its compensation and reward immediately following.

The main difference between our (worldly) shame and the (spiritual) bread of shame is that in our world we are ashamed of not meeting society's standards, and in spirituality we are ashamed of not meeting the Creator's standards. Imagine that you suddenly discovered that the entire universe, from before the Big Bang until the end of all time, is kind, generous, and giving. Sound great? Now imagine that you also discover that there is one single element in it that's selfish and wants to use everyone and everything else. Well, that must be the devil. Now imagine that you discover that this evil devil is you. What would you do? No person can bear it, of course. Then, to top it all off, you discover that the evil is not in your body, it's in your soul, in your desires, so even if you committed suicide you'd still be evil, because you can't put an end to your soul with a gun.

Naturally, when you discover something like that, the last thing you want is to remain yourself, and the thing you want most is to be a giver like the Creator. And the minute you want it, you get it.

Now you know that the *Tzimtzum* isn't a restriction imposed on you. It is the result of your own work of studying yourself. It is also a very rewarding and pleasurable event because it is the first time you receive the ability to actually be something else. You can choose not only between two options in this world but also between two entirely different kinds of nature. When you choose one, your senses will show you our world; and when you choose the other, your senses will show you the spiritual world. But you will be able to choose between them, and even jump back and forth from one to the other whenever you want.

Red Alert

Not every shame is constructive. When you're ashamed of not getting good grades, it doesn't make you any closer to spirituality. Only when your role model is the Creator Himself, the pure quality of giving, can you say that your shame is the bread of shame.

To sum it up, shame isn't a bad or good thing. It is the sensation of the difference between the person and the Creator. Because shame is such a powerful tool for progress, Kabbalists say that it is a quality reserved for very high souls. In our world it may be an unpleasant feeling. But to Kabbalists it is a blessing, a sign of progress, because it shows that they are learning more about the Creator, which enables them to compare themselves to Him. That's how Kabbalah works, the illness is the cure, as well: shame is both our bane and the power that drives us forward in spirituality.

Down Five Worlds

In Chapter 8, we explained that the worlds from the top of the ladder to the bottom, are *Adam Kadmon, Atzilut, Beria, Yetzira,* and *Assiya.* We also said that each world is made of five interior elements called *Partzufim.* Now let's talk about how they're made and how they work.

Don't be confused by all the names in Kabbalah; they refer to either bestowal or reception. Creator, Light, Giver, Thought of Creation, Phase Zero, Root, Root Phase, *Bina,* and others describe the will for bestowal. Creature, *Kli,* receivers, Phase 1, and *Malchut* are some examples of the will to receive. There are so many names because of the subtle differences in each—but in the end, they all refer to bestowal or reception.

Setting the Stage

Once Phase 4, called *Malchut*, experienced the bread of shame, her oppositeness from the Creator, she set up a condition before Him: "If you want me to enjoy, give me the ability to do it for *your* pleasure, not for mine, because I don't enjoy being an egoist." So the Creator gave her a *Masach*, the screen, to resist the entrance of the Light. Then she said to Him: "Thanks, now give me the ability to decide what to receive and what not to receive. I know that I can't receive anything and still be thinking of your pleasure, so let's start with little bits and pieces of Light." He gave her this ability as well.

Malchut began to receive the Light in five primary categories. Just like the visible Light is made of three basic colors—red, green, and blue—spiritual Light is made of five basic Lights—*Nefesh*, *Ruach*, *Neshama*, *Haya*, and *Yechida*. *Nefesh* is the smallest Light, and *Yechida* is the greatest.

Once *Malchut* receives the ability to split the Light into five sections, she begins to receive each of them, but only as long as she can do that while thinking of the Creator. Each time she receives a different Light of the five, she builds a special *Partzuf* to receive it. Thus, she completes her ability to sense the Creator at a certain degree by exploring the five Lights as much as she can without thinking of herself. And because there are five such Lights, each spiritual world contains five *Partzufim*.

Now you also understand why each such phase is called *Olam* (world), meaning concealment. This is the level to which *Malchut* can bare to enjoy the Creator's pleasure without thinking of herself. Naturally, the higher the world, the greater is *Malchut's* ability to enjoy the Creator's Light. This is also the great reward that comes with reaching the world *Ein Sof* (No End)—there are no limitations on reception of the Creator's pleasures.

On Track

Kabbalah ascribes each element in spirituality a gender tag; an element can't be neutral, but it can "switch" from being male or female. In general anything that gives is considered male and anything that receives is considered female. As in our life so in Kabbalah, things aren't that straightforward, and each entity contains male and female elements within it, and uses them according to need. Thus, although each element has a basic gender, it can function as its opposite sex when the need arises.

The Fixin' Machine

The spiritual worlds have what could be called a teaching mechanism built into them. They can teach you how to direct your desire to give back to the Creator. Although they run on "autopilot" meaning they unfold as a necessary cause and effect process, the guiding principle in each of them is "I will not receive unless it's for the Creator." When a person enters the spiritual worlds, this is what the spiritual worlds teach him or her: how to think more of the Creator and less of him or herself.

In that sense, the relationship between the worlds and the creature is like a group of construction workers teaching a rookie what to do. They teach each task by demonstrating it. Bit by bit, creatures can begin to "fix up their desires" and direct their reception to the Creator as an act of giving.

Red Alert

You may have a negative view of Upper Worlds and lower worlds. Creation is only this: a will to receive pleasure. *Upper* and *lower* do not relate to positions or places but to the *value* of desires. Higher desires are simply more altruistic than lower desires, which are more egoistic.

A Soul Is Born

When all the worlds were in their place, *Malchut* had learned to receive in order to give like the Creator. Now only one thing was left to know: why it all happened in the first place.

In Chapter 8, we said that Phase 3 completed the cycle of creation by receiving in order to give. You might say that the making of the worlds is like zooming into the process to see what happens in Phases 0–3. You can try it at home on your computer. Any software that allows you to focus on an object, such as Google Earth, will demonstrate how the same object seems more and more detailed as you zoom in on it. This doesn't change the object, but it certainly changes what you know about it. This is also why Kabbalists say that all the worlds, Upper and lower, are within us.

But in Chapter 8 we also said that the last phase (and the greatest desire) is to know the Thought of Creation. To understand the Thought of Creation, it was necessary to create a special *Partzuf*, which would exist in a special world, where this *Partzuf* could study the Thought of Creation of its own free choice. This is how the *Partzuf* of *Adam ha Rishon* was formed. Although *Adam ha Rishon* was not born in our physical world, it was quickly brought here, and was given the name Adam, after its task, to be *Domeh* (similar) to the Upper One, the Creator.

If you're wondering where Eve is in this picture, she is very much in there. In Kabbalah, Adam and Eve are two parts of the same *Partzuf*. When Kabbalists want to emphasize the reception in this *Partzuf* they refer to it as Eve, and when they want to focus on its giving capabilities they call it Adam.

This Guy Is a Saint

The world Adam was first placed in was *Atzilut*, where all the desires are corrected and work only to give to the Creator. In the world *Atzilut*, Adam acted on small desires—desires he was sure he could use with the intention of giving to the Creator, meaning altruistically. He was told he could do anything, as long as he didn't eat from the Tree of Knowledge, which represents the stronger desires, the ones Adam couldn't use with the intention to give to the Creator.

At this point, Adam was considered holy, a saint, unaware of his own uncorrected desires. But what Adam didn't know was that he was placed in the Garden of Eden and allowed to work with his small desires only as an example of how he should work with his coarser desires. So when they first appeared, he didn't know how to handle them, and sinned.

The Tree of Knowledge represents the strongest desires because the knowledge that the tree provides is the knowledge about the Thought of Creation, which creates the Tree of Life.

Well ... Not Really a Saint

When Adam finally decided to try to receive for the Creator with the intention to give to the Creator, he failed, and wanted to receive for himself. He discovered that he was totally egoistic in those desires, and this (bread of) shame made him cover himself, as the Bible has it, with fig leaves. Adam learned that he was naked, without a *Masach* (screen) to cover his bare (egoistic) desires.

But spirituality is a failsafe mechanism. Once a correction is made, you cannot breach it. As a result of Adam's mistake the *Tzimtzum* was reactivated and all the Light in *Partzuf Adam ha Rishon* left it, leaving Adam and Eve outside of the Garden of Eden. However, they were not totally alone; they had their memories (*Reshimot*) of the corrected state and the memories of their egoism. Those two seemingly bad memories are the most valuable tools for any person who wants to discover the Creator and correct the relationship that existed between Adam and the Creator and discover His full glory.

The Original Sin

In the Kabbalistic version, the story of the original sin has a twist or two that you may not know. Adam was commanded not to eat from the Tree of Knowledge so he would not entangle himself with desires he couldn't handle, but his internal female, Eve, told him that if he did eat, he would be able to give to the Creator even more than if he didn't. She was right, too, because in doing that, he would be using greater desires to receive in order to give to the Creator. But what Eve didn't know was that to give to the Creator with such strong desires, you need to have a very strong *Masach* to handle them. Adam did not have that.

You may justly ask, "Why didn't the Creator tell Adam that he couldn't handle such desires, did He want him to fail? What kind of a giving Creator lets his creation suffer?"

Red Alert

This is a good place to remind ourselves that all that the *Torah* (Five Books of Moses) and Kabbalah write about unfolds in the spiritual worlds, not in our world. Be careful not to ascribe spiritual qualities to apple trees or any other kind of tree, for that matter; it will not make you more altruistic.

To understand why the Creator did that to Adam, we must remember the Thought of Creation, and that this is what Adam really wanted. To teach Adam about his own desires, the Creator had to expose them to him, and how can you expose a desire to someone without letting him or her experience what that desire feels like?

From the perspective of the Creator no harm was done by Adam's sin because from His perspective, this is just another step toward teaching creation how to receive everything that He wants to give. The greatest gift the Creator can give to us is His Thoughts, so that's what He had to show us. Now that we have this memory in our *Reshimot* we can begin to correct ourselves and learn how to receive it.

600,000 Little Pieces

The first step in the correction of Adam's soul was to split it into "digestible" pieces, smaller bits of desire that weren't so hard to correct. For this reason his soul shattered into no less than 600,000 pieces. It continued to shatter and splinter and today we have as many pieces of his soul as there are people on Earth. Yes, you understand correctly. We're all parts of the same soul. In Part 4 we'll talk about the practical aspects of this fact.

Kab-Trivia

If you want to know how many people planet Earth can host, just become a Kabbalist and calculate how many bits of Adam's soul it takes to correct it. The more egoistic we become, the harder it is to correct each bit of soul, and the more we have to divide and multiply.

The splitting happened in the following way: when all the desires in *Adam ha Rishon* had a common intention to bestow upon the Creator, they were united as one. When the intention in the desires was reversed into an aim for self-gratification, each desire sensed itself separated from the others, and the single soul became divided.

All souls, therefore, are extensions of the general soul of *Adam ha Rishon* (literally translated as "the first man"). Because we are all born with a small portion, together we can correct the entire soul, as illustrated by the following story.

In Yehuda Ashlag's book, *Panim Masbirot*, a king needed to send a large quantity of gold coins to his son who lived overseas. He had no messengers that he could trust with a big sum, so he split up the gold coins into pennies and sent them by many messengers. Each individual decided it was not worth stealing such insignificant loot and delivered it. The large sum was reunited.

In the same way, many souls over many days can redeem the fragments after the apple incident. All the pieces combine to successfully complete the original task of receiving all the Light in order to give to the Creator. Your job is to correct your portion, the root of your own soul. This goal is individual. Everyone has free choice, and your soul is corrected according to your own effort.

Tricked into Receiving

In our world we have no choice but to be receivers. We don't know what true altruism feels like because we are all pieces of the soul of *Adam ha Rishon*, who became egoistic in the original sin. This is why Kabbalist Yehuda Ashlag explains that even when we do give, it is with some sort of self-interest in mind. He explains that we may be unaware of this self-interest, but that without it we wouldn't be able to perform any acts of giving in this world.

But there is a purpose to this state: it makes us totally opposite from the Creator, and therefore detached from Him. When we are detached from Him, we don't have His guidance, which makes sure that all our choices are truly free. Thus, when we ultimately decide that we want to be altruists, it'll be a truly free choice, and the spiritual world will reveal to us at once.

The Least You Need to Know

◆ Understanding the Thought of Creation is the key to understanding this world, and us within it.

◆ All people have a portion of the common soul of *Adam ha Rishon* to correct in themselves.

◆ The spiritual worlds teach you how to direct your egoistic desires toward good.

◆ Shame is the single most valuable tool for correction, if you know how to use it right.

Chapter 10

Decoding the Spiritual Language

In This Chapter

◆ Of course, it's all about the forces

◆ Understanding the Language of the Branches

◆ New meanings of old stories

◆ Prophecy and prophets

◆ Demystifying the language of *The Zohar*

To read about Kabbalah, you have to understand the language that it's written in. No, you don't have to learn Hebrew! (*The Zohar* and other texts are not written in Hebrew.) But you do need to understand the way Kabbalistic texts use stories to present ideas. Stories about people and the world become metaphors for concepts and ideas in the Upper Worlds.

The language of Kabbalah describes how forces from the Upper Worlds act on the objects of this world. Stories and the ideas behind them show how the universe is structured. When read in this way, stories about this world—the stories in the Bible, for instance—take on new meanings.

In this chapter, you start to understand how to unlock Kabbalah knowledge. You see that the roots and branches of Kabbalah language bring out more in the stories than generally meets the eye.

Roots and Branches

As we've explained in Chapters 8 and 9, the worlds are created by a series of causes and effects that stem from them. Therefore, *roots* refer to the spiritual forces, which create our world and the people in it. They exist in the spiritual worlds beyond this material one, but they influence and operate on our world.

def•i•ni•tion

In Kabbalah, every cause is considered a **root** and every consequence of the cause is considered a **branch**. The roots are also referred to as "parents" and the branches are considered their "children." The key concept in Kabbalah is that what happens in the roots will happen in the branches. Each object in this world is connected to a spiritual force.

The roots are like many unseen fingers pushing and prodding a piece of clay—our existence—into a certain form. They mold existence by guiding objects. These objects that the spiritual forces, or roots, guide are the *branches*. The branches exist in this world. They have material existence.

Like their names, which come from the world of botany, roots and branches are connected. Like a tree, one of them you see and the other you don't, yet both are connected.

A tree or plant cannot exist without its roots. Things that happen to the roots show up in the plant. If the roots don't receive enough water, the plant droops. If the roots are fertilized, the plant grows fuller.

Kabbalah describes the same mechanism in people. In the universe described by Kabbalah, what happens in the roots shows up in the branches. The spiritual world informs the earthly world, and just as a plant is affected by the condition of its roots, the forces in the spiritual worlds influence people and objects in this world.

In Chapter 9 we said that the substance (events, elements, and objects) in all the worlds is the same. We said that the only difference between them is in the spiritual level of the same elements: the higher worlds contain more altruistic elements and events. So clearly, the objects of each world relate to the objects above or below it. Forces from one appear in the next, and so on, though in a new way. The highest level, the Root or the Source, creates and controls the events through all the worlds, down to the "branches" in our world.

As Above, So Below

To indicate the difference in the quality of the substance in each world, the same elements in each world receive different names. The Upper World, for instance, contains angels, while our world contains animals. This does not mean that animals are angels. But if we keep in mind the world within a world concept from the previous chapter, we will recall that each element in reality contains five levels: 0–4. Level 3 of the will to receive in the spiritual world is called "angels," and the same level in the physical world is called "animals."

Animals and angels also perform the same function with respect to humans: "good" angels are forces that help our correction in a way we experience as pleasant, and "bad" angels are forces that help our correction in a way we experience as unpleasant. Similarly, "good" animals are helpful to us—domesticated—and "bad" animals are dangerous—wild animals. Of course, neither animals nor angels are good or bad; they're themselves. It's the qualities *we* ascribe them, according to our interests, that define them as good or bad.

The correspondence between the Upper and lower systems is similar to having an object, which you can sink in wax, in sand, in plaster, in cement, or in dough. The final result is different because of the differences in the substances. The shape or form, however, is the same. Even though the quality of the matter or its behavior are different, the final form corresponds to the object/shape that made it.

> **Kab-Trivia**
>
> Kabbalah explains that at the end of correction, when all our desires are corrected, even the angel of death will become a holy angel. It means that when we are corrected we will see that all the forces we thought were evil are actually good but presented themselves as evil to prompt us to correct.

But the matter is always opposite than the object/shape. If you press a flat board with a little dome in the middle against the beach sand, you will get a flat surface with a little crater in it. Similarly, the Creator is the object/shape and we are the matter. Because He is a giver, we are receivers.

Just like the dome and the crater, our will to receive is the exact negative of His desire to give. It contains all the elements that exist in Him, but in an inverted way: His white is our black, what's good in Him is bad in us. And since He is only good, we are only … you get the point.

As much as you and I might try, however, we cannot identify the higher degrees because our matter is opposite from the matter of the spiritual worlds. Their matter is purer—so pure that we cannot feel it. Yet the forms there are the same forms that exist here. It turns out that we and the Creator are like two people standing back to back and walking forward. The more we walk, the farther we grow. To find the Creator we have to stop and reexamine our direction.

A One-Way Window

The barrier to the spiritual world can be thought of as a one-way window. Even though you and I don't feel the spiritual world, it does exist and contains all the forms that exist in this world. So there is a spiritual "you," a spiritual table, and a spiritual chair. In other words, everything you find in this world has corresponding forces above. These forces operate on our matter to create it in more forms and in greater variety. When these forces operate on us, we suddenly have a "bright" idea of producing something.

Spiritual forms of reality don't exist physically in the spiritual worlds. For example, even though there is a spiritual "table," it is not an object in the spiritual world; it is only a force. It has no physical properties. Accordingly, people and objects in the spiritual world do not have names, as they do in this world. In the spiritual world, the force of "table" may be called "table" only because that's what it's called in this world, where that force has substance and form you and I call "table." In other words, spirituality has no words. It's only sensations of reception and giving and the intentions with which we do them. But to be able to discuss them with each other, we use the names given to their physical manifestations in our world, although we're actually referring to the spiritual force.

You and I cannot feel a physical sensation of the spiritual worlds. They are forces, not forms and substance. The reason is that the nature of the spiritual world is to give, and our nature is to receive. In other words, we are working in a totally opposite direction. It is not our nature to enjoy giving everything we have to everyone at all times. At the same time, we wouldn't be kidding if we said we wouldn't mind receiving from everyone.

That's how the Creator designed people.

The Bible: More than Meets the Eye

The *Bible* (or *Torah*) is sublime and spiritual but, frankly, it can be a bit long on history, with its lists of relations. You read about people marrying, divorcing, cheating on each other, and killing one another. A fair question might be: what's so spiritual about that?

In the framework of Kabbalah, however, the Bible doesn't tell stories of people. Instead, it presents relations between spiritual forces.

The Bible shows the process of the correction of souls through higher forces. This takes the souls on their path of ascent as they rise in their ability to bestow. Characters such as Adam, Noah, and Abraham are not thought of as people with personalities or as characters that lived somewhere and wandered around. They are considered forces that operate over desires that have to be corrected.

For example, there is the story of the exodus of Hebrew slaves from Egypt, when they were delivered to freedom. This freedom represents the acquisition of the first *Masach*, the crossing of the barrier. There are also darker stories, such as the story of David, who sent one of his warriors to war so he could steal the man's wife. When read from the perspective of Kabbalah, this story, too, is about the spiritual process of correction.

On Track

From the perspective of Kabbalah, nothing in the Bible refers to this world or is meant to improve your life here or give you any kind of bonus or security. It gives lessons only about spiritual forces and the correction of souls; it is designed *only* to elevate you to the degree of the world *Ein Sof*, similarity with the Creator.

Some stories may seem to have no rationality or sanctity in them. When reading them, remember that these are not events, but stories of forces. They are not to be understood or justified in earthly terms.

It helps to focus on the *intentions* of the act instead of the acts themselves. If a person sticks a knife in another, he might be performing surgery to save a person's life, or he might be trying to commit homicide. Consider that when a tailor cuts a piece of cloth, he doesn't ruin it, he corrects it by turning it into clothes.

The Language of the Branches

The Language of the Branches is the expression of higher forces that operate on our world. It is expressed in objects and in everything that happens. Where does it come from? It's like a computer screen: if you went behind the picture, you would not see the picture—you would see all the electronics that built it.

Let's say there is a picture on the screen, a beach. Behind the screen is not a beach, but a collection of electric impulses, forces and energies that create the picture on the

Word of Heart

You have not a blade of grass below that has not a sign above, which strikes it and tells it, "grow."

—Midrash Raba

screen. The picture is the "branch," and the electric forces that create this picture are the "roots." The connection you have with the electronic forces (root) through the picture (branch) is called the Language of the Branches.

The problem is that very few people "speak" the Language of the Branches. It is spoken by only Kabbalists, who also read books in this language.

Again, from the perspective of Kabbalah, the stories of the Bible are not about events or people that "happened." There is no "before" and "after" in the *Torah* (the five Books of Moses). Everything that's written there is above time, space, and motion. It didn't happen, it isn't happening, and it won't happen, unless you make them happen within you.

Here's a closer look at the stories in the Bible as read through the Language of the Branches.

Genesis

Before we begin to talk about the Bible stories, keep in mind that they are all written in the language of the branches. Not a single word in them refers to our physical world. Only when we read with this point of reference will we understand the text correctly. Even if we don't understand it, we will at least know that it is spirituality that we don't understand, not petty quarrels of people.

Word of Heart

First, you must know that when dealing with spiritual matters that have no concern with time, space and motion, and moreover when dealing with Godliness, we do not have the words by which to express and contemplate .... For that reason, the sages of the Kabbalah have chosen a special language, which we can call "the language of the branches."

—From *The Study of the Ten Sefirot* by Rabbi Yehuda Ashlag

Now let's talk about the Biblical creation story. The will to receive in the common soul (us) is called "Eve." The will to bestow, to give, is called "Adam." Egoism—the will to receive with the intention to receive—is called "the serpent," and we call it "ego."

The ego wants to take over all our desires and pull us toward egoism. This is considered that the serpent came to Eve—the will to receive—and said, "You know what? You can use your will to receive in a very good way." So Eve went to Adam—the will to bestow—and said, "You know, we have a chance to climb up to the highest worlds here. Moreover, this is what the Creator wants, that's why He made us receivers."

And she ate. The will to receive, joined with the serpent (egoism), ate the apple. Because they liked it, they thought, "Why not pull Adam into it, the forces of bestowal?" So she did. As a result, the whole body of *Adam ha Rishon* (the common soul), all his desires were corrupted by the serpent's intention to receive in what became the original sin.

Egypt and Abraham

Abram was born in Mesopotamia (today's Iraq), immigrated to Israel, and then, because of famine, went down to Egypt. This travel has a spiritual meaning because these places are degrees or forces. They actually tell the correction story of his desire.

Mesopotamia is a starting point, where Abram's desires are egoistic, like yours and mine. The land of Israel, called "desires to bestow," is the desire to give. Egypt is called *Mulchut*, the will to receive, and it consists of egoistic desires, with Pharaoh being the epitome of egoism.

Kab-Trivia

In Kabbalah, Israel is not a piece of land. Its name comes from two words: *Yashar* (straight), *El* (God, Creator). Therefore, to a Kabbalist, anyone with a strong desire to be like the Creator is considered a part of Israel.

When Abram first achieved correction, he changed his name to Abraham, broken down as *Av* (father) *ha Am* (the nation)—reflective of the great desires to receive that were to emerge from him. To match those desires, he had a will to give, which guaranteed that the desires will ultimately be corrected. Every time Abraham increases his will to give, he moves to Israel, and every time he increases his will to receive, he moves to Egypt. This is also why immigration to Israel is considered ascent and immigration to Egypt is considered descent.

The will to give by itself is powerless. You can truly give to the Creator only by receiving from Him. So Abraham asked, "How will I know that I will reach the same level of giving as the Creator?" Abraham couldn't receive because he was in a state of giving. The Creator put his seed in Egypt and told him he would receive the full measure of the will to receive. Abraham was delighted. After the exile, when the people mingle with the Egyptians and absorb their desires, the people will be corrected and know how to receive in order to bestow. This is the pattern of attainment for everyone and leads to the end of correction.

The Bible says that Abraham went down to Egypt because of famine. The famine was spiritual because he wanted to bestow but had nothing to bestow with. For Abraham, a situation in which he can't bestow is called famine, absence of desires to receive.

As a person gradually acquires a bigger will to receive, this is called experiencing the exile in Egypt. When you come out of the experience with great substance and vessels of reception, you can begin to correct them so they work in order to bestow.

Moses—the Point in the Heart

The next key Bible story from the perspective of Kabbalah is the story of Moses. Pharaoh enslaving the Jews has deeper significance than historical record.

Pharaoh, in the time of Joseph, dreamed that there would be 7 years of wealth, followed by 7 years of famine. Wealth is when you first discover a great desire for spirituality and feel great happiness. This is because you think that, through your ego, you can thrive spiritually. You are ready to read and learn and do all kinds of things. In that state, you think that you can acquire spirituality with the will to receive. Famine happens when you see that you cannot acquire spirituality unless you gain the attribute of giving. But you can't give, despite wanting to. You are caught in between. This is Egypt.

To bring about change, your "Pharaoh" grows. Your Pharaoh is your ego. It begins to show you bad things about the present state. If it is very bad, you want to escape or flee to spirituality. You want to go even if there is nothing appealing and attractive about it, even if the Red Sea is in your way (as in the story of Moses). When your ego shows you how bad it is, you will want to change. (In Hebrew, the Red Sea is called *Yam Suf*, the "sea of the end," representing the ego's final frontier. Beyond *Yam Suf* begins the spiritual world.)

The name Moses comes from the word *Moshech* (pulling). This is the point that pulls us out of Egypt, just like the Messiah, which also comes from the same word. Moses is the feeling within a person that stands against his or her ego and says, "Maybe we should come out." The big force that pushes is Pharaoh. The small force that pulls is Moses. This pulling is the start of your spirituality, the point in the heart.

Esther the Queen

This story describes the final correction of the will to receive, named *Haman*. *Mordechai* (the will to bestow) and *Haman* share a horse. *Haman* rides first, then *Haman* lets *Mordechai* ride while he walks with the horse. This shows how your will to receive ultimately surrenders before your will to bestow and gives up the reins.

Esther—from the Hebrew word *Hester*, "concealment"—is the hidden Kingdom of Heaven. She is hidden, along with Ahasuerus, the Creator, who is seemingly neither good nor bad. The person who experiences it doesn't know who's right and whether the Creator is good or bad.

Esther is also a relative of *Mordechai*, the will to bestow. *Mordechai*, like Moses but at a different spiritual stage, is the *Bina* point in one's soul, which pulls you toward the Light.

When the will to give appears, sometimes it cannot be seen right away. Sometimes it is hidden, like Esther the Queen. You may not know if the action is really giving. However, if *Mordechai* is the one riding, your will to receive can correct itself.

Kab-Trivia

When we celebrate the story of *Haman* and *Mordechai*, Purim, we are told we must drink until we cannot tell *Haman* from *Mordechai*, egoism from altruism. This is because at the end of correction, all desires are corrected and work in order to give to the Creator, so it doesn't matter which desire you work with, it'll always be with the intention to give.

Great Prophecies and Great Prophets: The Real Deal!

Prophecy is defined as a special degree of recognition of the Creator. One experiences these degrees on the way to *Gmar Tikkun* (the end of correction). In short, a prophet is one who converses with the Creator, and the greatest prophet is the degree of Moses.

Some prophets speak with the Creator, but through a veil. Only prophets in the degree of Moses, the highest degree (not the person), are in visible contact with the Creator.

Some people who "talk" to the Creator are placed in institutions—that's different! Neurological disturbances that create delusions are not the same as building a relationship with the Creator through spirituality. Before you can speak to the Creator, (if it is "real" speaking), you undergo corrections that take many years to complete. In those corrections, you acquire tools to understand what is true and false, good and bad, spiritual and corporeal. You understand this world and the next, life and death. In short, to talk to the Creator you have to cross the barrier and have a *Masach*.

Rabbi Ashlag defines spiritual attainment as the deepest possible understanding. It is a clear and vivid perception, measurable and conveyable so others can repeat, understand, and feel what is being conveyed. It is felt in the most healthy, clear, and direct way in human nature.

Another person can feel the same if he or she is on the same spiritual degree, using the information provided by the other person. This is how Kabbalists wrote their books.

Prophets, like all other Biblical figures, symbolize forces. In that sense, they are angels sent to help us correct, some in a more pleasant manner and some more harshly. At this very moment, there are forces operating on you, but you call them "heat," "cold," and "pressure." The same is true on more subtle levels, too. All of these are forces, called "angels." Angels operate upon us constantly. Prophets are considered angels because they have no freedom of choice in their prophecies. Like angels, they are pure driving forces, and every force is an angel.

Chariots of Fire

Eliyahu (Prophet Elijah) is a special force from above that helps souls complete their last and final correction. Rabbi Yehuda Ashlag calls the spreading of Kabbalah "the revelation of Eliyahu" because this force is the only means that can help us correct in the state we are today.

The biblical story of Elijah's ascent to heaven symbolizes corrections at the highest spiritual degrees. When we correct ourselves through spreading the authentic Kabbalah of the Ari and Rabbi Shimon, Ashlag says that we will discover the highest levels of spirituality.

Dry Bones

The story of bones that were made into humans is told in the Book of Ezekial. God led Ezekial to a valley that was full of a great number of very dry bones. God led him back and forth and asked, "Can these bones live?" Ezekial said to God, "You alone know."

Then, with Ezekial's prophecy and the Creator's life-giving breath, the bones took human form and became a vast army.

Rabbi Ashlag explains more in the introduction to *The Book of Zohar*. The bones are the only part that remains when the body dies because they correspond to the vessels of bestowal in the body (will to receive). Because these are vessels of bestowal, they do not need correction, so they don't have to die. After they are revived, a new (corrected) body (will to receive) stems from them.

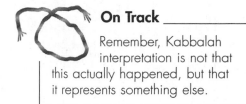

On Track

Remember, Kabbalah interpretation is not that this actually happened, but that it represents something else.

In the Belly of a Whale

One of the best-known stories in the Bible is the allegory of Jonah and the whale. The Creator asked Jonah to go on a mission to correct a wicked city. Jonah disobeyed the Creator and tried to avoid his task by escaping on a ship. At sea, a storm came, and Jonah told the crew to throw him overboard to appease the Creator. Jonah was swallowed by a whale and lived in its belly for 3 days and nights, at which point he prayed to the Creator. Even in the depths of the sea, behind the walls of whale blubber, his prayer was answered and he was (rather unceremoniously) spit up by the whale onto dry land.

The whale represents the collective *Malchut* of *Ein Sof*, the sum of creation's will to receive. The point called "the prophet Jonah" couldn't cope with his task, so he escaped because he didn't think he could succeed. Because he tried to avoid fulfilling his mission, a whale swallowed him. There, he was brought to the correction he was compelled to make.

Demystifying *The Zohar*

The knowledge in *The Zohar* is profound, but you need guidelines to "swim" through it. All *The Zohar* speaks of, even in fables, are the 10 *Sefirot* (*Keter, Hochma, Bina, Hesed, Gevura, Tifferet, Netzah, Hod, Yesod,* and *Malchut*) and their interactions. To the Kabbalist, the entries and their various combinations are sufficient to reveal all the spiritual worlds.

The Zohar was created by Rabbi Shimon Bar-Yochai (Rashbi). He had a big problem. He was debating with himself on how to convey Kabbalah knowledge for future generations. He did not want to expose people to the content in *The Book of Zohar* prematurely. He was afraid this would only confuse them and mislead them from the true path.

To avoid confusion, he entrusted the writing in the hands of Rabbi Aba, who knew how to write in a special way so only the worthy would understand. Because of *The Zohar*'s special language, only those who are *already* on the ladder of spiritual degrees understand what is written there. *The Zohar* is only for those who have already acquired some level of spiritual degree, who crossed the barrier. They are the ones who can understand the book, according to their spiritual degree.

Today many Kabbalists feel that many souls are too materialistic and egoistic to understand *The Zohar*. They need tools to bring them into the spiritual "zone" first. It's like a space shuttle that needs a big thrust before it can continue on its own engine. A supportive environment, teacher, and correct books give your spiritual understanding a "boost."

True Legends

There are different styles of writing in *The Zohar*. It was written in different languages, depending on how they wanted to express specific spiritual states. Sometimes the various languages create confusion. When the book talks about laws, people may think *The Zohar* is preaching morals. When it tells stories, people may see them as fables. Without spiritual attainment, it is difficult to understand what *The Zohar* is really about.

Some of *The Zohar* is written in the language of Kabbalah, and some of it is written in the language of legends. A true legend can be thought of as a "new used car." This doesn't make sense until you think about it, but consider these two stories from *The Zohar*, and you'll see what this means.

Two Men and a Donkey Driver

The Zohar contains a beautiful story about a donkey driver, a man who drives the donkeys of important men so they can carelessly walk and talk about their own affairs. But the donkey driver in *The Zohar* is a force that helps a person who already has his own soul.

In the story, two men talk about spiritual matters as they walk along from one place to another. Whenever they come to a dilemma they can't resolve, the donkey driver "miraculously" gives them the answer. As they progress (thanks to the driver's answers), they discover that their simple donkey driver is actually a heaven-sent angel who is there for just that purpose: to help them progress. When they have progressed to the final degree, they find that their driver is already there, waiting for them.

The Kabbalistic interpretation: the donkey is our will to receive, our egoism. You and I all have a donkey driver, waiting for us to enter the spiritual world so he can guide us. But just like the legend, we will discover who the donkey driver really is only when we reach his degree, at the end of our correction.

The Night of the Bride

Before the end of correction, there is a special state called "the night of the bride." The story in *The Zohar* talks about the preparation of the bride for the wedding ceremony. The bride is the collection of all the souls. It is a *Kli* that is ready to bond with the Creator.

When you reach this state, you feel that your *Kli* is prepared, supported, and ready for spiritual unity. The groom is the Creator. It is called "night" because the *Dvekut* (unity) is still not apparent. The Light is not shining in the vessels yet. Night means that the vessels still feel darkness, absence of unity.

When the night turns into day, the abundance of the end of correction is promised, but *The Zohar* doesn't tell us exactly why it is good—only that it is wholeness, Light, and peace. Still sounds promising, doesn't it?

A Tree of Life

Toward the end of the Middle Ages, a new kind of soul began to appear, whose will to receive needed a new approach to meet its needs. As always in Kabbalah, a new era calls for a new teacher. This is how Isaac Luria, the Ari, appeared.

The Ari didn't write his books. He taught his lessons and the students listened attentively. His best, and most dedicated student, Chaim Vital, put his mentor's words in writing. The most famous of the books put together from the Ari's words is *The Tree of Life*, which presents the Kabbalistic knowledge in a whole new way: more technical and systematic.

The Ari relayed his knowledge to Chaim Vital orally. Chaim lived much longer than his teacher, and his spiritual attainment evolved. He couldn't arrange all the writings, but he did the best he could. His children and grandchildren continued where he left off, and where he and his descendents didn't perfectly understand, Rabbi Yehuda Ashlag further elucidated the Ari's teachings in his *Talmud Eser Sefirot* (*The Study of the Ten Sefirot*).

We've Grown Up, Let's Talk Business

The writer of *The Tree of Life*, the Ari, marks the beginning of the last phase in the evolution of the souls. In the tradition of other Kabbalist writers, he was given the ability to disclose the great and unique things to his generation. The Ari teaches that his phase is the last generation, and Ashlag writes the same about his time. The Ari represents the last phase. From his time on, the wisdom of Kabbalah begins to emerge from hiding, though it still takes centuries. With him, a new *qualitative* process has begun.

Kabbalist writers can feel that their phase is the last before correction because they know it takes only a little *MAN* (prayer for correction) to reveal everything and bring the end to our world's troubles. There's just a fraction of an inch missing to make contact. Crossing the gap is up to us, and this is why Kabbalists try to spread their knowledge so more souls are corrected. They feel we are very close to completing our correction.

Ten Attributes

The words of Rabbi Shimon Bar-Yochai were written in *The Book of Zohar* by his student, Rabbi Aba. The words of the Ari were written by his student, Chaim Vital. But unlike his spiritual ancestors, Rabbi Yehuda Ashlag, known as Baal HaSulam (Master of the Ladder) for his *Sulam* (*The Ladder*) commentary on *The Book of Zohar*, wrote his books by himself.

The "flagship" of his work is his commentary on the writings of the Ari, known as *Talmud Eser Sefirot* (*The Study of the Ten Sefirot*). In six volumes and more than 2,000 pages, Baal HaSulam explains to uneducated souls of the twentieth and twenty-first centuries what the Ari actually meant when he dictated *The Tree of Life*. Baal HaSulam wrote his book specifically to people who want spirituality and nothing else. In his introduction to *The Study of the Ten Sefirot*, he states that his intended audience are those who ask, "What is the meaning of my life?"

The *Sefirot* are spiritual attributes. The 10 *Sefirot* represent the 9 basic attributes of the Creator—*Keter, Hochma, Bina, Hesed, Gevura, Tifferet, Netzah, Hod,* and *Yesod*—and the single attribute of the creature—*Malchut*. But the importance of the book is not so much in the vast knowledge it provides. It is in the way this knowledge is arranged: the exact format in which you need to study it in order to reach the spiritual worlds by yourself.

The Least You Need to Know

- Things in this world have a spiritual force that is behind them.

- The Bible and other Kabbalah texts are written in the language of the branches, using worldly names and terms to indicate spiritual processes.

- The stories of the Bible are not about people—they are about forces that act on souls.

- Prophets can speak with the Creator after a correction process where they learn details of spirituality. They can either "hear" or "see" Him, depending on their degree.

- The book written with our correction in mind is *Talmud Eser Sefirot, The Study of the Ten Seirot.*

Letters, Numbers, Names

In This Chapter

◆ Getting a handle on Hebrew letters

◆ Add numerical values for added meaning

◆ See the simple and not-so-simple symbolism of letters and names

◆ Discover your special name

Letters, words, and numbers are usually three separate things, but they are intricately linked in Kabbalah. Understanding their relationship gives greater spiritual meaning to each of them. In Hebrew (the base language of Kabbalah texts), each letter has a numerical value. Letters are used as numbers because Hebrew has no specific symbols for numbers.

The Hebrew language, and the way it is written, is a direct result of communication with the Upper Worlds. The language was created by Kabbalists, and they designed it in such a way that the letters of the Hebrew alphabet embrace all the knowledge of creation.

The combination of letters and the strokes of ink that make them up are laced with spiritual knowledge. Each letter and the names that they form have their own spiritual story to tell. Like much of Kabbalah, it's complex. But hang in there. The more you read through the material, the more you'll understand how the Creator is expressed in the letters of Hebrew.

The Hidden Meaning of Hebrew Letters

Because each letter in Hebrew corresponds to a number, any word or name can become a series of numbers. The numbers can be taken one at a time or added together. There is significance when words include or add up to the same numbers; the meanings of the words that share numbers are thought to be related in the deepest sense.

The letters are also felt to be the result of a spiritual sensation, or feeling. The direction of the lines and shapes in a letter has spiritual meaning.

As a result, Hebrew letters are also codes for sensations the writer receives from the Creator. When a letter or word is written, the author is giving us his or her conscious perception of the Creator. The Creator is acting on the writer as they write.

The color in writing is also a clue to the way creation (black ink) works hand in hand with the Creator (white paper). Without both of them, you could not understand the writing or the story of creation and what it means to you.

Cracking the Letter Code

The *Torah* is the major text of Judaism and the first five books of the "Old Testament" in Christianity, as well as a Kabbalah text. Believe it or not, this large book in its original form was recorded as a single word. Later, this single word was divided into more words, which are made of letters.

The letters show all the information that is radiating down from the Creator. There are two basic kinds of lines in Hebrew letters, representing two kinds of Light. The vertical lines stand for the Light of wisdom or pleasure. The horizontal lines stand for the Light of mercy, or correction. (There are also diagonals and circular lines that have specific meanings in each letter, and you can read more about this later in this chapter in the section titled "More About Shapes.")

> **On Track**
>
> Light of Mercy and Light of Wisdom are not really two kinds of Light, just as there are no two Creators. They are the same Light, but when the Light is used for correction we call it Light of Mercy, and when it is used for reception of pleasure we call it Light of Wisdom.

The codes come from changes in the Light as it develops your *Kli* (desire). The Light expands your desire. When Light enters your *Kli*, it is called *Ta'amim* (flavors), and when it leaves, it is called *Nekudot* (dots or points). Memories of entering are called *Tagin* (tags), and memories of departing are *Otiot* (letters). All letters start with a dot or point. A complete cycle of a spiritual state contains entrance, departure, memories of the entrance, and the memories of the departure. The fourth and last element creates letters, and the other three are written as tiny symbols (*Ta'amim*), tags (*Tagin*), and dots (*Nekudim*) above, within, and below the letters.

With correct instruction for reading the *Torah*, Kabbalists can see their past, present, and future states by gazing at these symbols in each of their combinations. But to see that, it is not enough to simply read the text. You must know how to see the codes.

Kab-Trivia

In his *Preamble to the Wisdom of Kabbalah*, Rabbi Yehuda Ashlag explains that *Ta'amim* enliven the *Otiot*, which are the vessels of reception. Traditional Judaism has turned the *Ta'amim* into singing notes, and in different parts of the world, Jews sing the same *Ta'amim* differently.

Certain combinations of letters can be used instead of the language of the Upper World when you describe spiritual actions. (The language of the Upper World consists of the *Sefirot* and *Partzufim*, introduced in Chapter 8.) Objects and actions shown through letters and their combinations, too, can give a description of the spiritual world.

The key to reading the *Torah* in this way is *The Zohar*. In essence, the book contains commentaries on the five parts of the *Torah* and explains what is concealed in the texts of Moses.

The letters represent information about the Creator. More precisely, they describe the individual's experience of the Creator. The Creator is infinite; we cannot confine Him to any boundary. Therefore, Kabbalists depict the Creator as white Light, the background of the paper on which letters and words are written. The creature's perceptions of the Creator emphasize different sensations that a person feels while experiencing the Creator, using letters and words. This is why traditional Hebrew writing is made of black letters over a white background.

Word of Heart

There are Emanator and emanated. The Emanator has four elements: Fire, Wind, Water, and Dust, which are the four *Otiot* (letters): *Yod, Hey, Vav, Hey*, which are *Hochma, Bina, Tifferet*, and *Malchut*. They are also *Ta'amim, Nekudot, Tagin, Otiot*, and they are *Atzilut, Beria, Yetzira, Assiya*.

—From *The Tree of Life* by the Holy Ari

So it turns out that the Hebrew letters are like a map of spirituality, whereby using the right combination can describe all the spiritual desires. The way they connect gives us the *Torah*.

Shapes

The dots and lines of Hebrew letters are shapes on the paper, which is blank and void. The paper is the Light, or Creator. The black ink on it is the creation.

If the Light descends from above—from the Creator toward creation—then there is a vertical line (|). If the Creator is relating to all existence (like the sweep of a landscape), there is a horizontal line (-).

The shape of Hebrew letters comes from the combination of *Malchut* (represented by black) and *Bina* (represented by white). The black point is *Malchut.* When the dot connects to the Light, it expresses the way it receives the Light through all kinds of forms and shapes, like a dancer moving and twirling and swirling through space. The shapes show the different ways creation (black ink) reacts to understanding the Creator (the white background).

Each letter is a sign of a combinations of forces. Their structure and how they are spoken express qualities of the Creator. You express the spiritual qualities you achieve through the shapes.

Symbolism

Hebrew letters also represent vessels or containers. Each letter symbolizes some aspect of the Light of creation. As you'll learn later in this chapter, the letters appeared one by one before the Creator and asked that they be selected to serve Him in creating the universe. Put simply, the letters asked to receive his blessing and give it to creation, just as a vessel receives water and pours it out to sustain life.

Word of Heart

Even if we take the subtlest word that can be used ... the word "Upper Light", or even "Simple Light." It is still borrowed and lent from the light of the sun, or a candle, or a light of contentment one feels upon resolving some great doubt ... How can we use them in context of the spiritual and Godly? ... It is particularly so where one needs to find some ratio in these words to help one in the negotiation customary in the research of the wisdom. Here one must be very strict and accurate using definitive descriptions ...

—From *The Essence of the Wisdom of Kabbalah* by Yehuda Ashlag

White symbolizes Light (giving) and black symbolizes darkness (receiving). For this reason, the properties of the Creator are absolutely white, symbolized by the white paper. Black is creation, you and me and this world, symbolized by the black ink. Alone, the Creator and creation cannot be understood at all. Together, they make letters and symbols that can be read and understood.

Think of it this way: without a creation, can we really call the Creator, "Creator"? To be a Creator, He needs to create. This Creator-creation dualism is the basis for all that exists. You can talk about something only from the perspective of the being that perceives that something.

The shapes of the letters symbolize a connection and bond between you and the Creator. They are not just black lines; they form clear shapes because they represent corrected relationships between creation and Creator.

This bond is built on contrast and collision. As creatures, you and I don't experience Light unless it collides with something. To sense Light, it must be stopped by something, such as your eye. The surface of an object (sound, light, or any kind of wave) collides with our perception. This stops it from continuing and allows us to sense it.

Because the paper is like the Light, it must be stopped with black lines (letters). That allows a person to sense the Light and learn from it. The black lines of the letters are seen as a barrier to the Light. This is because black (the color) is the opposite of Light. The Light strikes against the creature's *Masach*; it wants to enter the *Kli* and give delight. Instead of deflecting it, the struggle between the rejecting *Masach* and the striking Light creates a powerful bond, like spiritual Velcro. This collision is what the relationship between the Light and letters is based on.

In this way, the black lines of the letters limit the Light or restrict it. When the Light "hits" a line, it is forced to stop, and then the *Kli* (vessel, letter) can study it. It turns out that the only way to learn anything about the Creator is by stopping His light—restricting it and studying it. Ironically, it is precisely when you contain the Creator that you learn how to be as free as Him. In a sense, the *Masach* is like a prism: the rejection of Light breaks it into the elements that comprise it, and this allows us, creatures, to study it and decide how much of each "color we want to use."

The Letters in You

In Hebrew, there are five respective groups of letters, and their "relationships" between the palate and the throat (*Zivug*, if you want to use Kabbalistic terminology) enables you to create speech. Because there are five primary *Sefirot—Keter, Hochma,*

Bina, Zeir Anpin, and *Malchut*—there are also five openings to the mouth: teeth, palate, throat, lips, and tongue. You express the letters through these five openings. Even the lungs, which provide the air for our speech, are made of five parts, two in the left lung and three in the right lung. And here, too, it is because the basic structure of creation is made of five *Sefirot.* Note the following illustration of the Hebrew alphabet, in which the letters fall into three basic divisions.

א	= Aleph	1	י	= Yod	10	ק	= Kof	100
ב	= Bet	2	כ	= Chaf	20	ר	= Reish	200
ג	= Gimel	3	ל	= Lamed	30	ש	= Shin	300
ד	= Dalet	4	מ	= Mem	40	ת	= Tav	400
ה	= Hey	5	נ	= Nun	50			
ו	= Vav	6	ס	= Samech	60			
ז	= Zayin	7	ע	= Ain	70			
ח	= Het	8	פ	= Peh	80			
ט	= Tet	9	צ	= Tzadik	90			

Final Letters:

ך = Final Chaf   20

ם = Final Mem   40

ן = Final Nun   50

ף = Final Peh   80

ץ = Final Tzadik 90

The Hebrew Letters and Their Numeric Values

What's in a Number?

Hebrew consists of 22 letters. The letters describe creation's connection to the Creator. The first nine letters, *Aleph* through *Tet,* represent the lower part of *Bina,* the highest level that a creature can reach. The next nine, *Yod* through *Tzadik,* stand for *Zeir Anpin,* and the last four, *Kof* through *Tav,* stand for *Malchut,* the creature itself.

In addition to the "regular" letters, there are five final letters in Hebrew. If you look at the illustration, you see that they are not new letters; they bear the same names as letters in the original 22. There is a good reason for that.

⚑ On Track _____

You study the qualities of the Creator in the same way you determine an object's color. When you see a red ball, it means that the ball reflected the red color, and that's why we can see it. Similarly, when you reject (reflect) a fragment of the Creator's Light, you know exactly what you rejected. This is why the only way you can know the Creator is by first rejecting all His Light. Then you can decide what you want to do with it.

The original 22 letters are all in the world of _Atzilut_, the highest of the five worlds introduced in Chapter 8. Because the original 22 letters are in the world closest to the Creator, they describe a corrected connection between creation and Creator.

They do not describe the contact between the corrected world of _Atzilut_ and the as-yet-uncorrected state of the worlds _Beria_, _Yetzira_, and _Assiya_. So the five final letters make contact between the corrected state (_Atzilut_) and those of the uncorrected state, _Beria_, _Yetzira_, _Assiya_ (_BYA_). Because there are five phases in creation, there must be five final forms of contact between _Atzilut_ and _BYA_, hence the five final letters.

The letter _Bet_ is the first letter in the _Torah_ and the second letter in the Hebrew alphabet. It's the first in the _Torah_ because _Bet_ stands for the corrected connection between _Bina_ and _Malchut_, which is called _Bracha_, blessing.

Corrected connection between _Bina_ and _Malchut_ means that a blessing is received when _Malchut_ (creation, us) can connect to _Bina_ (Creator). We can connect to Him _only_ when we want to be like Him, and that's when it's referred to as a corrected connection. When _Malchut_ asks to be like _Bina_—that is, when you and I want to be like the Creator, it is called "a corrected connection" blessing (_Bracha_).

The numbers have different meanings because they relate back to the Upper World. For example, the number 7 is significant because the system that governs our world consists of seven parts, which are the seven lower _Sefirot_: _Hesed_, _Gevura_, _Tifferet_, _Netzah_, _Hod_, _Yesod_, and _Malchut_.

All the 22 original Hebrew letters are expressed in three different levels, corresponding to the three _Sefirot_: _Bina_, _Zeir Anpin_ (ZA), and _Malchut_. On the _Bina_ level,

⚑ On Track _____

Remember that Kabbalah is a scientific system that seeks to explain spirituality. As with most scientific systems, it divides and categorizes. The divisions of letters and numbers, and how they correspond to the divisions of the Upper Worlds and its divisions into the _Sefirot_ and _Partzufim_, is no exception, as you'll see.

the 22 letters are called big. On the *ZA* level, the 22 letters are called middle or medium. On the *Malchut* level, they are called small.

Units, Tens, Hundreds

The Hebrew letters are also divided into three numerical categories: the ones, tens, and hundreds of all arithmetic. This, again, is because of the division into big, medium, and small:

◆ The *Bina* level corresponds to ones and the category of big letters: *Aleph, Bet, Gimel, Dalet, Hey, Vav, Zayin, Het, Tet.* These are the nine (1–9) *Sefirot* of *Bina.*

◆ The *ZA* level corresponds to tens and the nine middle Hebrew letters: *Yod, Chaf, Lamed, Mem, Nun, Samech, Ayin, Peh, Tzadik.* These are the nine (10–90) *Sefirot* of *ZA.*

◆ The *Malchut* level corresponds to hundreds and the four small letters: *Kof, Reish, Shin, Tav.* These are the four (100–400) *Sefirot* of *Malchut.*

The obvious question comes to mind: what about the numbers above 400? The answer is that Hebrew is a spiritual language, not a math language. Everything about it represents spiritual states, and no more numbers are required to describe the structure of the world *Atzilut* (the "home" of the letters). In other words, with these 22 letters, you can describe *everything* from the beginning of creation to infinity.

Kab-Trivia

The words *Dror* (liberty) and *Kadosh* (holy) have the same numeric value (in Hebrew), and are therefore spiritual synonyms. Makes you wonder ....

So what happens when you want to express complicated numbers, like 248? You use three letters: *Reish* (200), *Mem* (40), and *Het* (8). And what if you want to write a higher number than 400, like 756? You use more than three letters: *Tav* (400) + *Shin* (300) + *Nun* (50) + *Vav* (6) = 756.

Of course, we can reach this number using many different combinations, but it is important to remember that if two words add up to the same number, they are spiritual synonyms and have the same spiritual meaning.

Now here's how this discussion of numbers relates to the evolution of spiritual desire explained in Kabbalah. When numbers represent the size of your *Kli*, the bigger they are, the more Light enters them. If there are only ones in your desire, that is, if you have a small desire, a small amount of Light is present. If tens are added and your desire grows, more Light enters. If hundreds are added and your desire reaches its peak, the Light symbolized by the letters fills your spiritual "vessels" (*Kelim*).

Things get tricky, however, as Kabbalah has an exception. Numbers can also represent the Light, not just the desires. In this case, ones (small Lights) are in *Malchut*, tens are in *ZA*, and hundreds are in *Bina*. This is because of an inverse relationship between Light and desire. This may be confusing, but it is because the greatest Light of the Creator enters into your *Kli* only when you activate your lowest desires.

Here are the numerical values of each level expressed in terms of the Light they represent and the level at which they fill your vessels:

◆ *Bina*—The Light (100); the vessels (1)

◆ *ZA*—The Light (10); the vessels (10)

◆ *Malchut*—The Light (1); the vessels (100)

God = Nature

Here's something else to think about: if you add the numeric values of all the letters in the words *the nature* (in Hebrew), they add up to 86. If you add the numeric values of the letters in the word *cup* in Hebrew, they add up to 86. And if you add the numeric values of the letters in the word *God* (in Hebrew), you guessed right—they add up to 86. That shows the equivalence of God and nature in Kabbalah that we noted in Chapter 3. Here's how it works.

We've already said that if two words add up to the same number, they have the same spiritual meaning. Therefore, the statement that Kabbalah is making here is very interesting (if a little complex):

◆ Nature and Creator are one and the same. The fact that we don't see them as such doesn't make it less true, just like the fact that we can't see bacteria with a naked eye doesn't stop them from affecting our bodies.

◆ A cup, in Kabbalah, stands for a *Kli*, meaning a desire to receive. Therefore, nature and our *Kli* are the same. Here, too, the fact that we don't sense it doesn't mean it isn't true, but the fact that they have the same value means that we have the opportunity to correct (change) our desires to match nature's structure.

◆ When we match our desires (*Kli*) with those of nature, we will also match them with the Creator (because nature and the Creator are synonyms). When we equalize our *Kli* with nature, we will discover the Creator.

In terms of an equation, it looks like this: if A = B, and B = C, then A = C.

The Secret Name of God

The name of all these "games" Kabbalists play with letters and numbers is *Gimatria*. Ancient Kabbalists perfected *Gimatria* to a point that they could (and did) describe the whole creation and the Creator-creation relationship using *Gimatria*, as the following sections demonstrate.

The Template of Life

Gimatria is an expression of the state of a *Kli* that discovers the Creator. The *Kli* discovers Him within its own structure. The *Kli* is made of 10 *Sefirot*. These 10 *Sefirot* are divided into the tip of the letter *Yod*, and then the letters *Yod*, *Hey*, *Vav*, and *Hey* again. This four-letter structure is known as the *tetragrammaton* (in Greek), *HaVaYaH* (in Hebrew), and Yaweh or JHVH or Jehovah (in English).

def•i•ni•tion

From Greek, literally meaning "four-letter word," **tetragrammaton** designates the sacred name of God.

The first *Sefira*, *Keter*, belongs to the tip of the *Yod*; the second *Sefira*, *Hochma*, to the *Yod*; and the third *Sefira*, *Bina*, to *Hey*. The next *Sefira*, *ZA*, contains six internal *Sefirot*: *Hesed*, *Gevura*, *Tifferet*, *Netzah*, *Hod*, and *Yesod*. All those *Sefirot* are contained in the letter *Vav*. And the last *Hey* is *Malchut*, which is also the last *Sefira*.

As a matter of fact, *HaVaYaH* isn't just the structure of one *Kli*; it is the structure of every *Kli*—and of everything there is, was, or will be. It is the template of life.

In Kabbalistic terminology, it is simply stated like this: "There is nothing in reality that is not made of 10 *Sefirot*." It's like a hologram—however small you cut it, you'll always get a structure of 10 complete *Sefirot*. This is also why these four letters comprise the word *HaVaYaH* (a generic term that means existence, being, and entity all in one).

Getting Personal

It's important to understand that there is a relationship between the letters, *Sefirot*, and *Kli* because, in Kabbalah, a person's name stands for a person's spiritual *Kli*. Abraham, for instance, stands for a very specific kind of relationship between the Creator and creation. Abraham stands for a soul that made a certain kind of correction. When he was born, his name was Abram. But after he made the correction of turning his desires from egoistic to altruistic, he changed his name to Abraham. The added *h* stands for adding the *Hey* of *Bina* to his name, the Creator's quality of altruism. This indicates that he has risen to that spiritual level.

The same process occurred with Jacob, who later became Israel. The same happens with every Kabbalist. Kabbalists name themselves according to their spiritual degree. It's not a question of changing the name on your driver's license; it's a little deeper than that. When you develop a certain relationship with the Creator, you will also know what to call yourself, though your friends will still call you Mark, Mary, Mitch, or Moses (well, maybe not Moses).

More About Shapes

The dot that begins a Hebrew letter is the point of *Malchut*. Next, a line is made. Stretching the line from above downward is considered expansion according to the Light of *Hochma* (wisdom). A line made from right to left is considered the expansion of *Hassadim* (mercy).

There is also a diagonal line, which signifies the connection between *Malchut* and *Bina*. It is the connection between the spiritual world and this world.

Through vertical, horizontal, and diagonal shapes, letters with a rich variety of meanings are created. The shape of every letter and its structure give all the properties and states of a spiritual object. Once you achieve these properties, you assume the name of that level.

Kab-Trivia

We already said that there is no bad in Kabbalah; it's all a question of how we relate to the situations we're in. Pharaoh is considered an evil force. But Kabbalists inverted the Hebrew letters of the name Pharaoh, and found that it really meant *Oref H* (the posterior side of the Creator). In other words, Pharaoh is really the Creator goading you harshly to progress to spirituality because you are not pushing yourself fast enough. If you push faster, you will find that Pharaoh is your friend.

Opening the Womb Door

To get a closer look at what the letters mean to a Kabbalist, let's examine a specific letter. Take the letter *Mem*, for example.

The letter *Mem* stands for *Bina*. *Bina* is the spiritual womb. It is also 40 in *Gimatria*. (That's why the early Kabbalists said it was forbidden to study Kabbalah before the age of 40—you can't really know what Kabbalah is about before you acquire the attribute of *Bina*. In fact, it was considered impossible because *forbidden* in Kabbalah means "impossible.")

Mem is something closed, something that can contain *Malchut*. When Kabbalists rise to *Bina*, it means that they become like embryos inside the Creator, letting His force work on them and correct them. It is then said that you, *Malchut*, rise to *Bina*, the Creator, and become enclosed in it.

As long as you need to let the Creator work on you, you remain inside the *Mem* until it's time to be born. When you are born, the doors of the *Mem* (made of the letter *Dalet*, which also means "door" in Hebrew) open and the spiritual baby is born.

A Point of Wisdom

Now take the letter *Yod* because it contains the whole of creation. *Yod* begins with a point. This point is not a part of the *Yod* itself, which is why it has its own name, "the tip of the *Yod*." Because you can't name the Creator by anything except what you perceive of Him within you, Kabbalists named the perception of the Creator "the tip of the *Yod*." It indicates that they can't say much about it except that it stands for the Thought of Creation, the desire to give.

After the tip comes the *Yod*. On one hand, *Yod* stands for all the power in the world, *Hochma*, the *Sefira* from which creation begins. On the other hand, it is the first will to receive. Because *Yod* represents direct contact between Creator and creation, giving and receiving, this letter stands for both the power of the Creator and the pleasures He gives.

The First Letter

Letters in Hebrew have personalities and feelings. They tell the story of the creation of the alphabet by the Creator Himself.

The Zohar has a beautiful story about how each letter in the alphabet stepped before the Creator and asked of Him to use it to create the world. They did that in reverse order, from the last letter (*Tav*) to the first (*Aleph*). The Creator answered each of them about why he couldn't create the world with them, until the *Bet* came.

The letter *Bet* entered and said to the Creator: "Master of the world, may it please You to create the world by me, because by me You are blessed above and below." This is because *Bet* is *Bracha* (blessing). The Creator said to *Bet:* "Of course, I will create the world by you, and you will be the beginning of creation!"

But there was still one letter remaining. The letter *Aleph* stood outside and did not enter to appear before the Creator. The Creator said to it: "Why do you not enter like all the other letters?" *Aleph* replied: "Because I saw all the letters leaving your presence fruitlessly without the desired answer. Besides, I saw You presenting the letter *Bet* with this enormous gift. It is not fitting for the King of the universe to take back the gift and give it to another!"

The Creator replied: "Although I will create the world by the letter *Bet*, you will stand at the head of all the letters. My unity will be expressed only through you, and all counting and deeds of this world will begin with you, and all unity is only in you."

So even though *Bet* was the first letter of the *Torah*, *Aleph* is the first letter of the Hebrew alphabet.

> ♦ **On Track** _____
>
> Don't worry about understanding the letters and their spiritual meanings. These will come to you as you climb up the spiritual ladder. Even if you can't speak Hebrew, Hebrew letters will become known to you because their essence is spiritual, and spirituality has no language.

What's My True Name?

All the letters exist within us and nowhere else. They are spiritual vessels, experiences that each of us will feel or have felt at some point in time.

The letters are *Kelim* (vessels) that perceive the Creator. When we learn the true meaning of the letters, we find the diagonal line of the *Aleph* connecting our world and the spiritual world. We find the closed *Mem*, the Creator's womb. And when we walk into the *Mem*, we find the *Samech*, the letter that supports all the fallen and guarantees that in times of hardship we will find the strength to continue.

We've already seen that each of the 22 Hebrew letters represents a certain property. The properties could be used for attaining closeness with the Creator, and once you have it, they give this closeness a name.

Every person has something called "the Root of the soul." As we climb the spiritual ladder and discover the letters, words, and numbers within us, we gradually come closer to our true selves.

The Creator created only one creation. This creation was divided into 600,000 pieces, which then broke into the billions of souls we have in the world today. As we climb the ladder, we realize that we are one body once more, and we find our place in it. This is the root of our soul.

Each root also has its own name, and when we reach the root of our soul, we discover our place in the system of creation and who we really are. And we describe it with a name that is just our own.

The Least You Need to Know

◆ Hebrew letters are thought to be the direct language of the Creator.

◆ Hebrew letters can be converted into numbers, and those numbers show the relationships of meanings between words.

◆ Hebrew letters are symbols of spiritual actions by the Creator.

◆ As you climb the spiritual ladder of Kabbalah, you discover the letters within you according to your spiritual state—and you discover your own true name.

Chapter 12

Reincarnation

In This Chapter

◆ Reincarnation according to Kabbalah

◆ The circle of life keeps spinning

◆ Body and soul's super adventure

◆ No soul is solo

◆ Soul questions (and answers)

Reincarnation as an event where a person lives and dies several times is the most common understanding of reincarnation. The notion of being reborn into a different identity is *not* reincarnation in Kabbalah. It is more personal.

In Kabbalah, a reincarnation is every time you make a step in spiritual growth. For example, if you correct yourself intensely, you can experience many lifetimes in a matter of minutes. On the other hand, when you go on without correcting your attitude toward others, you may never experience a single incarnation. This is how reincarnation is defined according to Kabbalah.

Body and Soul from a Kabbalah Perspective

Kabbalah recognizes people by spiritual characteristics. When Kabbalistic texts say a new person is created, they're not talking about arms and legs. They mean aims and desires. When the quality of your desires is transformed for the better, you would say, from a Kabbalistic perspective, that a new person, a more spiritual you, is created.

The body is merely a biological container. Organs, for example, can be replaced through transplants. Kabbalah sees the body as a vessel through which your soul can work. To correct your soul, your body must be present and active.

Word of Heart

This life is not eternal … for itself; it is rather like a sweat of life.

—From introduction to *The Tree of Life* by Yehuda Ashlag

Souls have only one desire while existing within physical bodies. They wish to return to their roots, the level they were at before their descent. Your physical body, with its desire to receive, pulls the souls back into this world. Your desire to be spiritual helps your soul return to its spiritual roots.

The Circle of Life

Souls come to earth in a cycle, going down and then up again. They join bodies, return to the Source—another Kabbalistic term for the Creator—and repeat the process. The number of souls is not infinite; they return again and again as they progress toward correction.

You experience many incarnations, or new souls, in several ways. It can be through a troubling experience that makes you ready to question your purpose or seek new answers. It can be through Kabbalah study. When you are ripe for spirituality, for example, you may discover *The Complete Idiot's Guide to Kabbalah*. This book can be the beginning of your conscious incarnations.

The incarnations that flow through you then return to the Source. Your "task" on Earth is to go through as many incarnations as possible so that your soul finds ultimate correction.

Why Do We Keep Coming Back?

Reincarnation is the repeated appearance of spiritual souls within the bodies in this world. This occurs as each soul reaches its individual end of correction.

Complete correction is a multilevel undertaking—a soul may not complete its task and will return to the Roots. On its next entry, because of the progress you may have made, it reincarnates further along on the spiritual trail.

The Creator wants you to be filled with spiritual pleasure, to be complete. That is possible only through great desire. Only with a corrected desire can you reach the spiritual world and become strong and active.

Word of Heart

And we must bear in mind that since the Thought of Creation is to bestow to His creatures, He had to create in the souls a great amount of desire to receive that which He had thought to give. For the measure of each pleasure and delight depends on the measure of the will to receive it. The greater the will to receive, the greater the pleasure, and the lesser the will, the lesser the pleasure ... So the Thought of Creation itself dictates the creation of an excessive will to receive, to fit the immense pleasure that His Almightiness thought to bestow upon the souls.

—From introduction to *The Book of Zohar* by Yehuda Ashlag

We've already determined that a desire is considered corrected only when it has the right intention. This is not automatic; the "right intention" is acquired through study. This is a process, not an instant fix. The souls continue to build to their goal, step by step.

Today, by the way, the study itself isn't enough to get you to spirituality. You need a group of friends to support you, and you need to try to help others reach correction. This way you bond with their desire for spirituality (point in the heart), even when they are still unaware of it. However, this help must not be compulsive, but an expression of love and compassion.

What's the Point?

The purpose of your soul's correction is more than just for its own needs. The picture is much bigger! The correction of your soul affects all souls because all souls are connected.

When you first come into this world, your soul is called a "point." We are all parts of one spiritual vessel or *Kli*, called *Adam ha Rishon* (the First Man). The soul of *Adam ha Rishon* was split into 600,000 souls, which come down to this world. This world houses a large number of bodies, each with its own soul.

If you do not build a spiritual *Kli* out of this point while living here in this world, your soul returns to its root in *Adam ha Rishon*. It is like a seed that did not evolve, unconscious and lifeless. The goal is for you to return to the exact same root in *Adam ha Rishon* from which you came down.

Where Does the Soul Go?

Location, as you and I think of it in time and space, does not exist in the Upper Worlds. What happens when the soul goes back to the Source? The soul may have some coffee and wait for the next body, but there really is no way of knowing. Part of Kabbalah is the understanding that there are some things you cannot know, and then acting according to that understanding.

Actually, the soul returns to its root in *Adam ha Rishon*. "Root of the soul" is the place of the soul in the system of *Adam ha Rishon*. This is a spiritual location that is very close to the Source, the Creator. You cannot find this spiritual location with the five physical senses.

What Is a Soul?

A soul is a spiritual force. In Kabbalah, souls are arranged in a pyramid, stacked according to their desires. Earthly desires are at the bottom, and spiritual desires are at the very top, where fewer souls are. As the desires move up, fewer souls are part of the level.

At the base of the pyramid are many souls with small desires (food, sex, sleep). These are desires that are animal-like. The next level has those that desire wealth, something beyond basic needs. At the next level is the desire to control others, through power. Even fewer souls are here. Next is knowledge—these souls are engaged in discovery. At the top of the pyramid are the few souls that strive for attainment of the spiritual world. All these levels make up the pyramid.

This pyramid is also within you. You have the potential to act in all these ways as well as to become spiritual. The pressure of the lower worlds must give way to the purest desire, the infinite desire for truth. Here you prefer to put effort and energy into increasing your desire for spirituality, rather than into earthly, egoistic desires. You don't have to do it all yourself—it is achieved through study, with groups and through spreading the knowledge to others.

Where Is a Soul?

Your soul and your body are unified. The body is the cover. You can think of your body as a shirt for the soul. Your soul connects you to all other souls and to the upper world, and this connection remains after your biological body is gone.

If you cultivate your altruism (thinking more about the unity of humanity and less about yourself), your effort becomes a spiritual *Kli* (vessel). A *Kli* perceives the spiritual world, beyond your five senses. You feel the Upper Force in your soul, not in your body.

When the spiritual understandings are intact, you do not feel the physical life and death so intensely. This is because your soul is in the spiritual realm. By focusing on the development of your soul, you can transcend biological (earthly) influences to the point that you are unaffected by them.

Rabbi Baruch Ashlag used to say that, to a Kabbalist, death and rebirth are as meaningless as taking your dirty shirt off and putting on a clean one. When his father, Rabbi Yehuda Ashlag, was asked where he wanted to be buried, he muttered in blatant indifference: "I couldn't care less where you dump my bag of bones."

When Is a Soul?

Time is our perception of the changes we experience as our soul develops. When your thoughts and desires change slowly, you feel that time is "crawling." When they are fast, you feel that time is "flying."

Time is sensed only when we experience change. Many changes make you feel that time is going quickly. When there are few changes, time is "crawling." When your spiritual void is full, there are no changes. You are then most like the Creator because you sense no beginning, middle, or end.

Three states exist for us: corruption, preparation for correction and correction, and bonding with the Creator. We experience the sensation of the passage of time when things are changing. The resurfacing of your *Reshimot*, or spiritual recollections, move you along. You first learned about *Reshimot*, reminiscences or recollections, in Chapter 8. *Reshimot* are desires before they are realized through the intention. These are "information cells" containing data about states and forms that occurred on our spiritual descent and that now determine our path as we return to spirituality.

From your first step on the spiritual ladder, you experience spiritual time. You completely identify with the spiritual process, and time is measured by the changes and actions concerning your contact with the Creator. The beginning, middle, and end are not separate events. Only your perception divides this Thought of Creation into three layers.

All souls were created at one time during creation. They are all tied together as parts of a single system, as one *Kli* (vessel) within *Adam ha Rishon* (the First Man). When Adam sinned, this structure shattered into individual souls, each confined to egoistic desires and oblivious, if not hostile, to others.

Souls join new bodies with added experience from their previous lives. They arrive in this life with renewed strength obtained during their previous life.

Soul FAQs

All of the souls that have come to Earth in the past 6,000 years have been here on previous occasions. It is like a dinner party where the guests keep going out and then coming back in. Each time they do, though, they have gained experience from their previous visits. They also learn something from one party and bring it to the next, which is held in a new house (or person). All their experience from past parties is applied to their present visit.

They are not new souls, but souls that may be dressed differently—with different attitudes and experiences. Their desires have strengthened and evolved because of their development in yesterday's party (life).

Who Was I?

Baal HaSulam writes in the article "The Freedom" that each generation contains the same souls as the previous generation, but in new bodies. So you know your soul has been on Earth before. The soul that is joined with your body could have been in a variety of persons, but there is no way to know because your soul is focused only on the present.

All of your memories are connected to one another. Everything you have ever experienced remains within you; nothing ever disappears. However, you cannot use it like a filing cabinet and pull out specific thoughts. Past memories appear on their own, in order to understand the present.

All souls are connected within a universal system. Because they are connected, memory is shared. Like a drop of water in a bucket, the souls don't keep their earthly identity.

Can We Identify People from the Past in Their Current Incarnations?

People from the past are part of history and heritage. Their souls can return to Earth. Kabbalists see the same soul reincarnated in Adam, Abraham, Moses, Rabbi Shimon, the Ari, and Yehuda Ashlag (all Kabbalist writers). It is as if the same soul covers itself in a contemporary Kabbalist. This allows each generation to get to know Kabbalah in its unique way.

However, Baal HaSulam was not born with the soul of the Ari. He was born and lived in his body as everyone does, with his own spiritual potential. In addition, though, he received the potential, the Light, the quality of bestowal called Ari. This is the spiritual force of the Ari. He then continued developing it with the method of Kabbalah.

You, too, can try to have all the souls your body joins within you. In that state, you will have other souls beyond your own soul. One of these additional souls will be called "the donkey driver," the soul that helps steer you along your spiritual path, which we mentioned in Chapter 10.

Can a Man Become a Woman, or Vice Versa?

No. Your soul may have been joined with a person of the opposite gender in the past, but it does not change your gender. Remember that reincarnation is not for whole bodies, only for the soul. Souls have no gender—they are simply a soul. It would be like assigning a cloud a gender.

A soul exists on Earth only while within a human body. The process of reincarnation can be understood only by attaining the spiritual worlds. In the spiritual worlds, souls

On Track

When Kabbalah speaks of a person being in this world, it is referring to a person's will to receive in a state of concealment from the Creator, with no intention to receive from Him or to give to Him. In other words, before we cross the barrier we are in this world. After we cross it we are in the next world.

are not burdened by the body. They can exist in our world and in the spiritual world simultaneously.

Was I a Dog?

As far as souls are concerned, Kabbalah distinguishes between animals and humans. Animals are animate, while humans are both animate and spiritual. As humans, you and I have the ability to give back to the Creator.

In the book *Attaining the Worlds Beyond*, there is a story about a lonely magician who creates things to keep him company. He creates a dog, which is very loyal and good to care for, but he notices that the dog will be loyal to any owner, not just to him. The dog could not reciprocate the specific care the magician gave.

Being able to reciprocate to the Creator is the gift of humanity. Therefore, reincarnation and evolution of souls deals only with human bodies. That's okay for Fido and Fluffy.

Is There Anything I Cannot Reincarnate As?

The progress of souls that develop with your help will live on. However, it is important to remember that *you* are not reincarnated; your soul is. Your soul is on its own journey—it has been in other places before you and will travel on when you are gone. Even though all objects have a spiritual force connected to them, your soul can't trade places with any of them.

> **Word of Heart**
>
> And there is much evidence pointing to a great wisdom called the secret of the reincarnation of the souls … the reincarnation occurs in all objects of the tangible reality, that each object, in its own way, lives an eternal life.
> —*Matan Torah* (*The Giving of the Torah*), from the essay "The Peace" by Baal HaSula

You cannot be reincarnated as an inanimate object, such as a stick or stone. Your soul cannot be joined with an animal, such as a lion, pet goldfish, bear, or ant. You can be only in another body of another human creature that is capable of continuing the process of attainment. But that still leaves plenty of options open, don't you think?

How Long Will I Continue Coming Back?

In his article, "What Degree Should a Person Reach," Rabbi Baruch Ashlag—Yehuda Ashlag's son and a great Kabbalist in his own right—asks, "What degree should one reach so as to not have to keep reincarnating?" He answers that the soul continues to come back until it reaches full correction and returns to its root. You don't have to correct anybody else, but you should try to give them the means to do it. If you've corrected yourself entirely, and did all you could for others, you will not continue to reincarnate.

The number of souls in the universal system is 600,000, and it is unchanging. There are 6,000 years given for all souls to reach attainment. As of 2007, there are 233 years left.

How long the souls continue to come back to Earth simply depends on how much progress is made toward their correction. You can think of it as your soul being on a journey, and you are the trail guide. If you get the campers (souls) to their goal, they won't have to come back next year to Camp Kabbalah. Or they will come back stronger and ready to progress more. Any progress is good progress.

The goal is to have all the campers (souls) reach the summit of a spiritual mountain where complete correction is achieved. They become more corrected as they go up. Until all souls reach the top, they will keep coming back into our earthly bodies so we can help them climb up. Studying Kabbalah increases the progress.

Kab-Trivia

A famous Chinese proverb says "Give a man a fish and you feed him for a day. Teach a man to fish and you feed him for a lifetime." This is similar to what we do when we help others to learn the knowledge of Kabbalah, which helps correct their souls.

Can I Recall Past Lives?

Kabbalists cannot consciously recall past lives, even under hypnosis, with voodoo, or with Ouija boards, You cannot sense past lives with your bodily senses.

You have gone through phases in your life: baby, youth, teenager—all leading to you today. "You today" cannot see "you last week" because "you today" covered it up. All the phases are there, but you can see only the present state, "you today."

Remember that your soul is measured not by events or faces, but by past states of spiritual progress. The progress in your soul's past is your starting point in this life. If you achieve a high degree of spirituality, the next person that joins with your soul will have an even better starting point.

What Remains from Previous Lives?

A previous life can also affect this one, usually positively. By simply existing, there is already some correction. This is because in every life cycle, we experience suffering, even if unconsciously. In that, we are no different from the rest of creation: the still, vegetative, animate, and human. Regardless of our feelings about pain, you and I still experience it.

Red Alert _____

You *do not* want to progress through pain. This is not the way. Pain only leads you to thinking you're a martyr, making you proud and driving you *away* from the need to become like the Creator. The only good thing about pain is that it indicates that you are not in the right direction, and shouldn't keep with it, or keep suffering.

You also experience pain in defined amounts. This pain leads to spiritual progress as you ask questions and seek change.

You can accelerate correction by making an effort to be spiritual. When you do, you feel pain consciously, and discover its root cause. You then decide to change your intentions in order to get rid of the pain.

So the past does affect the present. This is important because there is a need to constantly renew the links between all the souls. This fixes their connections in place and makes the unification of all the souls possible. This is called the correction of the collective soul.

Can I Do Anything to Affect My Next Life?

The connection between the present life and the next life is through the soul. The closer you bring your soul to the Creator in this life, the better it will be in the next. With the correction you achieve, your soul will be "further along" spiritually in its next visit.

The closeness you achieve with the Creator in this life makes your soul's "return journey" to Earth easier in the next life because your soul is further along on the path to complete correction.

People naturally head toward correction, either intentionally or by way of pain. When you prepare and change within, these changes remain with you for all time.

Everything you acquire (attributes, quality, knowledge) in this world passes away except the changes in your soul. It's like a seed that becomes a bud, then a plant. When the plant dies, its seed falls and sprouts another bud. What remains is the plant's energy. The spiritual energy that remains in us is a soul.

Kabbalah teaches that the ultimate measure of your life is found in the difference between the soul you received at birth and the soul that you have now. This comparison shows the extent to which you have elevated your soul in spiritual degrees.

Can We Recognize New Souls Around Us?

In their descent into the world, souls gather experience from past lives. This is called the path of suffering because suffering develops the soul. Each time it is reincarnated, the soul has a greater urge to seek answers to questions on its existence, its roots, and the importance of life.

> ### Word of Heart
>
> In our world, there aren't any new souls as the bodies are new, but only a certain amount of souls that incarnate on the wheel of transformation of the form, because they dress each time in a new body and a new generation. Therefore with regards to the souls, all generations since the beginning of creation to the end of correction are as one generation that has extended its life over several thousand years until it developed and became corrected as it should be. And the fact that in the meantime each has changed its body several thousand times is completely irrelevant, because the core of the essence of the body, which is called the soul, did not suffer at all by these changes.
> —*Matan Torah* (*The Giving of the Torah*), from the essay "The Peace" by Baal HaSulam

The purity of descending is in direct proportion to how much the souls require correction. Some souls are less developed than others. Developed souls have an enormous urge to recognize the truth. If given the right tools, they will attain recognition of the spiritual world.

It is considered in Kabbalah that you receive a "new soul" if you are suddenly awakened to the Creator. It is also considered a renewal of the soul. It's called "the point in the heart," where you feel a spiritual spark. The correction of your soul is an ongoing spiritual process that requires time and study.

The Least You Need to Know

◆ Souls continue returning to Earth until they achieve complete correction.

◆ Reincarnation includes only souls, not physical objects, plants, animals, or human beings.

- The spiritual attainment of your soul in previous lives is your starting point for this one.

- There is a set number of 600,000 souls in the universe, and they have been given 6,000 years to all reach correction.

- Your soul is connected to all others in the collective soul—actions of one affect all.

Part 3

Kabbalah and Your Life

By now, you may realize that Kabbalah affects your daily life. In this part, we'll discuss your relationships with the Creator, your family, your friends, your co-workers, and the world at large. And we'll discuss how these relationships can be affected daily by Kabbalah. By using Kabbalah's method of spiritual growth, you can enhance and add a new meaning to your relationships with those around you.

Then we'll move into Kabbalah's method of spiritual growth, which is based on an inner change that a person goes through. By changing your perception and attitudes, you can bring the upper force into your life and actions.

Chapter 3

Just Me and My God

In This Chapter

- ◆ Everything comes from above
- ◆ There is only the Creator
- ◆ Acting as if He doesn't exist
- ◆ Turning right, then left, to stay in the middle

Spirituality is a very personal, intimate process. On the outside, a Kabbalist looks like a completely ordinary person. And in most respects, Kabbalists *are* ordinary people, except for that extra niche in them—their relationship with the Creator. In this chapter, we glance into the spiritual processes that Kabbalists experience in their day-to-day lives.

When Spiritual States Begin

If you think back on your life for a moment, you'll find that it's made of many, many incidents that together form a chain of events. We don't experience them as events when they are actually happening, but when they are over, we look back and find that something started at some point and ended at another. The beginning and the end are the edges of the event. It can be any event, but some are more definable than others.

Let's say you take a test. You can analyze how you felt in the beginning, when you first learned you had to take the test, how you felt during the test, and how you felt when it was all over. But for Kabbalists, all things are connected to spirituality and can be considered spiritual events. A day with your children, a date, a thought, a lunch break, alone or with company—all are "events" in the sense that we can analyze them in spiritual terms, once we have contact with the spiritual world.

> **On Track**
>
> Kabbalists explain that all creations are sensing beings. In other words, all we have are our feelings and emotions. This is because the purpose of creation is for us to feel pleasure. Even our rationale exists only to justify, to rationalize our feelings. Therefore, if you want to study yourself, examine your emotions. See what gives you pleasure—you'll be surprised, and not always pleasantly.

When an event begins, you don't know that it's beginning, but you can learn to identify the beginning of an event by noticing the changes in your sensations. When your sensation changes, it's a sign a new event is looming. Take the example of the test. When you first hear about it, your emotions certainly change. Actually, in the case of an exam, your whole body would probably show the change—heart rate, breathing, palpitation, and sweating would probably all increase to some extent. This is certainly the beginning of an event. At that moment, you don't think, "I'm in the beginning of an event." You just experience it. Generally, it's only in retrospect that you see when the event started.

For the most part, Kabbalists develop a keen sense for detecting the beginning of events. They can sense them emerging and watch their own reactions to the situation objectively.

What Hit Me?

Kabbalists tell us that the first thing to do, once we realize that a new state (an emotion or sensation) has begun, is to say, "There is none else besides Him." This is a very important rule because if we say that there is none else besides Him, it means that we already recognize where the situation is coming from and who is giving it to us. This means that we can treat any situation in life as an opportunity for spiritual progress. And since the purpose of creation is to reveal the Creator, saying "There is none else besides Him" already connects us to Him and transfers the situation into the spiritual realm. This will make a huge and positive difference in how we experience things.

There Is None Else Besides Him

Let's see what that sentence, "There is none else besides Him," really means. At the end of the day, it means everything—the whole reality, its beginning, its middle, and its end. It means that there is nothing but the Creator and that we, too, are a part of Him, and all we need is to discover it.

So when we declare these words, it's as if we recognize His uniqueness and our inclusion in Him. It also means that the fact that we are not sensing that there really is no one else, and nothing else in reality, is due to our own faulty perception. By saying, "There is none else besides Him," and by admitting that, for now these are just words to us, we are acknowledging the limitation of our view. This is a very important stage because it is the first step toward correction.

In the Midst of the Act

Even if we realize that we are in the middle of an event in life and that it came from the Creator, we still have to resolve it, to do something about it. The fact that we acknowledge that the Creator is the operator behind whatever situation we're in—a test, a good lunch, a domestic dispute—doesn't excuse us from trying to resolve it as best as we can.

That's why Kabbalists always caution about over-studying. The principles of Kabbalah are taught by teachers and books. But the principles are *always* put into action in real life. Those who forget it will never cross the barrier and enter the spiritual world.

Getting to Work

During the event, we put the understanding "There is none else besides Him" aside. We don't forget about it, but we put it aside. We have to keep in mind that if He placed us in a certain situation, He probably wanted us to do something about it, or why would He have put us in it in the first place?

So the way to work during an event is the exact opposite of what we do at the beginning: now we have to say, "If I'm not for me, who is for me?", as if there is no Creator.

It is not that the Creator actually disappears or that we ignore His existence. But for us to learn as much as we can from a situation, about ourselves and about the Creator, we have to put forth our utmost effort to resolve it by ourselves. This will give us observations that are otherwise impossible to acquire.

We need those observations about ourselves and about the Creator because, to make a free choice, to become real (spiritually) grown-ups, we have to know all the options and choose whether we want to be like the Creator, altruists, or remain as we are born, egoists.

There Is None Else Besides Me

While we are in a state of "If I'm not for me who is for me?" the Creator doesn't disappear—there is still none else besides Him. He just moves away, so to speak, and lets us feel as if we are alone. Similarly, when little children play with toys and we want to help them grow, we let them play even when we see them failing the first or second times they try. This is very important for them because that's how they learn. That's what the Creator does with us: He lets us learn as if He's out of the picture. Put simply, we learn from the event we are experiencing.

> **On Track**
>
> Don't get discouraged if in the beginning of your studies concepts such as "There is none else besides Him" and "If I'm not for me who is for me?" seem obscure. A Kabbalah student experiences moments of great insights and intense bewilderment and confusion. But if you persist and insist, you will discover Him. Baal HaSulam calls those patient ones "heroes."

A Kabbalist works on two levels at once: on one hand, remembering that the Creator created the situation and completely controls it, and, on the other hand, working as if "There is none else besides me."

"There is none else besides me" is the essence of the scientific approach. This is the attitude that brought us our technological progress, with its advantages and disadvantages. Rooted in this approach, however, is our deepest desire—to know the Thought of Creation. Quite likely, this is why mathematician and physicist Stephen Hawking wrote in his book *A Brief History of Time*: "If we do discover a complete theory, it should in time be understandable in broad principle by everyone, not just a few scientists. Then we shall all … be able to take part in the discussion of the question of why it is that we and the universe exist. If we find the answer to that, it would be the ultimate triumph of human reason—for then we would know the mind of God."

When the Dust Settles

During the event, we work as hard as we can to succeed. In other words, we have a certain idea of the result we want to accomplish and we strive for it. However, the Creator will always have a different goal in mind than ours because He acts from the Creator's perspective, and we don't. So His goals are naturally not ours.

This is very important because if you look back at the events you've experienced in your life, you'll most likely discover that they never turned out quite the way you thought they would.

He Knew All Along

If the result is different from our original plan, and if the Creator knows everything because He created us, it must mean that, from the very beginning, our planning was wrong. Otherwise, our result would be as we planned and would be as the Creator planned.

But the fact that the final outcome and our planned outcome are different doesn't mean that we did something wrong. Naturally, we did the best we could in our current level of understanding. But the Creator shows us how things should unfold on a *higher* level. He *teaches* us. The reason things turn out not as we expected is that our efforts to do the best we can in a situation elevate us to another level.

Therefore, by the time the event is over, we have already climbed to a higher degree of understanding, even if we didn't notice it. In that degree, things seem different to us, so even if we arrive at exactly the result we first aimed for, now it seems dissatisfying. Our new degree dictates a new perception, and what seemed right yesterday, seems wrong today. This is why a dissatisfactory result doesn't mean we didn't do a good job. On the contrary, it means we grew to a new level of understanding.

> **On Track**
>
> We make the effort; He makes the change. That should be our motto in spiritual work. Our efforts, not our brains, teach us what the next degree is like. Our brains reflect our present level of understanding, which will change when we reach a higher level. This is why Kabbalists stress the importance of the effort, the desire, the *Kli*, not the knowledge one already possesses.

Returning to "There Is None Else Besides Him"

This brings us back to the conclusion that "There is none else besides Him." But now we *have proof.* We know for a fact that the result is not what we had planned and that He was planning and working behind the scenes all along, because we have climbed to a new degree, a new level of perception—His level.

There is a big difference between the "There is none else besides Him" at the beginning of an event and that same observation at the end of the event. In the beginning, it is something I "force" myself to follow, even though I don't actually feel it. But at the end, I not only feel it, but I *know* it because I've lived through all the possible situations in this event, and I know that it couldn't have happened the way it did, were it not for Him. This is real spiritual attainment.

To summarize the whole process, Rabbi Yehuda Ashlag offers a simple allegory. In the morning, we should remind ourselves, "There is none else besides Him." Then we go to work and do as best we can to provide for ourselves and for our families, as if there is no Creator. At the end of the day, we come home with our earnings and remind ourselves again, "There is none else besides Him." We should come to a point that we feel that if we had stayed in bed all day, the Creator would still care for our every need and would provide us with our earnings. When we come to feel that, it's a sign that we've completed this state and are ready for the next day (state). In other words, the result—our earnings—is predetermined, and our efforts, not our brains, open it to our understanding.

To understand this process more thoroughly, you need to know more about the *Reshimot*. This will be the topic of the next section.

Etched in My Soul

So that's it? When we attain (perceive, in the deepest sense of the word) that the Creator exists and does everything, is our work over?

Not quite. There is something called *Reshimot*. We already talked about *Reshimot* in Chapter 8, but here we can see how they actually work in our daily lives.

Do you know what you want right now? You probably do. But do you know what you will want tomorrow, in an hour, in a second? Can you *plan* what to want? You probably can't. That's because of the *Reshimot*; you can't control their order of appearance, so you can't know what desire they'll bring you next.

Remembering the Future

Let's remember for a moment what are *Reshimot*. The word *Reshimo* (singular for *Reshimot*) means "writing," as in registering or recording. When we were created, the Creator designed us in such a way that we started from the highest possible point, completely bonded with Him, and "slid" down from there, degree by degree, until we ended up in this world. All the steps we went down on are still written in us. We are unaware of them, but they are very much alive within us.

We still need to clarify why *Reshimot* exist to begin with. When we were first created, we were united with the Creator, and unity with Him is the purpose of creation. So you may rightly ask, "Why did He bring us down?" The answer is that He feels this unity, but He wants *us* to feel it, too. And the only way we will be able to experience unity is if we experience separation, too, and can compare them. You can't have black without white, hot without cold, wet without dry, and unity without separation.

But to make sure we don't get lost along the way and remain separated for all eternity, He records our decline within us, much as you stretch a long thread to show you the way out when you walk into a maze or a dark cave. These *Reshimot* are, therefore, our lifeline.

> **On Track**
>
> Don't bother with your next spiritual degree; the Creator has prepared it for you. Work on completing your work at your present degree, and the Creator will take you to the next level.

Changing the Future

So the concept of *Reshimot* is both good news and bad news. The good news is that our way up is paved and certain. The bad news is that if we don't like our way, if we're suffering along it, the *Reshimot* are predetermined and we're doomed to suffer until the final correction, right? Wrong. There is a lot we can change.

We are going "back to the future," so to speak, because we think of the next minute, hour, day, or year as our future. But the real future is our *Reshimot*, the degrees by which we have already slid down. So when a *Reshimo* first appears, it appears in the last state we experienced it, which is a broken state, separated from the Creator. (Remember the 600,000 little pieces from Chapter 9? Understanding Kabbalah becomes easy if you always keep in mind that we are one soul, shattered into 600,000 pieces, and that correction means putting the soul together.)

For this reason, every higher degree begins with a crisis: the present state is no longer satisfying, and the next is not yet corrected, so we're in a mess. This is also why our world is in crisis today, but we'll talk about it in Part 4.

As we work on our *Reshimot*, within whatever event the Creator hands us, our efforts gradually create our *Kli*, the desire that elevates us to the next level. But the fact that we work on our *Reshimo*, the fact that we experience all the sensations of separation and bonding, pains and joys of a state, doesn't mean we have to experience it physically or that it will take a long time to complete.

A good "spiritual worker" can complete a "before, during, after" cycle in a matter of minutes. Something that could take you years—and unimaginable pains—to complete on the physical level can begin and end in less than the time it takes you to take a shower.

And the neatest idea of all is the *Hitkalelut*. *Hitkalelut* means "inclusion." The fact that we are one soul, broken into billions of pieces has great benefits to it. Because you experience one cycle of event (*Reshimo*) and I experience another, if we have *Hitkalelut*, and thus feel *each other*, then I don't have to experience what you went through, and you don't have to experience what I went through. Our empathy spares us suffering. Think about it—caring for others' pains spares you those pains.

Three Pillars

One of the key concepts in Kabbalah is the Three Pillars concept, also known as Three Lines: right, left, and middle. Let's see what it means in our work.

Stumbling Leftward

There is a very important concept in Kabbalah: you tread either the path of light or the path of suffering. Because the purpose of creation is for us to receive pleasure, whenever we receive anything less than that, it is considered suffering.

The path of suffering is a state in which events find one spiritually unprepared, and then you don't know how to handle them. You don't remember to say, "There is none else besides Him," and then handle it as "If I'm not for me, who is for me?" and finally *know* that "There is none else besides Him." Instead, after you've suffered enough, the suffering makes you wonder why all this is coming to you and what you have done to deserve this. Only then do you begin to think about the Creator and get back on track.

But this is not the way to go if we want to be happy. There is an alternative, called "the path of light." This means that whenever a change occurs—not necessarily an unpleasant one, any change will do—one immediately thinks of the Creator and begins the "before, during, after" cycle.

By doing that, you not only speed up your progress, but you avoid all the pain you could have suffered had you treaded the path of suffering, without losing anything in spirituality. On the contrary, the time you have gained will make room for many more experiences to come, the whole journey will seem like an adventure tour instead of an ordeal, and you will look forward to life instead of dread what the future might hold. The next subsections describe how we progress on the path of light.

On Track

In Chapter 10, we defined Israel not as a piece of land, but as a desire aimed straight to God. Kabbalists say that Israel accelerates time. What they mean by that is that those who want to go straight to the Creator save a lot of time because their desire is always toward the Creator, so they are always on the path of light. However, note that this does not refer to the people of Israel in the physical world, but to those who have a point in the heart and want to reach the Creator.

Pulling Right

The end of the previous state is the beginning of the new state. This is how the *Reshimot* are linked together. We already know that after every state comes yet another state: when the state of lunch break ends, there is the state of getting back to work. This is how we progress. So what we do at the "after" stage of a cycle is very important because it determines how we'll begin the "before" stage of the next state. In simpler words, if we remember to ascribe whatever we experienced during lunch break to the Creator, when we go back to work, we will do it reinforced by a stronger tie to the Creator than before. This, in turn, will determine what we make of the rest of the day.

In the Three Lines, the right symbolizes the Creator, the light. So the first thing we do when a new state arises, which is also the end of the last state, is go to the Creator by saying, "There is none else besides Him."

In other words, in the beginning, I put my trust in the Creator. It's not that I believe that everything will go smoothly; I strengthen my faith that it comes from Him, that He does and controls everything, even though I don't feel it in this degree yet, because this degree is new to me and I still don't know anything about it. So this self-reminder that the Creator has everything mapped out is called "pulling right." I lean to the right line.

Red Alert

Don't let thoughts about the Creator take you away from life. There is no progress in spirituality unless you experience life to the fullest. The "during" stage in each degree *necessitates* that you will always do the best you can in every situation. You should only remind yourself of the Creator's doing when you are totally sure there is nothing more that *you* can do.

Right + Left = Middle

Now that we have strengthened ourselves with the power of the Creator from the right and believe "There is none else besides Him" comes the left line. The left line is an intensification of the will to receive, an appearance of greater egoism. When that happens, I naturally think, "If I'm not for me, who is for me?" because I think of myself, not of the Creator. In other words, I think that only I know best how to do and what to do.

But there is a very important rule here. Since the purpose of creation is for us to enjoy by becoming like Him, we will *never* receive more egoism than we can handle. Therefore, if we don't arm ourselves with great power from the Creator while we're on the right, we will not receive a lot of egoism from the left, and this will slow down our progress. So we don't need to work on our left line, our egoism; we can leave it alone. Work *only* on receiving great powers from the right, on strengthening your faith that there really is none else besides Him.

The worst thing you can do to yourself is sink into thoughts about your egoism. In Kabbalah, it is described by the verse, "The fool foldeth his hands together and eateth his own flesh." (Ecclesiastes, 4:5) Focusing on your egoism will lead you to feel sorry for yourself and will not take you any closer to the Creator.

Once you've taken all the faith you can from the right, you will receive the egoism from the left. You don't have to come to it, it'll come to you. When that happens, you work as described in the "during" stage: you do what you can while keeping in the back of your mind that "There is none else besides Him." And once you complete it and reach the "after" stage, you will realize how much joy you have given to the Creator and that He was guiding you all along. In doing that, you will have united both lines, and this is called the "middle line."

The Least You Need to Know

- Whenever you feel a change coming, think, "There is none else besides Him."

- Afterward, work as if there is no Creator and it's all up to you.

- In the end, remember that it was He guiding you all along.

- The states (events) in life change because they are surfacing *Reshimot*, memories from one's spiritual past.

◆ The end of an event is also the beginning of the next, the right line.

◆ Don't focus your mind on your egoism, focus it on the Creator, on altruism. When you are focused on the Creator, He will show you who you are and will guide you toward correction.

Chapter 14

Praying with Results

In This Chapter

- If you work at prayer, your prayer works for you

- Your prayer is your deepest desire

- Which prayers are answered?

- Praying for yourself and praying for all

Don't take this personally, but your soul is incomplete. However, it does not have to stay that way. You can seek assistance from something already complete. The Creator is complete, and He can also complete you. Actually, according to Kabbalists, there is nothing He would like more than for you to be whole. All you need to do is connect with the Creator.

You do this through prayer. When you pray, you ask the Creator to fill you. This may sound easy, but prayer is also considered work. This "work" sets Kabbalah prayer apart from other types of prayer, as you'll see.

Prayer in Kabbalah further differs from prayer in other practices because it does more than affect the individual. Prayer has the potential to touch humankind as a whole. Because each soul is connected to all other souls, praying for the group or for society can have proven positive effects.

Kabbalah prayer has no specific guidelines of when or where to pray, or of what to wear or rituals to perform as you do so. It depends only on the desire in your heart.

Know What You Want

In Kabbalah, you pray to fill a void or an absence of something. A lack can mean anything, a lack of money, of love, or of health. But when Kabbalists write about prayer, they are referring to a specific absence: the absence of the quality of bestowal, the nature of the Giver, the Creator. You cannot just ask for completeness in general. That would be like going to a restaurant and ordering a drink without specifying water, juice, soda, or tea. You must order the right "spiritual drink" to quench your spiritual thirst. The waiter is like the Creator. You must say exactly what you want.

On Track

It may seem strange that all you have to do is pray to get what you want, but not if you remember that there is none else besides Him. Kabbalists say that to get a full *Shekel* (coin), you have to give half, and the Creator gives the other half. Your half is the prayer, and His half is granting your wish.

To do this, your prayer must be very clear. You must know precisely what it is you want. When you request something, consider that you are speaking before the Creator. The Creator has the potential to make you the happiest person in the world. The Creator provides you with wholeness because the Creator is whole—nothing is lacking or deficient in the Creator.

When asking for fulfillment, carefully consider what is truly unfulfilled in you well before your prayer. This is thoughtful preparation. If the Creator fulfills exactly what you are missing, as He has the potential to, you will be the most perfect and complete person possible. You will not lack anything. Determining what you need beforehand is a crucial part of the praying process.

Your Desire Is Your Prayer

Although Kabbalists talk about prayer as a distinct action, something you must prepare for, it is actually a process. In truth, we constantly pray. Every desire in our hearts is a prayer. But if you start your list of desires with the material things you are lacking, you are off on the wrong foot. It is helpful to start out with a prayer *not* to be selfish. You are "putting a lid" on your earthly material desires and focusing on what can truly complete you: a relationship with the Creator.

You may remember learning about a *Masach*, or screen. When you build a screen, it enables you to reflect pleasure that you receive and give it to the Creator. This work is like a prayer to receive the strength to not be selfish. If your prayer is sincere, the strength is sent to you, and you can receive the Divine Light with the help of your screen.

The Light that you receive with your screen is twofold: first, it gives you *Hassadim* (mercy), which is the *Masach* we just mentioned. Once you have it, you can receive the other fold, the Light of wisdom and understanding, called *Hochma*. This light carries information about your present spiritual level and spiritual reasons for the events occurring to you. Once you understand the attributes of a spiritual degree, you take on its name. As you move up, every degree corresponds to more perfection and has a new name.

> **On Track**
>
> In Kabbalah, you pray for the strength not to move mountains, but to not be selfish. If you are sincere, you receive the Creator's Light and advance in spiritual degrees.

These degrees represent your spiritual progress. They help you focus on the Creator, understand His actions, and achieve the goal of creation. Selfishness enables you to do something only when you are sure to benefit or receive pleasure from it. During prayer, you must ask the Creator for help to contain the forces of selfishness.

This is the only direct path to the Creator. As you follow it, your connection with the Creator becomes stronger. You begin to understand what happens to you, why you experience certain feelings, and what you need to do about those experiences. This understanding propels you to your next spiritual degree.

Directing Your Prayers

Generally, most efforts made in our world are motivated by selfish needs. They are built on the ego. In Kabbalah, you do the opposite. You put down your ego in order to accomplish something. After battling your ego with good effort, you can turn to the Creator with your desires. A true prayer follows a genuine effort.

Don't expect to defeat your ego. You can't because it's you. To battle the ego means to try to go above it and to become giving, to see that everything you do stems from an intention to receive and, when you see you can't defeat your ego, to ask for the Creator's help in doing this.

If you make efforts to work on prayer, the Creator will hear your call for help. This process should be sincere because you cannot pull the wool over the Creator's eyes, so to speak. In a genuine prayer, you must …

◆ Know exactly what you want to achieve.

◆ Know that the Creator has what you want.

◆ Be convinced that He wants to give it to you.

Kab-Trivia

There is a famous allegory about a generous shop owner whose shop is always open, and everyone can walk in and take what they want. But his hand writes what you take, and his collectors collect. You can pay him by becoming like him, which is what he wants, or you can use what he gives you for yourself, and then his collectors come.

If those conditions are not met, you cannot accomplish the action properly. This is true in both the earthly and spiritual realms. The only difference is that in the spiritual realm, the desire for enjoyment is directed back to the Creator. A *Masach*, or screen, directs the enjoyment you receive back to the Creator, and you can develop that ability through prayer.

When bringing your desires to the Creator, remember that they cannot be selfish desires. They must be honest desires from your heart that ask the Creator to complete you. That is why the first prayer often is to not be selfish. It's the foundation upon which all other prayers can be built.

Which Prayer Gets Answered?

The Creator will satisfy your desires for progress if spiritual progress is your focus. This involves letting your desire for spirituality connect with every part of your existence. When you think of nothing else but progress toward the Creator and dedicate all your time and energy to this, your desires are answered.

Go to the Right Place

Knowing what prayers get answered requires taking the right prayers to the right place, just as you go to certain stores to meet certain needs. If you take a bicycle to be repaired at a doctor's office, you will get some funny looks. And if you are sick and go to the bike store, they may ask you to leave. Therefore, it is important to take what you need to the right place.

The Creator is the "right place." But that doesn't mean that the Creator will fix everything you take to Him. The Creator won't, for instance, change events that are happening on Earth. After all, He is the one who created them because there is none else besides Him, so why would He undo them?

With prayer, the Creator can and will change what is in you. This leads to spiritual ascent. This ascent leads to happiness and closeness to the Creator. In this area, the Creator can and will do anything for you. If you know what you are spiritually lacking, the Creator will fix it for you.

> ### On Track
>
> The most natural thing to do is to ask of the Creator to stop our suffering. If He is almighty, He can help me. Can't He? But Kabbalah explains that all the pains in the world come for only one reason: our own egoism. The fact that we are egoistic separates us from Him. This separation can be expressed in many ways, but they always feel negative. Therefore, the only prayer that produces a good response is the prayer to know the Creator, to be like Him.

The Creator can only change the events that are happening within *you*. But in Chapter 3 we explained that *everything* happens within you. So it's important to note that the Creator doesn't change the things going on outside of you because they are actually happening *within* you. It turns out that your relationship with the Creator is something very intimate and personal. Baal HaSulam defined it very concisely in a title of one of his articles: "Prayer Is the Work in the Heart."

One Prayer Is Always Answered

As we just explained, if you pray for spiritual progress, the prayer will always be answered. This is because prayer has to do with you, not the outside world. Spiritual repair is what the Creator does best. Actually, that's *all* He does. The Creator made the world so we could experience the pleasure of understanding Him. You do this through correcting yourself.

When you know you are missing something spiritually and you don't have the need fulfilled, you bring the Creator your requests. The Creator has the desire to bestow things to you, His creation.

From the Creator's side, it is unnecessary that you pray to be given benefit and pleasure. You don't need to ask to be "given" things because the Creator only gives—that is all He does, and He does it without a request.

The role of a prayer is not to convince the Creator to give; it is to prepare you to receive. It makes you look within you and see what you're looking for. In this way, you study yourself, you realize that you are egoistic, and you ask for correction. The minute you ask for that, you are corrected by the Creator, and you discover Him. Once you discover Him, you (obviously) know everything, and you don't need to pray any more.

Ironically, Kabbalists always say that the wicked are those who give to the Creator the most contentment. That's because those who feel that they are wicked ask for correction and that enables the Creator to give them correction, which is pleasure for Him. But if you are righteous, a total giver without a need in the world, what can the Creator give you?

Mind and Heart

The Kabbalists said, "What is the work of the heart? Prayer." Let's see why prayer in Kabbalah is considered work.

You have been created in such a way that you do not know what your own true intentions are. Desires come from your heart, but you have no power over them. The essential nature of your prayers cannot be fully understood. This is yet another way in which Kabbalah requires correction of the soul, and prayer is the only tool by which correction can occur.

You have to receive powers for correction from the outside. These powers exist beyond the bounds of your egoism. You must ask for such powers, and prayer is the means of asking.

Prayer is not what the lips utter, but the desires within your heart. The Creator reads the desires within your heart. So your work boils down to transforming your heart's desires. Yet you cannot do that by yourself; you must ask the Creator for it, which is why we mentioned earlier that a good first prayer is to pray not to be selfish. Direct your prayer to be given the only true desire—to feel the Creator.

The Zohar, the *Torah*, and all the other books of Kabbalah speak of those who attained the spiritual worlds with their desires and properties while living in our world. The Kabbalah method of prayer requires introspection, that you look inside your heart and truly ask yourself: who am I?

You don't learn this in prayer books. But if you work at this, you will reach the level of desires and requests of the authors of *The Book of Zohar* and the *Torah*.

To match your desires to those of the authors of those books, several steps are required. You must gradually come to understand that egoism is the source of all evil, and that people (including yourself) are egotistic. You must realize and feel this at the deepest and most intense part of your soul.

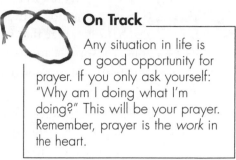

Get Ready to Receive!

The goal of the creation was for the Creator to bestow good upon His creations. There are no obstacles for the Creator to bestowing pleasure upon the created beings. The Creator created the lack, which is called a desire to receive pleasure, in order to fill that lack. Suffering is when there is absence of pleasure, or lack of pleasure.

The lack you feel should not discourage you because it was created with the intention to fill it. Because being filled by the Creator produces pleasure, your suffering is just an indication that you still need to learn how and what to receive.

Yearning for something makes receiving it even better. Have you waited a long time for something to find that it is more enjoyable? It is clear that if you give someone a meal, even if it is a feast, they will not enjoy it if they don't have any longing for the meal (hunger). In the same way, suffering makes us yearn for pleasure, making it that much more enjoyable when we receive completeness.

Fast-Forward Your Life

You may remember learning about *Reshimot* in Chapter 8. These are past states that you reexperience as you move toward closeness with the Creator.

You still progress in the same way you would without Kabbalah. This is because the events in your life are predetermined. By understanding Kabbalah and the concept of *Reshimot*, however, you learn how to experience things faster and advance toward the Creator intentionally. This is like "fast-forwarding" your life.

It is like a stick floating downstream, compared to a boat that you are rowing. Without Kabbalah, you will still make it downstream. However, with Kabbalah, you guide your progress and it is much faster. Eventually, you can be as close as possible to the Creator, which brings enjoyment to your life.

Personal Prayer and Praying for the World

Your prayer in Kabbalah can help in your own correction, but it can also help correct the entire world. This sounds like a big undertaking, but what makes it work is that all souls are connected. The more souls become corrected, the closer the whole world is to final correction, where all souls become like the Creator.

> **Word of Heart**
>
> A famous motto in Kabbalah says "One who shares in the suffering of the public is rewarded first."

To help the world become corrected, you must start with yourself. This is because reality, as we learned in Chapter 3, exists within you. So when you are corrected, you will discover that the whole world has become corrected along with you. Actually, Kabbalists explain that when you are corrected, you discover that the whole world has been corrected all along, and that you were the only disruptive part within it.

Private Correction

Spiritual progression is a personal path, and it is not necessary to reveal it to other people. If you do this, your prayer may be in vain. Learning about Kabbalah from others is necessary. But when it comes to subjects of prayer, meaning your requests of the Creator to correct in you, you should direct thoughts toward the Creator, and keep them to yourself.

As you move up the spiritual ladder, you attain new attributes with each new level of spirituality. You become more like the Creator. When these spiritual impressions are perceived, there are no words to describe them. Although Kabbalah provides a way to communicate about the Upper Worlds and move closer to the Creator, the experience is individual and so profound that it is indescribable.

You can achieve private correction when …

- ◆ You know you want spiritual correction.

- ◆ You know how to achieve it: through a *Masach* (screen), which comes with the right study—such that creates prayer.

Talking about your spiritual level is not recommended in Kabbalah. Talking about it will only confuse the listeners and expose you to their confused thoughts, which in turn, might slow down your progress. The bottom line? Help everyone progress, but don't pry in their relationship with the Creator.

Collective Correction

Private correction is individual, but it would not be possible without the help of other Kabbalists, past and present. If you are impressed by society, you may go to a place where your heart is impressed by society and you will succeed in "raising" your request there. Collective prayer is also the desire that all souls reach correction, not just your own. Because all souls are connected, the progress of each soul makes a difference to the whole.

When everyone does not seek correction, it is like having some students in a school class that have not read the textbook: it stops everyone in class from learning. This is why Kabbalists spread the word of Kabbalah through books and learning centers to help others correct.

Prayers for the Poor

Some religious practices ask that you pray for the poor or for the less fortunate. Kabbalah prayer, in contrast, deals only with yourself and your correction. Your job is to determine what you need in order to be complete. Then pray to advance in your completeness.

This does not mean that you do not care about other people, especially those who need extra help. Correction means becoming altruistic instead of egoistic. Therefore, caring for others is "built-in" in the prayer. If you are not praying to become altruistic then you are not praying for correction anyway.

Kabbalah encourages you to be involved in society. You can interact with people or give them a helping hand. But praying for others' condition to improve is not the purpose of Kabbalah prayer. If this is a concern of yours, use action instead.

Being poor, in Kabbalah, means being deficient, not having something. But why pray for something instead of working to get it? Because there is one thing that, no matter how hard we work for it, we will never get by ourselves: the Creator's quality of bestowal. So praying for the poor is wanting everyone to have the quality of bestowal

> **On Track**
>
> If there is none else besides the Creator, why does He send us pain? He doesn't. He is benevolent. He made us egoistic, and that egoism is what pains us because it is opposite from Him. So why did He make us opposite from Him? Because otherwise we wouldn't know what it means to be like Him. We wouldn't have anything to compare it with.

because that's the only thing they can't find on their own. This is why Kabbalists write that those who pray for the poor, for others, are rewarded first.

Prayers of Confession

Kabbalah prayer is about looking deep within yourself to see what you are spiritually lacking. Before you pray, you judge your soul and what it is missing. Then you ask of the Creator to fill this lack. This spiritual lack does not concern earthly actions or your beliefs or thoughts.

You find the lack by looking at your internal spiritual state and honestly seeing what you are missing. In other words, you compare your own qualities with those of the Creator, and confess to your situation. You may think that it is utterly impossible to compare yourself to a role-model like the Creator, but don't worry, He'll only show you that part of Himself that's not too far from you, so you can still ask, and receive correction for it.

Also, the Creator does not change according to your prayers. Instead, you are the one who changes and perceives the Creator's goodness in a different way. Prayer changes the way you look at the Creator. This is a very deep and practical concept that is applied to your day-to-day life.

Prayer Is Work in the Heart

Clothing, place, and time: these make no difference for prayer in Kabbalah. This differs from some prayer practices that may require certain clothing, body positions, ritual, or other factors. In Kabbalah, the only important factor is the internal desire of your heart. In prayer, that inner desire demands connection with the Upper Force.

Let's look at some other questions that differentiate Kabbalah prayer from prayer in other religious and spiritual disciplines.

Do I Need to Go Somewhere Special to Pray?

You do not need to go anywhere special to pray. In Kabbalah, there is not a holy place used for prayer such as a specially constructed building. The only real place you need to go is within your heart. You find your desire there. In prayer, you work internally and build similarity with the attributes of the Creator. What makes your prayer count is the desire in your heart.

Do I Need to Wear or Do Something Special to Pray?

You do not need to wear specific clothing to pray in Kabbalah. You could pray in what you are wearing right now. However, you would want to consider what you are spiritually lacking first.

Your body does not have to go through any rituals or rites, either—there are no particular movements, gestures, or dances in Kabbalah prayer. There is no particular way to sit or stand. In short, the body does not have any specific requirements to meet for prayer because prayer in Kabbalah is all about the heart.

On Track _____

It is not the body that needs correction. It's the soul.

For a Kabbalist, external things are unnecessary because Kabbalists concentrate on internal states. Connection with the Creator occurs only at the very deepest part of the heart. It is like a well dug deep in the ground, and you must connect with the source of water. The things happening on the ground level do not make a difference. In Kabbalah prayer, the important thing to remember is that you *do* need to prepare, but it is spiritual preparation, not physical preparation.

Do I Need to Pray at Certain Hours?

Night owl? Early bird? Wake up around lunch? There are no special times or certain hours for prayer. The time to pray is when you are ready to do so. It makes no difference what time it is because there is no schedule of prayer in Kabbalah. It depends only on the readiness of the desire in your heart. When that desire is ready, your prayer begins.

Some religions have certain days of the week for certain kinds of prayer or instruct you to pray at certain hours of the day. Others may follow the calendar: the sun and the moon. Others may have a direction that they face when praying or use objects to connect with their Creator. Kabbalah prayer focuses just on you—there is no schedule to follow. You pray at your own pace, as desired.

Kab-Trivia _____

One of the most famous group of Kabbalists, the Kotzk group in Poland, led by Rabbi Menachem Mendel, once tried switching the days, to see how it feels. They "moved" the Sabbath (Saturday) to Tuesday and behaved accordingly. After a while, when they gathered their impressions, they decided that it made no difference as long as they all did it together.

In Kabbalah, there is actually only one prayer. It is the request to connect with the Creator by sharing His qualities. You pray for the Creator to change your qualities in such a way that you will be close to the Creator and have contact with Him.

The Least You Need to Know

◆ A well-thought-out prayer for spiritual progress is always answered.

◆ Only states within you change, and these changes change your whole world.

◆ Prayer is the work of the heart.

◆ When you pray for others, you will be rewarded first.

◆ No specific clothes, body position, day, or hour for prayer is necessary in Kabbalah.

Chapter 15

Correction Is a Matter of Intention

In This Chapter

- ◆ How Light enters vessels
- ◆ The function of Light and intention
- ◆ How to correct your aim
- ◆ The Creator's concealment
- ◆ Maintaining intention for the Creator

In Kabbalah, it's your intention that counts—your thoughts and what's behind them. You need not worry about the physical world because spiritual development in Kabbalah takes place in the inner realm of life, and the inner realm is governed by intention.

In this chapter, we review how the Light enters the vessel—that's you. Then we take a closer look at how and why the Creator hides and what it takes to reveal Him.

Lights and Vessels

So let's go back a bit and review. Light is the Essence of all that the Creator bestows to all the worlds. It is existence itself granted by Him.

The Creator desires to fill your vessel with Light. In order for that to happen, however, you must desire it and intend it. In order to see how intention works in Kabbalah, let's look at the Light.

At the Source of existence, the Creator is in a state called "Simple Light." The Light shines over all the worlds that He created. But Light diminishes when it starts its journey to the lower worlds.

Without getting too technical, let's just say that from the Creator emanates the thought and desire to create the created beings so that they should benefit from His creations. The Creator's desire here is called the "Thought of Creation" or the "Upper Light."

The Light, in our world, is the Creator, and the Creator Himself is inscrutable to created beings—that's you and me. The relationship between the Creator and created beings takes place through the Upper Light, for the Creator wishes to fill created beings with pleasure.

How the Light Fills the Vessels

Simply put, the purpose of the Light is to create a created being that experiences the Light as pleasurable. In other words, created beings were created to receive Light, to be filled up by it and experience pleasure as a result. Kabbalists refer to created beings—again, that's you and me—as "vessels" for the Light.

At the same time, the Light creates in the created the desire to enjoy it. The amount of enjoyment a created being receives depends solely on the degree or measure of the being's will to receive the pleasure.

It's a little easier to understand if you think of it as being hungry. When your stomach is empty and you want to eat, filling your stomach with good food seems pleasurable. But after a full meal, when you're stuffed, the thought of more food—however delicious—is anything but pleasurable.

The Light creates a vessel and fills it. The pleasure that you and I sense from receiving the Light, called the "Light of Wisdom," is experienced as pleasure according to our willingness to receive. In other words, our desire is not yet independent; it is put there directly by the Light.

A spiritually advanced person is one who desires to benefit from all the Light that comes from the Creator. But first, the created being must know that the pleasure inherent in the Light is great. In other words, you must become filled up with Light and enjoy it. Then, to create a desire for the Light, you must lose it. This kind of experience produces a true desire for the Light.

Again, it's like eating. When someone gives you a food that you've never tasted, you may have no desire for it. In a sense, you eat the food because of the other person's desire for it, which he or she passed on to you by telling you that it's great and you should try it.

But once you've tasted the food and experienced pleasure from it, you want more, especially if the food is taken from you before you've finished it. This longing for the food that you now experience is independent of the person who originally gave you the food. It is now your desire, not the other person's.

The consequence in Kabbalah is that it is impossible to build your vessel in one go. In order for you to know and seek pleasure from the Creator, you must experience the pleasure in the Light and its loss. Here's the law in Kabbalah: the spreading of the Light within the created being's will to receive, and the Light's departure, make the vessel worthy for its task of receiving all the Light and benefiting from it.

Word of Heart

And while man has not attained perfection, these Lights, that are destined to come to him, are deemed Surrounding Lights. That means that they stand ready for him, awaiting his attainment of the vessels of reception. Then these Lights will clothe within the able vessels. Thus, even when the vessels are absent, when we delve in this wisdom, mentioning the names of the Lights and the vessels related to our souls, we are immediately illuminated to a certain degree.

—From *The Study of the Ten Sefirot* by Rabbi Yehuda Ashlag

Put a Lid on It

As much as we'd like it to be otherwise, the Creator knows that you and I are not exactly ready to receive the full force of Light. That's why there are four worlds above ours—*Atzilut, Beria, Yetzira, Assiya*, each with a decreasing amount of Light.

The worlds represent "filters" for the Light, and the farther the vessel is placed from the Creator, the more filters dim His Light, and the less Light the vessel can receive.

This progression of world under world with less and less light goes on until the state of almost complete absence of Light is achieved—until the creation of the world most remote from the Creator, where you and I are now.

By definition, spirituality is the desire to give (more precisely, the desire to receive for the sake of giving). Corporeality is the desire to receive into oneself, for the sake of oneself—egoism. That is the axis around which the whole of creation revolves.

It is possible to receive the Light only after acquiring a *Masach*, the screen you learned about earlier. This requires a transformation or correction of the egoistic desire to receive for the sake of oneself, to the altruistic desire to receive for the sake of the Creator.

This process of purification, correction, the acquisition of a screen, the replacement of egoistic properties into altruistic properties, represents the ascent up the ladder. Only by equating your properties to those of the Creator, only by acquiring the property of giving may you receive the Upper Light and enjoy it infinitely.

Surrounding Light

We live in complete spiritual darkness. The *Surrounding Light* shines on the outside and awakens our egoism and our will to receive, yet cannot penetrate this egoism. This is how we are awakened to spirituality.

To further awaken us, not necessarily to spirituality, but to any personal achievement, a part of the Surrounding Light must be inside us. But the Creator has given us the means to develop toward greater experience of the Light.

def•i•ni•tion

The **Surrounding Light** is the Light that desires to penetrate the created beings, but can't because of the absence of a *Masach* that enables us to receive it in order to give to the Creator.

For that purpose, the "point in the heart" is inserted into our selfish hearts. As we have said in earlier chapters, it is the awakening of this point in the heart that causes a person to question the meaning of his or her life and begin a journey to find the Light, a journey for which Kabbalah provides a detailed map. Intention is your driver.

Developing the Point in the Heart

This is where the concept of intention comes to play. The Creator wants you and me to experience pleasure. Therefore, He inserted into us a point in the heart that can develop a desire for the Creator. You and I, however, must develop that point into a desire to receive the Creator's Light and work diligently to develop the intention to receive that Light in order to please the Creator rather than ourselves. The teaching of the proper intention is the purpose and task of Kabbalah.

Through Kabbalah study, you become aware of your selfishness. You also become aware of your true nature, which fosters your desire to receive pleasure without considering other people's opinions, thoughts, and desires.

Your desire to experience the Creator is developing, and Kabbalah enables you to change your selfish intentions into altruistic ones.

Between Mechanical Actions and Intentional Actions

Intention lies behind doing, and simple doing is not enough. In spiritual and inner development, mechanical observance is not enough, which may be why people who observe religious traditions out of habit may find it difficult to come to terms with the fact that the act itself doesn't promote them spiritually.

Kabbalists want to develop the intention placed within the gestures and commandments, but first and foremost, within the thoughts behind them. They do not contemplate gestures and commandments as such. Commandments simply performed for the sake of performance do not transform you or promote spiritual growth.

You can be observant and still be selfish. To transform spiritually, your attention must be focused on the intention behind a commandment, not on its physical observance. This is what is meant by the sentence "A commandment without intent is like a body without a soul." It is spiritually dead.

The process of correcting selfishness is called "the spiritual observance of the commandments." You are endowed with desires so that you may develop your intention to use them "by turning them toward the Creator."

Corrected Aim, Increased Desire

People want to be rewarded for anything they do. Even when working to attain spirituality, we want to be rewarded because we are made of a desire to receive pleasure and cannot operate any other way. Yet, behind every act there is also an aim. Our first, inherent aim is to receive for ourselves—egoism. Our will to receive determines that we will be rewarded for every act.

But this is not egoism. Egoism is when the reward is a benefit for myself. If you think about it, a reward can also be someone else's pleasure. But when I think of my own pleasure, this is egoism. When I'm an egoist, without self-gratification, our egoism will not permit me to make even the slightest movement.

We begin our spiritual work from zero, as if the Creator had shone on us from afar with the illumination of Surrounding Light. This illumination compels us to act, and we decide to give up all the beauties of this world in favor of a spiritual sensation.

We do not even know what exactly we want to receive because the Light shines on us from a distance without clothing our vessels. At this point, the Light merely gives us the sensation of the future pleasure we will find in spirituality, which we cannot find in the world around us.

It is a process similar to the way children grow. Let's say that a boy wants to be a fireman when he grows up. He doesn't know what it means to be a fireman; all he knows is that they drive these big red trucks very fast and have neat helmets on their heads, and they generally look way cool.

In a sense, being a fireman "shines" to the boy from afar; it shines with "Surrounding Light." But when the boy grows and sees what it really means to be a fireman, the hours, the pay, the danger, the training, then he can really measure "the Light," meaning the pleasure he'll get out of it, and decide if this is what he wants to do in life.

Take Aim, Hit or Miss, Take Aim Again

The right aim is the single most important and most difficult thing that a person must do. It is built under various influences of the Light of the Creator on one's ego, which occurs during the study.

Gradually, you formulate the right aim. You study, correct, and intensify it. At the same time, however, you constantly realize that what seemed like the right aim yesterday now appears disguised as egoism. And tomorrow you will again find that yesterday's aim was the wrong one, and so on.

That's because any deed performed with an intention "dedicated to the Creator" is spiritual, while the same deed performed with a "self-aimed intention" is material and selfish. And it's very difficult, if not impossible, to keep your aim true all the time, since your desire constantly grows and becomes more difficult to correct.

For this reason, the Kabbalist analyzes all thoughts, actions, and events according to their impact on his or her spiritual path. In other words, the Kabbalist analyzes everything in terms of the intention behind his or her thoughts and actions. That's how the Kabbalist gauges the importance of all factors in his or her progression in relation with the Creator. This is the only direct path to Him. As time goes by, the connection between you and the Creator will clarify itself and become more sustained. Thanks to this process of analyzing intention and learning from the selfishness you find, you begin to understand what happens to you and why you experience certain feelings and what you need to do.

These new induced states are used as a springboard that propels one to the next spiritual degree-level. In other words, your desire for the Creator will intensify as your aim becomes increasingly true (altruistic).

The Recognition of Evil

When the Surrounding Light shines on us, we begin to see our real essence. It is a process called "the recognition of evil." But before the Light shines on us, we always try to justify ourselves. We think we are always right. Once under the Light of the Creator, however, we begin to see the evil in ourselves, which drives us to ask for help of the Creator, the Source of that illumination.

If our request is genuine, the Creator will change our natures. But the will to receive doesn't change—the aim changes from "for me" to "for the Creator." That change is called *Tikkun* (correction).

Just like being a fireman shone to the boy in the earlier example, the Surrounding Light shines on us and gives us the sensation of a better future, without actually showing us what that future is. Yet there are times when we are disconnected from this light, as if the Creator has left us. It is not that the Light was actually "put out." It's just that sometimes we are so immersed in our egoism that we cannot even feel the tiny ray that exists in our world.

Kabbalists call this sensation "darkness." The problem with darkness is not so much that it is unpleasant but that without Surrounding Light, we cannot see a future for ourselves, not even a blurry one. Today, when our egoism has reached unprecedented levels, it is no wonder that depression is the most quickly spreading disease, and especially in the Western world, where egoism is at its worst. (More on that in Part 4.)

Working Toward Intentions

The work of the Kabbalist is to carry on despite the seeming absence of the Light. It is impossible to continue with their inner work when in such situations, and the only thing they can do then is to continue with a mechanical performance of whatever they were doing, such as attending classes and helping to disseminate Kabbalah.

But you can develop the right intentions, even with mechanical action. The right intentions appear progressively along with the study of Kabbalah. In essence, Kabbalah is the science of intent, enabling one's heart to long for spirituality.

Double and Single Concealments

You do not immediately understand and sense the Creator. Instead, you go through various concealments of the Creator—first through the double concealment, then through the single concealment, and then to the revelation of the Creator.

What is "concealment"? What does "the Creator's concealment" mean? What exactly is concealed from us: His nature, properties, intention, desire, direct and indirect actions with regard to us? Why?

def•i•ni•tion

Double concealment is the state you experience when you cannot feel the Creator. You know He exists, but you are totally unable to feel Him.

This world, our corporeal world, is at the level of *double concealment*, where only the "will to receive" is sensed. In the state of double concealment, a person does not feel the Creator and cannot perceive anything as coming from Him. The Source itself is concealed. Indeed, the sensation a person has is that the Creator is absent. In that state, one cannot feel that it is the Creator who does everything.

This does not mean complete concealment, however, for there is a certain revelation: "The Creator exists and conceals Himself from me. He pays no attention to me, but He exists."

How can double concealment even be possible? If you think about it, you've probably experienced it as follows: imagine that someone is after you, wants to harm you, and is hiding from you all the time. You acutely feel it, but where is he? He must be somewhere nearby, but you do not know how to find him.

Double concealment is when bad things happen to you; you see what causes them, but you know that something else is actually hiding behind those things that appear to be the cause of your misfortune. In other words, you know he's there, but you can't feel him and you can't find him—you experience only the bad things he sends you through his messengers.

The next stage in experiencing the Creator, then, is *single concealment*. At this point, you recognize that the state you are in is the result of the Creator's own actions, not some outside force. The single concealment is the concealment of the correct connection with Him. In other words, the connection already exists, but it is incorrect and, therefore, the Creator is still concealed.

def•i•ni•tion _____

Single concealment is the state of feeling that the Creator exists, that He is behind all your experiences, and realizing that the concealment is the Creator's own doing.

Why Concealment?

All that concealment is purposeful and needed. If you felt all these desires and lacks in your current state of the will to receive, all you would feel is misery. Spiritual desires are such massive lacks that the pain would be intolerable. They are a sense of the true eternal you, the spiritual you, ready to awaken to an entirely new world.

There is a second reason as well. Just as your desires have corresponding pleasures with them in the corporeal world, spiritual desires have corresponding pleasure in the spiritual world.

This creates an entirely different problem. If you were to sense the pleasure associated with spiritual desires as you do in this world, you would instantly be a slave to the pleasure. You would be more than happy to become corrected and bestow all day and all night, as long as the pleasures here are equally enormous as the desires. But you would be bestowing only in order to receive the pleasure and not to bond with the Creator. The intention would be wrong, and, as a result, the pleasure wouldn't last.

So where does all of that leave us? Back with intention.

The spiritual desire you begin to experience, the point in the heart, is actually the "embryo" of your desire to take pleasure

On Track _____

Kabbalah does not speak about ordinary people who never think about connection with the Creator. If the person falls to this state and completely forgets about the Creator, the state is no longer called double concealment, and there is no spiritual term for it. The person has simply declined to the animal level and has no connection with the Creator.

in relationship with the Creator. To fulfill that desire, you must find a way to change your intention. At the same time, you must do this without experiencing the pleasure associated with the new intention, or you risk simply falling back into giving in order to receive for yourself.

If your intention is strong enough, you succeed in that difficult task. You begin receiving the Creator's gifts, and they evoke in you love for Him.

Reward and Punishment

Let's cover one final concept in intention, for understanding the nature of reward and punishment from the Kabbalistic point of view leads to total responsibility for your states and intentions. In simplistic terms, you come to the Creator's single revelation. The nature of reward and punishment is revealed with the existence of connection to the Creator.

From the Creator's point of view, there is no reward or punishment. He does not possess a desire that a human would act one way and not the other; He wants us only to enjoy ourselves as much as possible. The Creator's task is to lead us to a special inner state so that we can receive from Him all the good and all the enjoyment that are set aside for us as a result of achieving the purpose of creation.

The Creator does not aim to punish or encourage us for our past deeds. He only constantly leads us toward the purpose of creation.

If you start seeing the Creator in this way, reward and punishment acquire special direction and meaning. Reward and punishment are then no more than intentions: reward is the intention for the Creator, and punishment is the intention for you. If you still can't feel it, you're under concealment. With the right intention, you experience everything that happens to you or comes to you, both good and bad, as a reward. And with the wrong intention, everything that happens to you feels like a punishment, even though it is actually a sign of the Creator's teaching.

All of our life's experience, which come to us from the Creator, are all teachings from the Creator—they are thus all good, and come from Him who does only good. Such classifications as reward and punishment simply do not exist because everything displays only positive and benevolent ways in which the Creator treats the creations.

On Track

While it is beyond the scope of this book, it is worth mentioning that once we realize there are no rewards and no punishment, we realize that the Creator loves us and all creations, has always loved us and all creations, and will always love us and all creations. As you might have guessed, this is the final, and highest state—eternal love.

Keeping the Intention Day-to-Day

Of course, none of us immediately understands and senses the Creator, not even in the double concealment. Instead, we go through the various concealments of the Creator—first through the double concealment, then through the single one, and to the revelation of the Creator.

Finally, there is the comprehension of eternity, perfection, and infinite love for the Creator, the One who always treats us and the whole of humanity with constant love and the desire to give the utmost enjoyment.

So what do we do? We study Kabbalah, as will be described in Chapter 16. And we work on keeping our intention focused on the right aim. This takes constant attention and inspiration. It might mean stealing a few minutes at work to read an inspiring word. It may mean calling a study partner. It may mean reading inspiring quotations before sleep. It likely means all of those things, for that's the kind of effort it takes to maintain total responsibility for how you perceive the Creator and His actions. But first and foremost, it simply means thinking about these things.

Yet even with all the inspiration in the world, how can you discern between wrong and right intentions? It is done under the focused guidance of Kabbalistic books, a teacher, and a group. This is why Kabbalah study can be so intense, as we will see in the next chapter.

Going to Sleep with the Right Intention

The most important time of day is before going to sleep. Before you go to sleep, read a few sentences or a few words of something that inspires you. Listen to music. Half an hour or 15 minutes—it doesn't matter how long. That's enough. When you go to sleep with spiritual thoughts, your thoughts will continue to work within you through the night, and you will have gained time and effort without even thinking about it. Moreover, when you wake up in the morning, you will "automatically" begin it with thoughts about spirituality instead of the day's chores.

Rabbi Baruch Ashlag would open his father's notebook for just a few moments every night; that was enough for the expansion of the Light in the soul.

Powerful Kabbalistic Quotes

Following are some quotes of prominent Kabbalists to help inspire you during your day or before you go to sleep. Read them one at a time, then contemplate. There is no rush; these quotes work best when you think about them for a while.

All of man's engagements are guided by a single, intrinsic premise, and the internality dresses within all people. It is what they referred to as "Nature," whose numeric count is the same as *Elokim* (God). And this is the truth that the Creator concealed from the philosophers.

—Rabbi Moshe Chaim Lutzato (The Ramchal) (1707–1747), *The Book of the War of Moses*

Man's future will indeed come, in which he will evolve to such a sound spiritual state, that not only will every profession not hide another, but every science and every sentiment will reflect the entire scientific sea and the entire emotional depth, as this matter really is in the actual reality.

—Rabbi Abraham Yitzhak HaCohen Kook (1865–1935), *Orot Kodesh, A (Holy Lights, A)*

One who feels within, after several attempts, that one's soul within is in peace only when engaging in the secrets of Torah, should know for certain that this is what one has been made for. Let no preventions—corporeal or spiritual—stop one from running to the source of one's life and true wholeness.

—Rabbi Abraham Yitzhak HaCohen Kook (1865–1935), *Orot Kodesh, A (Holy Lights, A)*

The *Torah* was given to learn and to teach so that all will know the Lord, from least to greatest. We also find many books of Kabbalists alerting of the importance of the study of the wisdom that everyone must learn.

—Rabbi Yitzhak Ben Tzvi Ashkenazi (???–1807), *The Purity of Sanctity*

Indeed, if we set our hearts to answer but one very famous question, I am certain that all these questions and doubts will vanish from the horizon, and you will look unto their place to find them gone. This indignant question is a question that the whole world asks, namely, "What is the meaning of my life?"

—Rabbi Yehuda Leib HaLevi Ashlag (Baal HaSulam) (1884–1954), *The Study of the Ten Sefirot*

Even when one does not have the vessels, when one engages in this wisdom, mentioning the names of the Lights and the vessels related to one's soul, they immediately shine upon one to a certain measure. However, they shine for him without clothing the interior of his soul for lack of the able vessels to receive them. Despite that, the illumination one receives time after time during the engagement draws upon one grace from above, imparting one with abundance of sanctity and purity, which bring one much closer to reaching perfection.

—Rabbi Yehuda Leib HaLevi Ashlag (Baal HaSulam) (1884–1954), *The Study of the Ten Sefirot*

The Least You Need to Know

◆ The *Masach* is what gives us the intention, allowing the Light to fill our vessels.

◆ To transform spiritually, you must focus on the intention behind a commandment, not on its physical observance.

◆ The Kabbalist analyzes all thoughts, actions, and events according to their impact on his or her spiritual path.

◆ There are four phases to our relationship with the Creator: double concealment, single concealment, reward and punishment, and eternal love.

◆ Maintaining proper intention for the Creator takes daily focus and inspiration.

Chapter

16

Studying Kabbalah

In This Chapter

- ◆ Past practices
- ◆ Books from authentic sources
- ◆ Choosing the right teacher
- ◆ The power and practice of Kabbalah groups
- ◆ Virtual Kabbalah study

The study of Kabbalah has changed dramatically over the years, and not just in the opening up of the once mysterious and secretive wisdom to the masses. Kabbalists are connected in the most technologically advanced and media-savvy ways. As a result, the books, teachers, and groups required to get the most out of Kabbalah study are easy to find today.

For the most part, you can go right to the authentic source texts of Kabbalah from your own home and in your own language. You can even find a teacher and a virtual group when you get to that point in your spiritual development. In this chapter, you learn how to study and live Kabbalah the modern way while staying true to the wisdom in the traditional texts.

"The Wisdom Must Be Open to All"

From the early Kabbalists (Adam and Abraham) and through the writing of *The Zohar* and up to the Middle Ages, Kabbalah was primarily passed through word of mouth. The small texts that did exist may have been the starting point of study, but Kabbalists primarily shared their spiritual experiences with each other as they discovered the Upper Worlds.

At the same time, Kabbalists prohibited the study of Kabbalah by people who had not been prepared for it, unless they did so under special circumstances. They treated their students cautiously, to ensure that they studied in the proper manner. They intentionally limited the number of students.

Although we have made the point that Kabbalah study is open to all, we have not related how important the study of Kabbalah is today. To Kabbalists, in fact, wide dissemination of the wisdom of Kabbalah is a *must*. That, as much as anything else, accounts for the tremendous interest in Kabbalah today.

It is written, "For they shall all know Me, from the least of them unto the greatest of them." (Jeremiah 31:33) This refers to wide dissemination of the wisdom of Kabbalah throughout the world, as a means to know the Creator. Kabbalah seeks to spread the message of the Creator not in the religious sense, but as a message of bestowal of the Creator, as a way to bring humanity and this world into equivalence with the Creator.

The reason is that Kabbalah is based on the need for all souls to correct, and places great importance on the collective. The greater the number of people studying Kabbalah, the greater the overall effect. In the math of Kabbalah, 1 + 1 is more than 2. When masses of people study, the quantity itself improves the quality of the study. Studying in the evening for half an hour or an hour is enough because millions, if not billions, of other people are doing the same. All of these people become spiritually connected, even if they don't feel it, and the mass has its effect on the entire world.

Even tiny changes in millions of people produce great changes for the better in society as a whole. (More on that in Part 4.)

As a result, today's method of Kabbalah study appeals to a mass audience, not just to a few ultradedicated students studying in the wee hours of the morning with their Rabbis.

Word of Heart

One learns in the place one's heart wishes.

—Ancient Kabbalists' maxim

Studying Kabbalah the Correct Way

Only two things are necessary to study Kabbalah correctly: a desire to know it, and proper instruction. And proper instruction is achieved by three means:

◆ Proper books

◆ Proper group

◆ Proper teacher

If a person studies Kabbalah in the right way, he progresses without forcing himself. There can be no coercion in spirituality.

The aim of study is for a person to discover the connection between him or herself and what is written in the book. That is why Kabbalists wrote what they experienced and achieved. It is not to impart knowledge of how reality is built and functions, as in science. The purpose of Kabbalah texts is to create an understanding, assimilation, and feeling of spiritual truth.

If a person approaches the texts in order to gain spirituality, the text becomes a source of Light and corrects him. If he approaches the texts in order to gain knowledge, it is mere information for him. The measure of inner demand determines the measure of strength he gleans and the pace of his correction.

If a person studies in the proper manner, he or she crosses the barrier between this world and the spiritual world. He enters a place of inner revelation and reaches the Light. If the student does not achieve this, it is a sign of insufficient effort, in either quality or quantity. It is not a question of how much study, but the focus of the student's intentions. Of course, crossing the barrier doesn't happen overnight, but it should be the end result of the study.

Embracing Kabbalah does not work by avoiding nice things so that one's desire will not be kindled. It is a mistake to believe that by putting on a nice appearance, you will achieve spirituality. Correction does not come from self-punishment or from false pretence of correction.

The Kabbalah way absolutely rejects any form of coercion. If you experience any external pressure from others or any obligatory rules or regulations, it is a sign that the action is intended not by the Upper Worlds, but by someone in this world. In addition, inner harmony and tranquility are not prerequisites for attaining spirituality; they will appear as a result of the correction.

The Kabbalah way grants a person an inclination to spirituality, bringing him to prefer it to materialism. Then, in relation to his spirituality, he clarifies his desire. Accordingly, he either retreats from material things or not, depending on his attraction to or necessity for them.

> ### On Track _____
>
> Material desires appear successively, not all at once. If you felt a desire for money, it doesn't mean you won't feel it again tomorrow. You probably will, and even stronger. But the fact that desire for money appeared, disappeared, and reappeared is a sign you are working correctly, that the reappearance is a surfacing of a new *Reshimo*, from a new degree. It's a sign you completed your work on the previous degree and thus cleared the way for a new degree of desire to appear.

Fasts, Retreats, Cries in the Woods

Kabbalah has changed not only in who can and cannot study, but also in its practices. As you'll recall from Chapter 6, some of the original Kabbalists, such as Rabbi Shimon Bar-Yochai, were essentially hermits. But even that was not because they chose that lifestyle; they were persecuted or forbidden to engage in Kabbalah. The Ari, for instance, was a rich merchant when he arrived as a Kabbalist in Zephath. Kings David and Solomon also were neither poor nor hermits, but they were great Kabbalists.

As a result of the opening up of Kabbalah study, Kabbalah is a vital part of today's popular culture. Kabbalists do not have to abstain and practice asceticism. They live in the world and experience it.

Rabbi Ashlag, for instance, believed in manual labor. When he came to Israel from Poland, he brought with him machines for processing leather. He wanted to start a leather factory, work during the day, and study at night. He also brought up his children in this manner. When his eldest son, Baruch Ashlag—who later became a great Kabbalist in his own right—turned 18, Rabbi Ashlag sent him to work as a construction worker. He, too, would work during the day and study at night.

Yet there is a contradiction that anyone who follows Kabbalah faces. On one hand, earthly life is meaningless, and a serious Kabbalist ascribes no importance to it. On the other hand, it is a Kabbalah imperative to live within the flesh and feel it.

Many teachings and religions in the world talk about abstinence. The more one diminishes one's corporal pleasures and the more one secludes oneself, the better it is for one's spiritual ascent. Kabbalah is unique because its method suggests the opposite: leave mundane and earthly things as they are, stop messing with your body and its habits, and deal only with the point in the heart. Rather than working to diminish your desires, Kabbalah suggests that you leave them alone, because restraining desires will not correct your soul.

Kab-Trivia _____

Why is Kabbalah traditionally studied before dawn, in the wee hours? When people sleep, the local "thought-field" is quieter, and there are fewer disturbances resulting from people's thoughts. Kabbalists also study in these hours because they have to work in the morning, just like everybody else. A true Kabbalist, after all, is permitted neither to live without a steady job nor to be detached from worldly life.

Your only concern should be to increase your point in the heart. Build a soul out of it, and your soul will teach you. You then will advance correctly.

Books, Teachers, Groups

Correction does not happen without study and effort. It can take great effort and always has, as illustrated in the following bit of history.

The Creator made a ladder for our ascension, and it appeared in Jacob's biblical dream. Rabbi Yehuda Ashlag used the same allegory of a ladder in the 1950s, when he completed his commentary on *The Zohar*. He called it *HaSulam* (*The Ladder*) commentary and said that, like any ladder, his commentary helps you climb to where the good stuff is found.

If you have an attic filled with good materials, all you need is a ladder to get there. "And my commentary," he said, "is just like any other ladder."

Rabbi Ashlag wrote that only through effort will we manage to start moving toward the Creator.

For that reason, the Creator sends us books, teachers, and groups of study companions. The rest of this chapter describes each of those tools of Kabbalah study—books, teachers, and groups—and how they work.

Learning from Authentic Sources

Spirituality can be attained by studying the right books, meaning books written by a true Kabbalist. Reading the right books is like being led by a tour guide in a foreign country. With the aid of the guidebook, the traveler becomes oriented and better understands his new whereabouts.

We need books that are suited to our souls, books by the Kabbalists of our generation or the previous one, because different souls descend in each generation, and each generation requires different teaching methods.

The Power of Books

There is a special force in books of Kabbalah: any person who studies those books under the right guidance can attain the spiritual degree of the author.

Students who take a leap of faith and follow the ways expounded by the writers of authentic books of wisdom can bond unconsciously with the spiritual. Students who delve into a text of wisdom rise, and the spiritual level of the author is revealed.

Whenever you read the works of the righteous, you bond directly with them through the surrounding Light. You are then enlightened, and your vessels of reception are purified and imbued with the spirit of the Creator.

Living in our world, we absorb various pictures and impressions. Because of that, we can all describe what we feel. But Kabbalistic books describe the experiences of a person who feels this world and the upper spiritual world at the same time. They describe the writer's feelings of a world that others do not sense.

That is why Kabbalah books and Kabbalist writers are unique. A Kabbalist teacher is not only a person who feels the Upper World, but also a person who can describe emotions in a clear language so that others can feel and understand them. By studying books by Kabbalists, we nurture the missing senses within us, the ones that must be developed in order to feel the Upper World. After all, there is no time in spirituality. This way, we can all attain the sensation of the eternal Upper World and live willingly in both at once.

How to Read Kabbalah Books

There are many books of Kabbalah, written in various styles and forms, and written by Kabbalists in various degrees of attainment. That is why it is crucial that we know which books to study.

When a Kabbalist grasps spirituality, he feels it experientially, just as we experience the occurrences and incidences of this physical world with our physical senses and feelings. Because the objects in the spiritual realm are totally dissimilar from the objects of our physical world, it is difficult for Kabbalists to find the right words.

It happens in our world, too. We are not always able to explain our feelings, and at times we end up using vague words and gestures.

This is why Kabbalah books are difficult to understand. Until we have a connection to spirituality, what we read is just words, without any understanding of the meaning behind them. Don't become frustrated if what seemed clear yesterday becomes very confusing the next day. Depending on your mood and spiritual state when you are reading, the text can appear full of deep meaning or be entirely meaningless. Don't give up if the text appears to be vague, strange, or illogical. Kabbalah is studied to help you to see and to perceive, not for the sake of gaining specific knowledge.

Remember, too, that Kabbalah uses the language of the branches, described in Chapter 10. The spiritual world and our own world are parallel. There is not an object, phenomenon, or force in this world that is not a consequence of the Upper World. Therefore, Kabbalists use names taken from our world in order to describe spiritual objects, for these objects are the roots of our world.

An ordinary person, as yet without a "spiritual screen," relates to books of Kabbalah as fairytale stories that happen in our world. But one who is already a Kabbalist is not confused by the words, for he knows precisely which "branch" they stem from and which consequence in our world correlates to the "root" in the spiritual world. That is how Kabbalah books are written and must be read.

> **Red Alert**
>
> One of the most common mistakes beginners make is ascribing spiritual forces to branches, instead of focusing on the roots. For example, because we have a spiritual state called "water" (*Hassadim*, mercy), we also have water in our world. But that doesn't mean that if you drink water you become merciful.

The Right Books

Not all books claiming to be about Kabbalah give accurate information or a pure presentation of Kabbalah. Because Kabbalah has picked up many associations in its development (some of which are not accurate, as described in Chapters 1 and 5), it is important to review the books you read with a thoughtful approach. Today, the same rule of caution applies to Internet sites.

To make this easy, most dedicated Kabbalists recommend abandoning all books on the subject of Kabbalah other than *The Zohar*, the writings of the Ari, and the writings of Rabbi Ashlag. That may be the best approach for the serious, lifelong Kabbalah student.

For most anyone else, however, look for introductory books based on those writings, such as those listed in Appendix B. We wrote *The Complete Idiot's Guide to Kabbalah* to provide an introduction to the root sources so that readers can make enlightened choices for further study.

Choosing the Right Teacher

But what is the correct way of studying and how do you make sure you study properly? Students who study correctly work on themselves and their inner beings, and they generally are guided by a teacher.

def•i•ni•tion

When Kabbalists talk about **faith,** they do not refer to blind faith, in which we follow some belief because we have been taught to believe something. It's the opposite of blind faith. In Kabbalah, if you don't perceive the Creator even more clearly than with your physical senses, then you have no faith.

Experiencing the Creator is an act of *faith* that usually requires a teacher. The teacher guides the student and induces faith in him. The student rises to the spiritual level of the master and bonds with the teacher's wisdom and thoughts.

In fact, today, a single individual cannot enter the spiritual world. This would be like one individual beginning to develop the whole of physics or chemistry and then developing the technology to apply them. It would be similar to living like a Neanderthal without using all that humanity has achieved thus far. In other words, it would be senseless.

That's why a beginning student needs a teacher who has already attained the Upper World and can show the student how to attain each step to develop toward the Upper World. The teacher is a spiritual connection to the student, but the student will understand that connection fully only after attaining the Upper World independently.

Unity with the teacher occurs in the preliminary stages because both are on the worldly level. But unity with the Creator is possible only when you experience the Upper World. The teacher is your leader in that journey. Contact and unity with a teacher lead to contact and unity with the Creator.

Follow Your Heart

Teacher and student have a special bond, sometimes sticking together for years or even most of their lives. When students find a "match" with a teacher, they may remain near the teacher so that they can continuously learn more about Kabbalah and develop further spiritually as their teacher develops further spiritually.

This does not mean that a student cannot become a great Kabbalist without remaining next to the teacher one's whole life. Two such examples are Rabbi Yehuda Ashlag and Rav Kook both giant Kabbalists who did not remain with their teachers but left them and went on developing and carrying out their personal vocations as spiritual leaders. The important thing is to find the right teacher and be diligent in the study. When you have crossed the barrier, your own connection with the Creator will guide you further.

Red Alert _____

The teacher's role in Kabbalah is very subtle. The teacher must direct the student away from him, and toward the Creator. There is no way a person can avoid the attention and admiration students shower on a teacher, unless the teacher has already transcended the ego and entered the Upper World. And how do you know your teacher is the right one? Follow your heart!

How do you find such a teacher? Kabbalah has a very simple answer: follow your heart. Study where your heart desires and where you feel you belong. This is not a place where you are being persuaded to think this or that, or a place you're pushed toward. It is a place you choose of your own free will and choice. The spiritual development of Kabbalah can take place in no other way.

When you detach yourself from persuasions, from anything external, from your upbringing, and from everything that you have heard in your entire life. When you feel in your heart that you have found a teacher and place of study, you should stay. That is the only valid test, and nothing else matters.

A Genuine Kabbalah Teacher

A great Kabbalah teacher is given the title "Rav." A Rav may or may not be a Rabbi, a person ordained by a rabbinical school. In Kabbalah, a genuine Rav distances himself from the disciple and directs the disciple toward the goal—the Creator. The Rav does not make a Rebbe (parish leader) of himself, but guides and leads without making a saint of himself.

Word of Heart

When Michael Laitman asked his teacher, Rav Baruch Ashlag, if the Rav could prove he was the right teacher, Ashlag replied: "I have no answer for you. It is something you will have to answer in your own heart. You should believe no one. I do encourage you to go and look elsewhere, and if you find a better place for you, that's where you should stay."

The disciple must develop a connection and a special relation to that teacher. Thanks to that connection, the disciple can gradually resemble the Rav and ultimately become a Rav on his own.

The Rav and the disciple are two degrees: the disciple is at a certain level of attainment, and the Rav is on a higher level. Being a disciple is more difficult than being a Rav because the disciple is at a lower degree. The disciple must realize who the Rav is and what should be learned from him.

To be a disciple means to see the wisdom that the Rav possesses, realizing that you do not yet have that wisdom. To gain the most from study with a teacher, the disciple must reach the conclusion that the attributes he or she seeks can be acquired only by cleaving to the person with the higher degree.

In the past, the disciple needed to cleave in the full sense of the word: physically—to become like a part of the body, to be like a supporting organ—and spiritually—to try to think, experience, and aspire to live as the Rav does. Today only the spiritual cleaving is necessary because it is impossible to be physically close to a Rav who might be thousands of miles away. What is physically impossible is a sign that it is also spiritually unnecessary.

As Rabbi Baruch Ashlag said: "Criticize and doubt everything. The most important objective is to be freed from prejudice, from education, and from public opinion. Free yourself from anything extraneous and try to absorb the way your nature tells you. That would be the truest, because any education and any external opinion is coercion."

That advice is particularly important when you decide to gain the fullest power of Kabbalah study and become part of a group.

Learning Within a Group

All of the great Kabbalists studied in groups. Rabbi Shimon Bar Yochai held a group of students, and so did the Ari. A group is vital in order to progress. It is the primary tool of Kabbalah, and everyone is measured by his contribution to the group.

A person who studies alone can use only one's own vessel to receive the Light of the Creator. Those who study in a group, even if they sometimes argue, create a spiritual vessel that consists of all the participants, and everyone begins to enjoy its illumination.

Appendix C provides some contact addresses for existing groups in the United States, Canada, and Israel, which study under a Kabbalist teacher and with genuine books. Also, in today's high-tech world, a group doesn't have to meet in a physical location. It can be a group of like-minded people who share a common (spiritual) goal, and they can meet on the Internet. Such a group can be contacted at this e-mail: info@ kabbalah.info.

The Power of a Group

The group provides strength. Everybody has only a small desire for spirituality. The way to augment the will for spirituality is through joint desire. Several students together stimulate the Light and provide a unified field that is stronger as a whole than each individual on his or her own.

The reason, in Kabbalah terms, is that we are all parts of the same soul (remember Adam?). Mixing the parts together recreates the collective vessel and brings us closer to the corrected state, where there is more Light. This Light affects each person in the group, and this way, all the group members become corrected both individually and as a collective.

A group is like a partnership. You can fall and have nothing left of the previous spiritual situation, but the group will continue to exist and hold your desire for you. Your share in the group continues to exist, regardless of your present state.

Kabbalah Group Dynamics

Rabbi Yehuda Ashlag said that you must think of your group members as great (in spirituality). This will help you absorb spiritual powers from them when you are in personal decline. This is similar to the law of connected vessels, by which water always flows to the lowest place. If you think of the Light, or spiritual power, as water, then all you need to do is feel lower than your friends. Their Light will flow into you, and more Light will flow into them from Above.

In this way, everyone contributes to the collective progress: the ones in decline contribute by feeling lower than their friends, and the ones who feel strong contribute by drawing more Light from above. This facilitates perpetual progress of the entire group. Although the group members may change roles according to their personal spiritual states, the group's progression is endless, and always toward enhanced spirituality.

Thus, the group is the first and foremost power. Friends influence one another for better or for worse. There are processes and movements in the group: apparent strangers can enter the group, and, after some time, they are no longer considered strangers. At the same time, people who were in the group might suddenly be pushed out, as though a centrifugal power threw them out without a reasonable explanation. They can be people who have already given everything they were supposed to give to the group.

On Track

The information in this book builds the foundations for your journey toward perceiving the spiritual forces of the Upper Worlds. Yet it is only the beginning. At later stages in your ascent, progress can be made only with the help of a teacher and a group, either in person or online.

This melting pot gradually builds the condition by which any person who endures, despite the egoistic personal discomfort, will ultimately break through to the spiritual world. A lot of internal hard work is needed here. But those who take that path begin to feel their inner changes and note how the understanding of their world changes daily.

A great group consists of people who agree to achieve the goal of merging with the Creator. At early stages, members of such a group must apply the law of love to each other. For only a group can break through the selfish shells of its individual members, using the Law of Commitment. Here's how it works.

Each member of the group becomes responsible for all. At the same time, the whole group becomes responsible for everyone on the way to achieving the goal. Everyone tries to give up his personal desires and fulfill the needs of the others.

As a result of this work, everyone becomes assured that he won't lack anything; the others will take care of all his needs. The sensation of commitment compensates for the selfish desire to receive. Because of that, a group member can serve the others and love them. Commitment is a foundation for people's love to each other.

This is particularly important when the student experiences the inevitable backlash. This happens when the student's egoism grows, which is a natural part of the progress in the study. The growing egoism gives the student further material for correction, but the first reaction of a student when the reinforced egoism meets the quality of bestowal (Creator) is the backlash.

Yehuda Ashlag writes that such a student stops believing or altogether forgets about the Creator and becomes disenchanted. It seems to the student that those who aspire to the Creator are poor, sick, despised, uncivilized, and stupid hypocrites. Those who do not seek the Creator and rely on their own minds and animate instinct seem to be prosperous, healthy, calm, clever, kind, amiable, and self-assured.

> ### On Track
>
> It is very important that every Kabbalah student will have a duty in the group. In times of decline, the simple duties bring you back to the group. You perform the simplest task, such as writing e-mail memos, or washing dishes after a group meeting, and the work itself affects your soul. Because you have to force yourself to it, your soul asks why is it worth the effort, and the question itself draws Light on you and revives you. Neat, huh?

When the Creator invokes such a feeling, the person wishes to forget that suffering comes from the Creator. This leads him to loss of faith in the Creator's rule over the creations. The student believes that everything happens at the whim of fate and nature.

This is all part of the Creator's double concealment (see Chapter 15). This is when the student can and should rely on the group for help and guidance.

Having the Right Attitude

But how will you be able to receive help from the group when you need it? How do you make the most of group study?

You receive help only if you can nullify your ego and submit to the opinion of the group in everything: the goal, the idea, the way to attain the idea, the values, and the order of importance. Only then will you make your mark on the group and become like it, meaning that you take responsibility for how you have created the group.

This does not mean that you become mindless. Kabbalah study must be your choice. It is written, concerning the verse "therefore, choose life" (Deuteronomy 30:19), that the Creator puts one's hand on the good fortune (fate) and says, "Take this." This means that the Creator brings a person to a group, puts his hand on the good fortune, and says, "Take this." The rest of the work is one's own free choice. In other words, to be brought into a group means that you come to study along with others and absorb from them what you need for spiritual progress.

This is done by a very simple means: you take from the group *only* their appreciation for your goal of unification with the Creator. This is what the verse "Love thy friend as thyself" relates to; this is what makes them your friends.

If you listen to them, and if you appreciate your friends in the group, then you will absorb the message of the greatness of the Creator, meaning the greatness of bestowal. You can then really become a group of Kabbalists.

Virtual Kabbalah Study

Kabbalists are standing by … it's almost like a call center these days. The general public cannot have a teacher standing next to each of them, but teachers are available to anyone, anywhere.

Advanced communications connect groups with Ravs. To the Kabbalist, everything develops according to what is needed for the final correction, and perhaps that is why communication has developed in the way it has.

Television, books, radio, and the Internet are all readily available anywhere. You need not live in any particular place to have access to a good teacher and a dedicated group.

Rabbi Yehuda Ashlag recognized this and noted that teaching must be suitable for today's world. Seminaries can't be opened everywhere, but wherever a group can organize, a seminary, in effect, exists. The group can receive guidance through the Internet to both have a guide and increase the contact among its members.

The Internet offers an ideal way to learn about Kabbalah. You can read articles at your own pace, and many of them have been translated in ways that are easier to understand than the original text. Some sites, such as www.kabbalah.info, offer a question-and-answer forum where you can write in questions and have them answered by those knowledgeable in Kabbalah. (See Appendix C for information on this and other websites.)

The Least You Need to Know

- ◆ Proper instruction is the only thing required to learn Kabbalah correctly.

- ◆ It is important to learn from authentic sources and understand their language.

- ◆ The true teacher guides you to the Creator, not to him or herself.

- ◆ The greatest power in Kabbalah study is working in partnership with a committed group.

Kabbalah Music

In This Chapter

- ◆ Music works when words don't
- ◆ What counts in Kabbalah music
- ◆ Music of the world to come
- ◆ Kabbalah compositions explained

Kabbalists have always written music as part of their spiritual expression. It's an inseparable part of their spirituality and stems directly from their spiritual degree.

Because there are no words in the spiritual Upper Worlds, music fills in where words fail. For a music-sensitive student, music can be just as beneficial and powerful as any book—at times, even more so.

Kabbalah texts can be very cumbersome because they describe the Upper Worlds that cannot be sensed directly. Because of the power of music and the limits of words, music serves as an enhancement to Kabbalah study and a way to review its methods.

When Words Fail

Starting to perceive the Upper World, a Kabbalist enters a different dimension. An entire world is revealed before you in its entire beauty and wealth. It is something that does not exist in this world.

The Kabbalist perceives an entirely different picture: forces that bring our world into action and souls that are not attached to bodies. Past, present, and future stand before the Kabbalist in the present. The Kabbalist experiences all of this and lives fulfilled with the eternal, perfect sensation, with a feeling that encompasses the whole universe.

Words are not enough to express this deep emotional experience. How do you describe something that can't be seen or touched? The worlds of Kabbalah have to be "felt" by the Kabbalist.

When words fail, music can provide insights beyond our common understanding. Music has the power to "move" us and to make us sense things that are beyond words.

> **Word of Heart**
>
> When the lower ones begin their life by song, their spiritual ascent to the soul's root, the Upper Ones add them power in order for the lower ones to attain the Upper Light of Wisdom that has reached and became revealed in *ZON* of the World of *Atzilut* and in the angels preceding it. This way, the lower ones increase the powers and luminescence of the wisdom in the Upper realms.
>
> —From *The Sulam Commentary on The Zohar* by Baal HaSulam

The Spiritual Power of Music

Kabbalists use writing to explain to others the levels of spirituality they have reached. In their books, however, Kabbalists only advise us on how to attain an impression, sensation, and discovery of this reality. They write about the kind of actions that you must perform inside of yourself, with your own strength, desires, screens, and *Reshimot*—with everything inside of your soul.

The books say, in effect, "Perform certain actions and you will feel." They do not, however, say *what* we will feel because it is impossible to convey the feeling in words.

It is similar to offering a new food to someone and saying, "Try it, and you'll see what it's like!" Whether it is bitter or sweet, you only hint at what the person is going to sense or how he will experience the sensation. Yet the sensation itself is experienced only by the person receiving the offer, not by anyone else.

That is why it is difficult for Kabbalists to convey what they feel, what they face, what is revealed before them: what the concealed world is like. Only one medium some-how expresses the impressions and delight of a person before whom the Upper World has revealed itself, and that is sound. This is why, in addition to writing articles and very deep, intricate material, Kabbalists also write melodies and songs. It is one more way to express the sensations of a Kabbalist in a more concise manner, directly from heart to heart, through sounds, without words, so that these sounds would enter our heart and change us in some way, somehow tuning us into perceiving the Upper World.

Red Alert _____

Even sounds cannot convey impressions of the Upper World precisely, for we do not have the same *Kelim* (desires), the same sensory organs, or the same inner attributes as Kabbalists who attain and sense the Upper Worlds. Sounds give us an impression of the Upper Worlds, a similar sensation yet a weak duplicate.

A Heart-to-Heart Resuscitation

Kabbalah music expresses the states of mind and soul of the Kabbalist. The melodies are composed to describe the experience of two opposing stages in spirituality. The first is agony, a result of drifting away from the Creator. The feeling of drifting away from the Creator produces sad music, expressed by a prayer appealing for closeness. The second emotion is delight, felt as a result of getting closer to the Creator. This feeling of closeness to the Creator produces joyous music, expressed by a thanksgiving prayer.

If you listen to Kabbalah music, you hear and feel the two distinct moods in the music. They are the longing and desire for unification with the Creator when you are drifting away, and the love and happiness you feel when discovering or rediscovering the unification.

The two moods together express the Kabbalist's relationship to and unification with the Creator. Even though the melody may bring one to tears, one loves to hear it because the melody expresses distress that has been dealt with and has been fulfilled.

The music bathes the listener in a wondrous light. We do not need to know anything about it before listening to it because it is wordless. Yet its effect on our hearts is direct and swift. Hearing it over and over again is a special experience.

If you feel the music, you won't need to imagine the forms in spiritual worlds, described in books. These forms don't exist except within you and, therefore, mislead you. What is so special about the music is that everyone can understand it, even if we have not reached the composer's spiritual level. Listening to music composed by Kabbalists gives us all the opportunity to experience their spiritual sentiments.

Melodies of the Upper World

The melodies in Kabbalah could be described as melodies of the "World to Come," as they serve the purpose of bringing the Upper Worlds to this world. Singing evokes blessings from above so that they manifest in all lower worlds.

In the words of Rabbi Elazar Azikri (1533–1600), "Those who aspire shall sing praises unto spiritual heights, unto the Upper Ones and lower ones, fastening all the worlds with the tie of faith." (Remember, faith isn't blind faith; it is a tangible perception of the Creator.)

A Song from the Source

In order to understand what the Kabbalistic composer wants to express in the melody, you merely need to listen, and your understanding works automatically. By listening to the melodies of a Kabbalist, you have the opportunity to be affected to a certain degree by their impressions of the spiritual worlds.

> **Word of Heart**
>
> When a person acquires the quality of *Bina*, mercy, he or she feels calm and serene. Rav Baruch Ashlag expressed it in his gentle melody to the words from Psalms (116), "For thou hast delivered my soul."

There is a soul in each of us, and the soul of a Kabbalist resembles a musical instrument that already plays properly and feels properly, similar to the biblical King David's violin. This is not a regular violin, but the inner *Kli* (or vessel) of a Kabbalist's soul, inside of which he feels reality in a certain way and can express it through sounds. So King David could write the Book of Psalms fully composed of the impressions of the Upper World.

Climbing Up the Notes

You can use Kabbalist tunes to connect to the spiritual roots from which they were written without having to work hard. Just relax and listen to the music.

Yet there is information in the notes themselves. The notes in Kabbalah are not random or "free form." They are composed according to Kabbalistic rules and are chosen according to the way a soul is built. They are a way to climb the ladder. You (the listener) feel them penetrating deep within your soul, unobstructed. This happens because of the direct connection between your soul and the roots of the notes.

Go back to Chapter 11 and think of the spiritual nature of Hebrew letters and their representation of numbers. The most important thing in Kabbalistic music is not the notes themselves, but all the fine nuances that exist between them.

Just to give you a sense of it, in Chapter 11 we said that there are *Ta'amim* (flavors), *Nekudot* (dots under, within, and above the letters), *Tagin* (crowns on top of the letters), and *Otiot* (letters). These represent the finest nuances formed over the entire impression from the Light—impressions, for instance, of *Reshimot* leaving the spiritual vessel and entering it again.

Word of Heart

Singing is the song, the call of the soul, that contains the entire *Torah,* the entire Upper Light. The song, to which the Upper and the lower ones in all the worlds awaken. The song, like a spring from above, a repose of the Upper One, the Divine mercy. The song that adorns the Holy Supernal Name, *Malchut,* the receptacle of the Creator. And this is why it is the Holy of Holies.

—From *The Sulam Commentary on The Zohar* by Baal HaSulam

It is the same with sounds. Musicians who understand how to play Kabbalistic melodies are few and far between. The difference between the one who plays correctly and one who plays nicely lies in the extent to which one understands where important things are. What's most important lies not in the sounds, but in the tiniest symbols, in how the sound begins and ends.

The author, Rav Laitman had a wonderful student who played the violin. "I'm ready to play only on the condition that you will hold my hand," he told his Rav. And this is right—Kabbalah music is about conveying the right feeling, not the accurate note.

Original Kabbalistic Music

We have an enormous gift of melodies from the last great Kabbalist of our generation, Rabbi Yehuda Ashlag. These melodies express all of the steps and all of the sensations of the Upper Worlds.

By listening to these melodies, you come closer to the true sensation of the Upper Reality, spirituality. You gradually draw closer, as though you are entering the Upper World. Rabbi Yehuda Ashlag wanted us to come closer to this state. This is why he left us his melodies.

Actually, as is often the case with Kabbalists, the writing of the melodies started from a practical need. When Yehuda Ashlag came to Israel in the early 1920s, students came to him and asked of him to teach. When he realized he was about to start a group, he wanted to provide them with melodies that were nothing they were used to from home. He feared that when they listened to them, they would think thoughts they used to think before their studies. So he composed new tunes to old words from the Bible, to sing on Sabbath meals and other festive occasions.

He composed melodies to songs such as "To declare Thy lovingkindness in the morning, and Thy faithfulness in the night seasons" (Psalms 92:3); "A God that hideth," which is a famous Sabbath song; and others. Sometimes he would simply hum a tune and declare that it reflected a certain verse or a psalm from Psalms, but no direct connection to the words was made.

In all, Ashlag composed just over 20 melodies. His son, Baruch Ashlag, also composed a few melodies, and there have been many renowned Kabbalists who have composed music and written poems. Prominent examples of such Kabbalists are the Holy Shlah; Rabbi Yehuda HaLevi; Rabbi Shlomo Elkabetz, composer of "Lecha Dodi" ("Come, my beloved"), probably the most famous Jewish melody; and, of course, the Holy Ari.

On Track

Three CDs of the Kabbalistic music from Rabbi Yehuda Ashlag and Rabbi Baruch Ashlag have been recorded, as Rav Laitman heard them from his Rabbi, Rabbi Baruch Ashlag. You can listen to the melodies free of charge at www.kabbalah.info/engkab/mmedia.htm, or buy them at www.kabbalahbooks.info. You can also download them at no further charge.

For every person, regardless of how much he or she knows and how long he or she has been studying Kabbalah, the sounds are the shortest, most direct, and simplest means for experiencing something from the spiritual. This is true even when you still lack the inner attributes and capacities acquired during the study.

Following are descriptions of and commentaries on some of his songs. These melodies allow you to experience some of the concepts covered in earlier chapters. Most of these melodies relate to Rosh Hashanah (the New Year) and Yom Kippur (the Day of Atonement). The melodies were written to express the inner state of a person who exists at the spiritual degree called Rosh Hashanah or Yom Kippur. As you read and then listen, reflect on these melodies as a means for entering the Upper World.

Tzadik Ke Tamar Ifrach ("The Righteous Shall Flourish Like the Palm-Tree")—Psalms 92:13

This melody expresses the desire for spirituality and the joy of attainment, a sense like that expressed in the chapters in Part 1 of this book.

Basically, there are two states in every Kabbalistic song. One is the state of the *Kli* when it is detached from the Creator and requires correction; the other is when the soul (*Kli*) that you have has received its correction and attained delight and excitement. Here the music expresses this delight.

The first state allows you to experience a state that you know is a part of the spiritual journey. This is because a righteous person begins from discovering the evil in him or herself—the lack of correction and separation from the Creator—and eventually comes to justify the entire process through which he or she passed.

Tzadik Ke Tamar expresses the corrected state, where one seemingly enters the King's palace—the Upper World. The melody bursts out the joy of reaching adhesion with the Creator.

This song is special because it expresses gratitude not for the state attained, but for the ability to justify the Creator in the entire journey. You feel in the melody the causality and the pressing necessity of all the states you passed through. You understand that all of them were prearranged from above, by the Creator, so that you could attain this elevated state.

LaMenatzeach Al-Shoshanim ("To the Leader Upon Lilies")—Psalms 45:1

A lily is *Malchut* (the receptacle of the Creator), which contains all the vessels, all the desires, the totality of one's life. This song expresses the entire process of correction as described in Chapters 13 through 16.

"A lily among the thorns" (Song of Songs 2:2) means experiencing all one's desires and using them to be like the Creator—for bestowal, altruistically. You must reach this state through the thorns, through many discernments, interruptions, and clarifications. That's the beginning of the journey.

It is only from within *Malchut*, from the most inner point in the heart, that you begin to feel the Creator, a feeling of unification and true love. This is the end of the journey.

In between, you experience in the melody the middle, the revelation of hatred and fear, confusion and lack of confidence, dependence and every possible complaint, everything that one can imagine. With all this, you turn to the Creator and blame Him for everything.

You are initially built in an opposite form from Him, as an egoist, who only thinks about himself and wants only to take advantage of the entire world and of the Godly force and use it for his own needs. In the process of Kabbalah study and work, you discover to what extent you are opposite in form (qualities) from Him.

When all the forces of evil—egoistic desires—are revealed in you, and you are able to conquer them, you reach what is called Goodness. What do you then say to the Creator? "My heart overfloweth with a goodly matter" (Psalms 45:2). There is only one good thing in the world—adhesion with the Creator, with bestowal, with love.

"I say my deeds are for the King" (Psalms 45:2). Everything that is inside you is now directed to the King. You praise not yourself, but the Creator, because you discover that by acquiring His attributes and understanding them, you ascend to the same levels as the Creator. You open up and see the whole picture. Then, as the melody goes, you praise Him, connect with Him, cling to Him, and love Him.

"Thou art fairer than the children of men" (Psalms 45:3). You become a hero, and all of creation is below you; you take ahold of it in order to work in the same form of bestowal as the Creator.

This kind of work is a song that can be "sung" only by one who has indeed reached the end of the way, the final correction.

Rav Laitman's teacher, Rabbi Baruch Ashlag, was especially fond of this song—*LaMenatzeach Al-Shoshanim*. He sometimes sang this song alone in Tiberias. Laitman would hear his teacher singing from the next room on the long winter nights. Rabbi Ashlag would be in a special state from the song, deeply absorbed in contemplation, detached from reality, yet attached to this flowing song, to the forces, the levels, and the states that this song expresses. It's a song of love, of unity with the Creator.

Word of Heart

Singing is the secret of attracting the Light of Greatness and Wisdom, coming from its root in the spiritual height, over the … line called "night." This is why "Those who sing at night, sing for all in whom this song resounds," as it is said about the greatest poet of all times, King David, the author of Psalms, who used to write at night: "And he rose while it was still night." The revelation of the Light of Wisdom in man is his spiritual ascent, and such an ascent is possible only from darkness; it is performed only at night.

—From *The Sulam Commentary on The Zohar* by Baal HaSulam

Chamol Al Maaseicha ("Have Compassion on Your Creation")—A Song Title in the Prayer Book for the New Jewish Year

This melody expresses the experience of daily relationship with the Creator, as described in Chapter 13. It asks for forgiveness and pardon.

As usual in spiritual work, there are two opposite conditions. For those who have crossed the barrier there is but one state, "There is none else besides Him." Those who are still in a state of unconsciousness experience the state called "If I'm not for me who is for me?"

To those who are on the way from this world to the Upper World, the two states are revealed at any given time: the state of the creature and the state of the Creator that work together. On one hand, it is the Creator who apparently arranges everything, but on the other hand, it depends on the creature.

When you reach the state where "If I'm not for me who is for me?" and "There is no one else besides Him" converge and become one, you then have a real prayer, composed of two opposing discernments, and you feel that you cannot decide. This is when you ask of Him to have compassion on His creations.

How can it be that the Creator controls everything in a human, yet on the other hand, humans still feel that they exist outside the Creator's control? Listen to the melody to experience the opposition and request to be on the right path.

Ya'ale Tachnuneinu ("Raise Our Pleas")

"Pleas" mean the prayer of the many. "Many" means when a person discovers that he is still composed of different forces that are not like the Creator. This melody is a Kabbalistic prayer, as discussed in Chapter 14.

This is a prayer in which you judge the forces in you that are not like the Creator, experience those forces, scrutinize and parse them one by one and, therefore, reach a state where you raise *MAN*. *MAN* is a request, a plea of the Upper Force to come and correct the opposing forces inside you and give those feelings one desire and one intention—to please Him. You plead that you will feel one flow, that all the opposing forces inside you will lead you to the Creator, to the quality of bestowal.

In states of either morning or night, in states when the Upper Force shines on you and when it does not, you plead that your prayer shall be whole until it is answered. It is answered when all the requests and desires are united in you, and all your vessels become one great vessel in which you can reach adhesion with the Creator.

Ya'ale Tachnuneinu is sung on Yom Kippur, the Day of Atonement, in a state when the empty vessels are revealed. From these pleas, as we raise requests for correction, we receive the Light that reforms from above, and when the vessel is corrected, it reaches a state in which it is filled with all the light of love and adhesion.

Kel Mistater ("A God That Hides")

Kel Mistater is sung toward the end of *Shabbat* (Sabbath), at the end of the day. The end of Shabbat is the time when the *Shechinah* (Divinity) that comes during the spiritual ascent starts to purposefully depart, leaving one in darkness. The purpose for the lack of fulfillment is so that the fulfillment received on *Shabbat* will serve during the following week as the driving energy for an independent attainment of what the Kabbalist received as a gift on *Shabbat*.

Shabbat is called "a gift." As it is written in the Talmud, "The Creator said unto Moses, 'A good gift have I for Israel and *Shabbat* is her name. Go and tell them.'" A gift is something that is not given to you as a reward, for you have not labored for it. A gift is given by the Creator out of love.

This is a song of concealment, a concept introduced in Chapter 15. The Upper Force comes from above, and a person is inevitably awakened by it. There are times in studying Kabbalah when you experience various sensations, phenomena that you do not yet deserve according to your level of spiritual attainment. This is a gift.

Now you may be granted your ascent, your revelation, but after some time, this sensation begins to wane. Then you may say, "The Creator is hiding. You, the Creator, have revealed Yourself to me in the state of *Shabbat* as a gift, and now you go away from me again in your hiding. I understand that this is necessary so that I can come closer and reveal You even on 'low' days, at the time of Your concealment, on week-days, when I am in the state of weekdays separated from sanctity. But I must ensure that all days of the week connect to the degree of *Shabbat*."

Kel Mistater is the song of a person who has experienced the Creator and expresses the sensations of all 10 *Sefirot*. The impression and inspiration that these ascents evoke within a person are truly profound. Their tremendous spiritual power justifies the special efforts Rabbi Ashlag made in creating these new melodies.

These melodies are taught even to the beginners so that they become inspired by the songs and experience the inspiration and delight, even though they have not yet attained this experience in practice.

The Least You Need to Know

- ◆ Kabbalah music makes it more easier for you to experience the spiritual worlds.

- ◆ Kabbalistic songs express the interplay of two moods: anguish over moving away from the Creator and joy over moving toward the Creator.

- ◆ All you need to do, in the end, is relax, listen to the music, and try to be absorbed in the emotions the Kabbalists reveals in their music.

- ◆ Kabbalistic songs cover the entire knowledge and experience of Kabbalah and correction.

Part 4

Kabbalah in Today's World

You know what Kabbalah is and how it got started, but how does it relate to today's world? In this part, we'll explore the reasons for the global crises we are facing from the Kabbalistic point of view.

You may be asking, "What's in it for me?" Well, we'll also discuss your role in the big picture and how you can help heal your own environment and the world at large.

Remember, we are all one soul. What happens to me affects you directly, so you have the ability to impact someone on the other side of the world. This final section will help you understand how to use your connections in society, through Kabbalah, to make the world a better place.

Chapter 18

The Global Village and the First Man

In This Chapter

- The world in crisis
- We are all part of one soul
- Change the whole by changing the parts
- What great desires can give you (and what they can't)
- To change the world, change yourself

It is hardly news that humanity is in a crisis. Many already feel it and many declare it. In fact, even the crisis has become a kind of a fad. There are movies about it, some of which have become blockbusters; there are books about it, some of which have become bestsellers; and there are proponents of it, some of whom have become celebrities.

But the bottom line is that there really is a crisis, and many people feel empty, frustrated, and disoriented. The worst part is not that we don't feel as happy today as we did yesterday; it is the sensation that we have lost control. It seems more and more difficult to make our tomorrows brighter. And that's the real crisis.

A physicians' proverb says that an accurate diagnosis is half the cure; the entire healing process depends on it. In this chapter, we explore the roots of our crisis and the way to cure it. This chapter introduces the concepts, and the rest of the chapters discuss in more detail the ideas presented here and their practical implementation.

I Sneeze, You Get a Cold

When miners dig coal in China, the air in California gets polluted. When emissions from American cars dissolve in the air, the ice in Greenland melts. And when the ice in Greenland melts, the sea level rises.

It boils down to this: when I sneeze, you get a cold. And when you sneeze, I get a cold right back. In other words, we are all part of the global village, and our actions affect one another.

United We Stand, United We Fall

Of all the values you and I hold dear, the one we probably cherish most is privacy. We'd all like to have a piece of private property.

> **Word of Heart**
>
> This entire reality, Upper and lower, is one … was emanated and created by a Single Thought. That Single Thought … is the essence of all the operations, the purpose, and the labor. It is, by itself, the entire perfection … the "One, Unique, and Unified."
>
> —From *The Study of the Ten Sefirot* by Rabbi Yehuda Ashlag

Back in Chapter 6, we said that there are five levels of desire: inanimate, vegetative, animate, human, and spiritual. We also said that there was once a single soul, called Adam, which broke into a multitude of fractions, which then dressed in physical bodies in our world. This is why we have so many people on planet Earth.

In truth, however, no matter how far we feel from one another, we are still that one soul, Adam. If a brain cell is oblivious to a blood cell, it doesn't mean that it can live without it. Without the blood cells bringing food and oxygen to the brain, the brain cells would die—and so would the blood cells. So would we.

We may not like it, but united we stand and united we fall because united we are, already.

Accountability as We Grow

Think about this: as you grow, you assume greater responsibilities. A newborn baby is responsible for nothing. How can it be? Because it cannot think about things and process them, because it cannot understand the world it experiences, a baby cannot be held responsible.

But an older child is already responsible for something, even if it's just to remember to put the sandwich in the lunchbox or to take the dog out at the end of a school day. A youth is already responsible for many more things, and a young adult is expected to take full responsibility for his or her life.

As we grow, we usually marry and have kids. Then we become responsible for others, too.

But what if we were responsible for every single human being on Earth? What if that responsibility was not only to the people alive today, but also to all things—people, animals, plants, and minerals—that have ever lived since the moment Creation was first thought of and to all eternity? This is the meaning of spiritual responsibility.

Now, this responsibility may sound like a heavy load, but what if that responsibility was not the result of some mean schoolteacher who wants to give his students an assignment they can't succeed in? What if it were simply the result of love?

We love our children, so responsibility for their well-being is welcome. What if we felt the same kind of love and care that we feel to our children toward the whole world and everything in it—toward all the creatures that ever lived, that are alive today, and that will be alive at any time in the future? That immense love is spiritual bliss. Kabbalah helps us experience this immense love, and make it inherent in our nature.

600,000 Parts

Remember how we started? First there was Adam, one soul. Adam was a good soul, wanting only to give to the Creator. But he misjudged his ability to give to the Creator, and that mistake cost him—and, consequently, us—heavily. He broke. His soul shattered into 600,000 pieces, which continued to break until today, when we finally have billions of pieces, all of which are tiny bits of the original soul.

Kab-Trivia _____

Here's the Kabbalistic explanation for the overpopulation on our planet. Our egoism keeps growing and becomes increasingly difficult to correct. The only way to correct it is by "splitting" it to tiny bits. For egoism to correct, it needs to "dress" in a physical body. Thus, the number of people in the world is the number of fragments of the common soul (Adam) we currently need to complete its correction.

The Common Soul

The beauty of it is that each of us is both a particular soul and a piece in the puzzle of *Adam ha Rishon*. Within us are all the pieces of that first soul, just as every cell in our body contains all the genetic information to create a whole new identical body or a part of a hologram contains the entire image.

But to realize that we are one soul, we have to want to feel this way. This simple rule runs throughout Kabbalah and spirituality: no coercion. In other words, you don't get what you don't want to get.

The cells in our body don't "think" about how they work together. They just function as one common body. We wouldn't make it past the first week of pregnancy if it hadn't been this way. Indeed, biology provides a perfect model for what Kabbalah describes as the common soul.

When a baby grows in its mother's womb, the minute cells begin to differentiate, a beautiful thing happens: they begin to communicate and cooperate with one another. The more differentiated they become, the more they are forced to cooperate. A liver cell can't do what a kidney cell does, so the kidney cleans up the toxins that the liver can't, and the liver creates the new cells that the kidney can't. This way, they are both different but cooperating—and every part of the body benefits as a result.

What About the Rest of the World?

Just like our bodies, our souls can work cooperatively. We can live as separate units, just as there are unicellular creatures, but we all know that unicellular creatures are at the low end of nature's pyramid. On the contrary, the creatures at the top of the pyramid are made of many kinds of cells, where each cell can do only one thing and all the cells function as a single unit.

Kabbalists of the past, especially the ancient past, had to attain spirituality all on their own, hence the fantastic nature of their achievements. But it's different today. Now that Kabbalah is open to all and studied by many, it's a safe bet that most of us will attain as much individually as any of the great Kabbalists of the past. As a unit, however, we can achieve far more than has ever been achieved before.

For this reason, contemporary Kabbalists stress the importance of dispersing the knowledge about Kabbalah. They want the world to know so that more "cells" will join in the collective work of the soul, the spiritual body.

Fix Me, Fix You

There are many "side effects" to the fact that we are made of one shattered soul. One of them is that if I correct myself, I also correct my part in you. And vice versa. If you correct yourself, you also correct your "you" in me.

To bring it all down to Earth, let's take three separate people as an example: Jack, James, and Mary. One day, Jack begins to feel his point in the heart and begins to correct himself. Jack has a little piece of James and a little piece of Mary within him, and the two others also have little pieces of the others in them. They are "cells" in the same spiritual body, and each cell contains all the genetic information to create a whole body.

When Jack corrects himself, the Jack in James and the Jack in Mary is corrected, too. Of course, the other two don't feel it because they're not Jack. Subconsciously, however, the Jack within them begins to urge the other two to start checking out this new concept of spirituality.

Little Points in Every Heart

Now, Jack doesn't really give anything to the others. He *inspires* them to check it out for themselves. His transformation serves as a model for theirs. This is because the basic structure of every human being is the same. We all have points in the heart, so we don't need to receive anything from anyone. We need to merely listen openly, and then our own point in the heart will open. We've already talked in Chapter 3 about the importance of the social influence in determining the direction of our growth. If we want to become rich, we have to surround ourselves with people who want money. If we want to become lawyers, we surround ourselves with judges and advocates, and listen to what they say.

Red Alert

If we are in an environment of people with a negative approach—to society or to themselves—we will inevitably begin to think like them. The way to make sure we progress in a positive direction is to surround ourselves with people who are on that direction, too.

We learn more than just techniques by talking to people we want to resemble. We absorb their spirit. Absorbing the spirit is the most important thing in everything we do, and it's the whole difference between success and mediocrity, or even failure.

Same goes with becoming spiritual. The best way to do it is to surround yourself with people who want spirituality, too. We all have more egoistic desires within us than anything else and just one tiny speck—a point in the heart—of spirituality (true altruism).

So if many others talk to me about spirituality, I get inspired and think that everyone but me has loads of spirituality. Of course, it isn't true, but it does have the effect of making me want spirituality much more strongly and accelerating my progress.

The Little Me in You

Let's go back to our friends, Jack, James, and Mary. Let's say they meet and become best friends. Thanks to Jack's first awakening, they now all want spirituality. Their points in the heart are wide awake, and they want it so much that it's all they talk about.

They read books and discuss them. They watch videos and try to follow the charts of spirituality that the teacher shows on the screen. They play at fantasizing what it would be like if everyone—literally, everyone—wanted nothing but to do good to others.

Now let's say that Jack suddenly has other thoughts. He begins to wonder if it's all really out there or in him, and maybe someone just made it all up. But because he continues to play the game, just like we all pretend to be things we're not or at least better than we actually are, his friends don't see his situation.

They continue to be impressed and continue to impress each other. Because they keep pushing themselves toward correction, their parts in Jack become more corrected, too. As a result, the James in Jack and the Mary in Jack affect Jack the boy, and his point in the heart reawakens, and he continues with new strength.

Save the Whales ... and Everything Else

Today many already realize that man is the only destructive element in nature. The reason for this is that we are not really part of nature. Our bodies belong to the animal kingdom, but our minds don't. Our minds are the reflection of our higher self, the spiritual self, which is still hidden from us.

Animals don't need to be taught how to behave because their behavior is hard-coded in them, written in their genes before they are born. If we were made of only the animal part in us, we'd be the same. But we're not, and therein lies the problem.

When babies learn to crawl, we must watch so they don't hurt themselves because their bodies can do things that their minds cannot monitor. For the children to be safe, they don't need to develop their bodies even more; they need to develop their minds so their minds will know what to do with their bodies.

The General and the Particular

There is a rule in Kabbalah: "General and particular are equal." It means that what is true for an individual is true for the whole, and vice versa. Just like a single baby, the whole of humanity must develop its mind so that its body—the collective body of humanity—will not damage itself.

Regrettably, we are slow learners. And this is why we are harming the whales and every creature and place on Earth, extinguishing its life and exploiting its minerals. In the process, we're also harming ourselves, probably more than we're harming any other creature. Just look at the rate of degenerative diseases today, and you'll see what we're doing to ourselves.

We can't save the whales—or anything else, for that matter—simply by not hunting them. We have to correct our minds first, and our minds can be corrected only if we correct the spiritual element in all of us.

The Higher Degree Rules

In Kabbalah, the basic rule that governs here is called "The higher degree rules." Spirit is above matter. There is probably no dispute about that. All religions are based on that statement; so are science and psychology.

To change your world, you have to go to the place that corrupts it, and that place is the human mind. As long as humans were only sophisticated animals, the world was fine. It was not in danger. When we began to want to control it, when we started developing our egoism, that's when troubles started, not just for ourselves, but for the world at large.

If we correct our spirits, our bodies will act naturally, in harmony with the whole of

Word of Heart

A will in the Upper One becomes a mandatory force in the lower one.

—From *The Study of the Ten Sefirot* by Rabbi Yehuda Ashlag

nature and, hence, with the Creator. Then we won't have to worry about saving animals. Nature will do it. After all, it had been doing it for millions of years before we came, and far better than we have ever succeeded.

The Greater Your Desire, the Meaner You Are

There is a rule in Kabbalah: "He who is greater than his friend, his desire is greater than him." It means that if Jack has a greater desire than James, Jack's desire is greater than Jack himself. In other words, in the correction process, we're always one step behind our desires.

This is a deliberate process. It isn't that our desires grow. They only appear one by one, from lighter to heavier. When I finish correcting one desire, the next desire in line appears.

Remember the *Reshimot?* They form the desire-sequence that leads up the spiritual ladder. That is why Jack, who corrected his previous desire, is greater than James, who hasn't corrected this level of desire. But Jack's desire is greater than Jack himself because it is leading him to the next degree. More on that in just a bit.

A Time of Raging Desires

We've already said that desires grow from generation to generation. This generation has the worst and strongest desire in the history of humanity. Kabbalists graphically demonstrate what they think of this generation with the words, "The face of the generation is as the face of a God." Desire is running rampant to the point that people simply cannot find satisfaction anywhere—hence the soaring depression and violence rates in today's society.

But this generation isn't merely greedier than their fathers were. Today, for the first time, there is a desire to know how things really work. This is a desire of the mass of people, too, not just the exclusive domain of science and philosophy. More people don't settle for the answers provided by traditional means. They want to find out for themselves, and find out for certain. Taking someone else's word for it just doesn't do it for them any longer.

> **Word of Heart**
>
> There is a magnificent, invaluable remedy, to those who delve in the wisdom of Kabbalah. Although they do not understand what they are learning, through the yearning and the great desire to understand what they are learning, they awaken upon themselves the Lights that surround their souls.
>
> —From *The Study of the Ten Sefirot* by Rabbi Yehuda Ashlag

These people need a method to reveal the overall design, and that method is Kabbalah.

Knowledge Is a Factor of Desire

As long as we are not using the method that can satisfy our deepest desire, to know the designer of the world and to learn from Him why He did it and how, we will not be happy. But as we've said before, the more we want, the more we develop our brains to provide us what we want.

Technology isn't going to stop just because we have a new desire. But as long as our technology is not accompanied by the study of the Upper Worlds, it will only make us feel worse. There isn't anything wrong with technology itself. It's just that it has become imbued with hopes that don't belong there. We think it can make us happier by making our lives faster, easier, more exciting. But all it can really do is show us more easily and more quickly that we are empty inside.

For knowledge to make us happy, it needs to be used for spiritual research. When we do that, what we know will open up new sides of itself that will make us see our world in a light we never dreamed existed. The Upper World isn't a different place; it's a different perspective.

The Meaner You Are, the Greater You *Can* Be

In light of what we've just said about growing desires and scientific progress, we can now begin to see our current situation from a spiritual point of view. In the past, people were not as mean, as egoistic, as they are today.

The gradual emergence of the *Reshimot* accounts for the change. When *Reshimot* of smaller desires appear, they don't seem like such mean desires. Today, however, the last and most egoistic kind of *Reshimot* are appearing.

As with everything in Kabbalah, this is not a bad thing. It's a springboard for greater achievements. If we play our cards right—if we funnel these desires into the only constructive direction there is—the sky (or shall we say, heaven) is the limit.

A Great Desire Means Great Pleasure

We can't control which desires surface, but we can control what we do with them once they do. People still want money, power, and knowledge. But people are also getting frustrated and depressed because, underneath the surface, the foundation of all those desires is spiritual. People want to control *everything*, they want to know *everything*.

Granted, most of us don't feel those desires. But we have them nonetheless because it's human nature to want *everything*. The only reason that we don't feel them is that we're realistic enough to know we will never have them.

In Kabbalistic terms, this is called "A man does not wish for the King's daughter's hand." Even so, knowing that I can't have the king's daughter doesn't mean that, deep down, I wouldn't like to. Frustration naturally arises.

But the truth is that even if I did have the king's daughter, I wouldn't be satisfied. A desire that great really stems from the spiritual. It can be completely satisfied only through spiritual means.

If we direct these desires toward the root from which every desire and every pleasure comes, then we would experience the satisfaction of these desires immediately after we experienced the desire itself. It would be like a never-ending chain of desires and pleasures endlessly linked.

What would we do then? Probably sit back and enjoy the ride.

It's Not Who I Am, It's What I Do with Who I Am

We don't have to worry about the kind of desires that surface in us. Deep within, we are all potential criminals of the worst kind you can imagine. But that doesn't mean that we have to act on those desires. Most of us don't.

But if we acknowledge those parts of ourselves, if we can begin to realize that we're selfish, that's a very good start. We can then really start a change in ourselves and in the world around us.

No good thing ever came out of another good thing. Something good always grows out of a crisis because crises are a window of opportunity for change. It is simple mathematics to see that because the present crisis is the worst, the opportunity for growth and for progress is greater than ever.

What You Really Need to Fix

Now we're left with just one question: "What do I need to do?" That's the beauty of Kabbalah. You don't need *to do* anything, you need *to think*. Every now and again, hook up with Kabbalah, read something about it, watch a lesson on video, talk about it with friends. That's enough.

Nature created us egoists, and nature will change us. But for the change to happen, we need to want it to happen. That's all we need to worry about—wanting to change.

The Least You Need to Know

◆ The world is in a time of crisis in which many people feel empty and frustrated, and are seeking something more.

◆ We are all part of the single soul of Adam.

◆ Because we are all interrelated, like the cells of the body, we can change the whole by changing the parts.

◆ The desire to know how the world works and to understand the unseen secrets is greater than ever.

◆ The opportunity for growth and change is greater in this time of crisis.

Chapter 19

The Malady: Trapped in the Ego Cage

In This Chapter

- ◆ The next critical shift in thinking
- ◆ The one question science and religion can't answer
- ◆ The maladies of depression, drugs, and violence
- ◆ The collapse of society and the environment
- ◆ Maladies as a sign that a change is coming

Given that we are all actually one, that our desires are growing, and that we need to make the most of our desires rather than suppress them, let's see where we go next.

This chapter focuses on what happens when you misuse the ego. We'll look at the current state of humanity and spirituality, as a way to get a temperature on where we are, where we're headed, and what we can do about it. Don't worry, it has a happy ending.

Humanity at a Crossroads

Throughout human history, there are times that mark a critical shift in the course of human events and thinking. The last such period was the Renaissance, which marked a dramatic change in the way people thought and in how they considered religion, science, art, and human society.

Around that period, the great Kabbalist Rabbi Isaac Luria (the Ari) declared his time as the beginning of the last generation. Kabbalists have marked the end of the twentieth century, too, as the beginning of another major change, a time of some tumult.

> ### On Track
>
> In Kabbalah, everything has a positive meaning. If you can't see a term or a state as positive, it's a sign you haven't grasped it to the fullest. In Kabbalah, generations do not refer to physical life cycles, but to changes in consciousness, in correction. So the last generation isn't the end of humanity, but the end of our unconscious progress, and the beginning of our conscious and enlightened progress toward correction. When we are corrected, we will not need to change anymore, which would be from the Kabbalistic perspective, the last generation.

When You Can't Find Decisive Answers

A malady is something bad because it points to a dysfunction in one or more of our systems. If we think of our time in terms of human comfort, we shouldn't really see anything wrong. We live longer. We have plenty of food (at least, in North America and in Europe). On the whole, we can afford to buy more than our parents and grandparents. And we have far more options on which to spend our extra income.

So what's the problem?

It's this: until not so long ago, we had hope that, in time, and with the help of science, technology, and medicine, the answer to all society's ills would be revealed. Today, however, virtually all fields of science or society are in some state of confusion. There are so many schools of thought that it's difficult to find which one to follow and which of them is the most promising.

> ### Word of Heart
>
> You can't run a race properly when the finishing-post hasn't been properly positioned and fixed in place.
>
> —Francis Bacon, English philosopher and statesman

Moreover, every field of science is so connected to other fields that you can't study one without the other. At the same time, there is so much information in each field that you can't study many fields because you'll end up being expert in none.

What to do?

All Questions Can Be Answered Except One

Don't worry. Science has its ways, and it will provide answers. The only problem is that it will provide more answers of the kind we already have. It's not that these answers aren't true. They are. But science tends to answer *the wrong question*.

The reason there is a crisis in the world today is not that science has gone wrong. It's that both science and religion, the two most common places we look for answers, are failing to answer the underlying question we are really asking: what is it all for? If all the abundance I have doesn't make me happy, if it doesn't fill my heart with joy, then what's it all for and what do I need it for?

Science makes no pretense to answer that question. It tells you how life is organized, but it doesn't tell you why it exists. Religion, any religion, tells you that if you do what you must in this world, you'll be rewarded in kind after you die. No science and no faith tell you the whys of life, death, rewards, and punishments. Nothing tells you why those things exist, only that they exist. And if you happen to be one of those who are asking, you're probably quite frustrated.

Plague of the Twenty-First Century: Depression

Frustration, especially when prolonged and relating to life's essential questions, has all kinds of bad effects, one of which is depression. And depression is soaring to unprecedented rates in the United States and other developed countries. In 2001, the World Health Organization (WHO) reported that "depression is the leading cause of disability in the United States and worldwide." The WHO stated that one out of four people will suffer from a mental disorder during one's life.

In the past 50 years, there has been a significant increase in the number of people suffering from depression. What's new is that depression is starting at younger ages. It is expected that mental disorders, primarily depression, will continue to expand and gradually become one of the leading causes of human ailments.

According to the *New England Journal of Medicine*, "Annually, more than 46 million Americans, ages 15–54, suffer from depressive episodes." And the *Archives of General*

Psychiatry announced, "The use of potent antipsychotic drugs to treat children and adolescents … increased more than fivefold between 1993 and 2002," as published in the June 6, 2006, edition of *The New York Times*.

Moreover, depression is one of the key causes of suicide. Every year, more than a million people take their own lives, and between 10 and 20 million people attempt it. Suicide attempts are particularly increasing among youths.

Great Desires Need Great Pleasures

A person can stay depressed only so long. Eventually, he or she will look for a way out of it. Because we can't suffer forever, we have three options:

1. Lose all hope that it'll ever get better and commit suicide.

2. Detach our emotional capacities, usually by using drugs or alcohol.

3. Find the cause of the depression and step out of it.

The problem lies in an inability to satisfy the desire to know what stands behind this world—namely, the Creator, or Nature. In other words, if people want to be happy, they must know not only what gives them pleasure but, first and foremost, why they are alive to begin with.

We are depressed for a good reason. We can't find the answer to the question that troubles us most: why are we born, and what is the purpose of our lives? Of course, most of us don't feel this question consciously, but it is still there, nagging in the back of our minds.

When our desires were less evolved and overblown, meaning before the end of the twentieth century, we settled for worldly pleasures: food, sex, money, respect, power, and the highest, most esteemed pleasure one could seek: knowledge. But this new desire that's nagging in the back of our minds wants something more than this world has to offer. It wants to know why this world exists and, most of all, what the world's existence gives to us.

This last kind of wish is the greatest desire. By "greatest," I don't necessarily mean that it is the most intense desire. It is greatest because it is the most comprehensive. We can think of it like this: in construction, you may want to be the electrician, the plumber, or the floorer. If you want to be something higher, you may want to be the foreman. But if you want to know why everything is designed the way it is, why one type of material is used instead of another, and in which order materials are put together, you have to be the architect.

In Kabbalah, the desire to know how everything works is called "the desire to know the Thought of Creation." This desire is considered the greatest desire because it is greatest in *value*, not in intensity.

On Track

There are benefits to quality and benefits to quantity, and we need to make the most out of both. When a lot of people want the same thing, it impresses us and we, too, begin to think that it's worthwhile. This is the power of quantity, and this is why we disseminate Kabbalah. On the other hand, when you study, think less of the hours you spend doing it, and more on what your thoughts are while doing it—how much you ponder correction, altruism and unity. This is called "the quality of the study."

Show Me Where I Get My Fill

That kind of desire, as we've said in many other situations, requires a sense of wanting or motivation. In his essay "The Peace," Rabbi Yehuda Ashlag states …

> It is well known to researchers of nature that one cannot perform even the slightest movement without motivation, without somehow benefiting oneself. When, for example, one moves one's hand from the chair to the table, it is because one thinks that by putting one's hand on the table one will thus receive greater pleasure. If one would not think so, one would leave one's hand on the chair for the rest of one's life without moving it an inch—and all the more so with great efforts.

In other words, the ego is not the malady. The malady is the disorientation and misplaced desire. Because we don't feel a sense of purpose and pleasure in what we do, because we feel disoriented and unsure of what really fulfills us, we don't know where to find what we want. So we feel "stuck" and "stagnated."

There is great potential in our situation. We can harness all this locked energy into fantastic progress, if only we find where to channel it. And it should be channeled to the World Above—not toward the stars, but toward a higher form of existence, one that coincides with nature, with the Creator. More on that soon.

Word of Heart

He who has a strong enough Why can bear almost any How.

—Friedrich Nietzsche, German philosopher

Increasing Drug Abuse

In the last decades, drug abuse has turned from a marginal phenomenon to a major social problem throughout the world. It affects all socioeconomic levels. Every teenager is aware of the possibility of using drugs, and even kids as young as elementary school age are exposed to drugs.

According to a March 2003 fact sheet published by The White House Office of National Drug Control Policy (ONDCP), Drug Policy Information Clearinghouse, 42 percent of Americans admit to having used drugs at least once in their lifetimes. In Europe, there are 3.5 million known cocaine users, many of whom are people with higher education.

It's not that drugs themselves are bad. In the past, drugs have been used primarily for medicine and for rituals. Today, however, people use drugs at a much earlier age and primarily to alleviate the emotional void that they feel.

Actually, it isn't all that obvious that drugs should be illegal. After all, if all I do is smoke marijuana in the privacy of my home, and no one knows about it, and I don't risk anyone by driving under the influence, why shouldn't I be allowed to smoke it? Indeed, in some countries, the less harmful drugs are permitted, and even where they aren't, use of such drugs is often not taken too seriously or is even overlooked.

But there is a deep reason why society at large does not make drugs legal: it's against the purpose of creation. Consider this question to see why: how can you be the architect of reality if you are disconnected from it?

Deep down, people feel that it is not good to be detached from life. You may ask, "Why not? Am I really missing out on much? If I'm already depressed, why not at least pass the time more easily, and less painfully?" Because there is a reason for the depression that underlies drug abuse. Actually, not so much to the depression, but to the frustration that created it.

The Creator has no intention to detach us from reality—only to use reality in such a way that we are compelled to ask questions about life and about ourselves. If we are detached from reality, whether through drugs, alcohol, workaholism, or any kind of addiction, we lose the chance of progressing to a higher level of reality.

Acts of Violence

Each person is unique. In distress, we each act differently, and some act violently. Violence can take on any form. It can appear as terrorism. It can appear in many forms in schools, in households, or on the road (as in "road rage").

If you've read carefully up to this point, it won't surprise you if we tell you that violence is spreading because of the growing frustration some people feel from their inability to find the answer to the question that is really "bugging" them deep down: "What is the purpose of my life?"

Naturally, when the ego grows, I become less tolerant to others. If I disagree with them, I will want them either under me, controlled by me, or gone completely. It's just the ego's natural way.

In an article titled "Peace in the World," Rabbi Ashlag wrote, "Each and every one of us stands ready to abuse and exploit all the people for his own private benefit with every means possible, and without taking into consideration that he is going to build himself on the ruin of his friend." This is a law that cannot be breached, according to Rabbi Ashlag. Humans feel that all the people in the world should be under their own government, exist for their own private use, or give them unbridled respect. Ashlag also wrote, "If one could do it without much effort, he would agree to exploit the whole world with all three together: wealth, government, and respect. However, he is forced to choose according to his ability and capability."

The Last Resort

The result of our growing egoism is that we are becoming resolved to more aggressiveness and violence. Governments are spending absurd sums on armaments instead of helping their poorer citizens. In many countries, violence has become a legitimate means of resolving differences and, as a result, many citizens defend themselves with the force of arms.

Organized militias claim to protect certain interests or areas that want independence from the central government. For the most part, the soldiers in those militias end up exploiting the citizens they are meant to protect.

The greatest irony is that the richer countries are selling arms to the poorer countries, precisely those that are supposed to spend the least amount on arms and the greatest amount on welfare. Every year, the G8, the richest countries in the world, sell more than $12 billion in arms to the poorer countries. In many cases, those arms are then used against the richer countries that sold the weapons in the first place.

But violence isn't just terrorism. It is everywhere. While writing this chapter, four deadly attacks with firearms occurred in U.S. schools in a single week. Schools must now literally defend themselves against killers that raid them simply for the purpose of the indiscriminate killing of children.

Even If You Kill Me, I Don't Go Away

In all this havoc of egoism, we are forgetting the roots of creation. We *are* one soul. It doesn't matter how many innocent people die; we will still be one soul.

In writings that were given the name "The Last Generation," Rabbi Ashlag wrote that if we don't change the course of events, we will experience a third and a fourth world war. The relics, he wrote, will still have to do the job and correct our egos. We must realize that there is a crisis, and we must deal with it in the only way possible: through rising to the level of nature's altruism.

The correction we must make is the same correction we've been discussing throughout the book: becoming altruistic, giving, like Nature. That means that we have to realize that we are a united soul. So even if we kill each other, the burden of the dead doesn't go away. The correction must and will still happen, just through another person.

> **Word of Heart**
>
> What man actually needs is not a tensionless state, but rather the striving and struggling for some goal worthy of him.
>
> —Viktor E. Frankl, Austrian neurologist and psychiatrist

No one comes into this world without a reason, just as there are no cells in a body without necessary function. If we hurt or even kill each other, we hurt or kill the body we live in. Just like cancer, violence and bad intentions make the whole body of humanity ill, until the body dies and the cancer dies with it.

Collapsing Society

Given the picture we've just painted, it is easy to see that we are living in a collapsing society. If you need any more evidence of the malady, here are a few more examples:

- ◆ **Degenerated diseases are on the rise.** The population in the richer countries suffers from more degenerative diseases than people in poorer countries. Thanks to modern medicine, combined with modern technology, people live longer.

With the rise of heart disease, for instance, it can seem that those extra years are spent trying to stabilize our blood pressure and monitor our diet to manage our cardiovascular problems, diabetes, or weight.

◆ **Families are splitting apart.** Divorce rates are soaring, and more children grow up in single-parent families.

◆ **Obesity is on the rise.** In the United States and other developed countries, many are overweight not because we can't find wholesome food, but because we use food to compensate for another lack, which food can't satisfy. The inner void drives us to fill our tummies, but that doesn't make us fuller inside; it only makes us feel emptier.

◆ **Poverty and hunger are increasing.** "According to official measures of poverty, in the year 2003, 12.5 percent of the total U.S. population lived in poverty; 10 million households—31 million individuals, of whom 12 million were children—risked hunger or faced food insecurity; and 3.1 million households—including 2 million children—suffered from actual hunger," wrote Professor Ervin Laszlo in his book, *The Chaos Point* (Hampton Roads Publishing Company, 2006).

◆ **Water shortages are becoming rampant around the world.** Statistics from the United Nations Educational, Scientific, and Cultural Organization (UNESCO); the Food and Agricultural Organization (FAO); and other U.N. and world bodies show the details with striking clarity. Professor Laszlo writes in *The Chaos Point*, "Just 50 years ago, not a country in the world faced catastrophic water shortages. Today about one-third of the world's population lives under nearly catastrophic conditions, and by 2025 two-thirds of the population will have to cope with such shortages."

◆ **The environment is collapsing.** In February 2006, James Lovelock, the scientist and leading environmentalist who created the "Gaia hypothesis" (that the entire biosphere is a like a living, self-regulating system), published a book titled *The Revenge of Gaia* (Penguin Books, 2006). He claims that we have passed the point of no return and that the earth is doomed to become a vast desert, except for the poles, where the climate will be livable.

Red Alert

A short Kabbalistic allegory shows how egoism is killing us: egoism is like a man with a sword that has a drop of enchantingly luscious but lethal potion at its tip. The man knows that the potion is a venomous poison but cannot help himself. He opens his mouth, brings the tip of the sword to his tongue, and swallows.

Just as the human body is controlled by its brain, the highest level in the body, Earth, is controlled by humankind, the highest level on Earth. And just as physical pain indicates that something is wrong with our bodies, the natural phenomena we are witnessing indicate that there is something very, very wrong with the whole system of life on Earth. If we understand the reasons for the natural catastrophes that are occurring at an increasing rate, we might be able to change our course, before the grim predictions of the scientists come true.

The Final Frontier

Today, at the dawn of the third millennium, we are faced with a new situation. It is the first time that we are being attacked by an enemy that is nowhere to be found yet exists everywhere. We are fighting our egoistic selves. The malady lies in our minds and in our hearts, and that's the only thing that needs to be corrected.

It is a new frontier, but when this war is over, there will be no other frontiers because when we defeat the ego, we will find that we have no enemies. Moreover, we will discover that we never had any enemies. They were all a figment of our imagination, set to fool us by the Creator.

> **Word of Heart**
>
> We have clarified that it [the malady] comes from a sublime cause, directly from the Creator, who is the root of all creations. When it sits within our narrow egoism, its action becomes ruin, destruction, and the source of all the ruins that were and will be in the world. Indeed, there is not a single person in the world who is free from it, and all the differences are only in the way it is used, whether for the desires of the heart, for rule, or for honor. This is what distinguishes people from one another.
> —From "Peace in the World" by Rabbi Yehuda Ashlag

The wars helped us grow, as individuals and as a society. Through war we developed medicine, technology, social structures, and governments. The history of the human race is a history of wars. But we couldn't do it any other way because the only way the ego knows is the way of war. Without someone to surpass, the ego stays passive, and we remain passive along with it.

But with the new direction, the enemy will be the ego itself, and we will learn how to use society to combat our own egoism. In doing so, we will learn how to cooperate, share, support, and love one another. Now, for the first time in history, humanity has a common enemy, regardless of sex, race, age, and faith. Along with the common enemy, comes the common weapon, the wisdom of Kabbalah, built specifically as a means for correction of the ego.

The next chapter talks about diagnosing the ego as the problem on the personal level.

The Least You Need to Know

◆ Now is a time when humanity is shifting, with science and technology unable to answer the question of all questions: what is life for?

◆ Frustration from finding the answer to the question about life's purpose leads to escalating depression rates, violence, and alienation.

◆ Symptoms of our malady are the frightening rates of our social and environmental collapse.

◆ The problem lies in the human ego.

◆ The Creator created these maladies so we could see that in the end, nothing good comes from egoism.

Chapter 20

Diagnosis Is Half the Cure

In This Chapter

◆ The interconnected nature of nature

◆ What you see outside is what you are inside

◆ Distinguishing between egoism and luxuries

◆ Egoism as the engine of change

In the last chapter, we presented the ills of society. As discouraging as it might be, and as much as we may not want to think about it, it's much healthier to acknowledge the crisis and boldly cope with it.

As we said in Chapter 18, to cure the crisis, we must first diagnose it. This is half the healing. With that in mind, in this chapter we start looking at what we can practically do to find the root of our problem, and how Kabbalah allows us to take personal and societal action. We also review how Kabbalah views perception and show how you can put that information to use. As you'll see, by recognizing the evil in society and, more important, the evil in yourself, you'll be on the way to making the world a better place.

The Nature of Nature

As we outlined in the last chapter, nature is approaching a catastrophe along with us. To understand the origin of the crisis, let's analyze the rudiments of nature itself. We start with the nature of human nature, as viewed from the perspective of Kabbalah.

Humans: Naturally Self-Destructive

Of all nature, only human beings relate to others with malicious intentions. No other creature harms, degrades, or exploits another creature; derives pleasure from the oppression of others; or enjoys another's affliction.

The egoistic use of human desires, with the intention to elevate oneself at the expense of others, leads to a precarious imbalance with the surrounding world. Human egoism is the only destructive force with the ability to destroy nature itself. The danger to the world will persist until we change our egoistic approach to society.

Egoism of a part leads to the death of the whole. Look at it from a biological point of view. If a cell in a living organism begins to relate egoistically to other cells, it becomes cancerous. Such a cell begins to consume surrounding cells, oblivious to them or to the needs of the whole organism. The cell grows out of control and eventually extinguishes the entire body, including itself.

Kab-Trivia

As a rule, the less dangerous illnesses are also the most common. The common cold is probably the best example of that. Conversely, extremely deadly viruses, like the Ebola, are very rare, because they kill their victims before they spread the virus around.

The same applies to human egoism with respect to nature. While developing for itself, detached from the rest of nature and not as an integral part of nature, human egoism leads everything to death, including itself.

Cells can exist, develop, and multiply only by interacting as a single whole. This altruistic interaction functions in every being except in humans. The Creator gave human beings the freedom of will to fully perceive the need for altruism and to keep this comprehensive law of nature voluntarily—or not to.

As is well recognized in the media, globalization has compelled us to see the world as an interdependent whole. It may sound trite to say we're all connected, but trite or not, it's true. It's also true that many of the world's ills have developed because of the interconnectedness of societies. So will the solutions. They will come about only through the coexistence of all parts of nature and while each part works to sustain the entire system.

It is evident that humankind's problem is to balance each person's excessive desires with nature, to become an integral part of it and act as a single organism. Put in Kabbalistic terms, humankind's task is to become altruistic.

Life's Principle

Altruism, one of the primary principles of Kabbalah, is defined as care for the well-being of one's fellow person. Research of altruism reveals that not only does it exist in nature, but it also is the very basis for the existence of every living thing.

A living object is one that receives from its environment and gives to it. Every living organism comprises a combination of cells and organs that work together and complement each other in perfect harmony.

In this process, the cells are obliged to concede, influence, and help one another. The law of cell and organ integration according to the altruistic principle of "one for all" operates in every living organism.

Conversely, different natural elements, such as plants and animals, consist of different measures of a desire to be filled with power, vitality, and delight. The intensity of this desire creates nature's various levels: inanimate, vegetative, animate, and human.

def•i•ni•tion

Altruism is connectedness for a higher purpose than the individual element in the collective. For example, altruism among cells in an organism means that each cell does what is best for the body, even if it means the end of life for that cell, instead of each doing as it pleases. Kabbalistic altruism means working to increase the connectedness, the ties among the parts of the world.

Don't forget that each of the four levels—inanimate, vegetative, animate, and human—exists within each element in nature. Even a rock has a human part to it, as do plants and animals. What determines their outward appearance is the dominant level in them. In humans, the dominant level should be the human level, and because it's the highest, it controls all other levels. So you can see what happens when this level is malfunctioning. In Kabbalah, the human level is that part in us that has free choice. If we can develop a part within us that is totally unaffected by society, our past, and calculation of self-gratification, we will truly be free—from our egos.

By attaining nature's unity under the principle of "one for all," we begin to perceive the uniqueness of humanity and its place in the world. The peculiarity of humans, compared to the rest of nature, lies in the power and nature of human desires and in the continuous evolution of human desires.

Human desires are the motivating force that propels and develops civilization. The trick is to use Kabbalah as a way to turn the developing egoistic desires into altruistic desires.

The World as a Reflection of Inflated Egos

How do you do that, especially given that human desires have led to the maladies outlined in Chapter 19?

You look at the world and see that it's corrupted and wonder what to do; then you turn on the tube and forget it all for a while. The corruption you see outside and on the TV, however, is simply a reflection of the corruption and egoism inside yourself.

From a Kabbalistic point of view, the best thing you can do is see how the reflection on the outside is a reflection of yourself on the inside. Let's see how.

In Chapter 3, we discussed the nature of perception. We said that the five human senses cannot perceive everything and how Kabbalah develops a sixth sense, or *Kli*, which is the intention to use the desire to receive in order to give to the Creator.

We also showed how the senses perceive not the thing itself, but a copy of the thing. For example, you do not hear the sound itself; you hear a representation of the sound as a result of vibrating air acting on the eardrum, which, in turn, "interprets" the sound to the brain.

From that foundation, we also suggested that what you perceive is influenced, if not determined, by what you already know. What you experience is on the inside, not on the outside.

Red Alert

Correction works *only* from the inside out. We shouldn't fall into the trap of thinking that by changing our social and ecological environment we will be making any real change. As long as we haven't corrected our egoism, the world cannot truly be a better place, welcoming to its inhabitants.

So what you and I see outside, in society, is as much a reflection of our internal state as it is an external reality. You and I are the society in which we live. Society wastes because you and I waste. As we'll see in the next chapter, the best thing you can do about the maladies of the world is to change yourself.

Before we head in that direction, however, one last look at human desire is necessary to show our evolving desire is not only part of the problem, but also the solution.

The Evolution of Desires

With the exception of humans, all of nature consumes only what it needs for sustenance. Humans crave more food, more sex, and more physical comfort than they need for their sustenance. This state is especially true in desires that are uniquely human, in the (endless) pursuit of wealth, power, honor, fame, and knowledge.

When Basic Needs Become Egoism

Desires for things that are necessary for existence are not considered egoistic, but natural because they come as nature's commands. These desires are present in the inanimate, vegetative, and animate, as well as in humans. Only those human desires that exceed what is necessary for existence are egoistic.

In addition to the fact that the human desires grow exponentially, they incorporate pleasure from degrading others or seeing others suffer. These desires are unique to human nature, and they are the real egoism. We experience them through our connections with others, and this is why the only way to correct our desires is to work on them with other people, as discussed in Chapter 16.

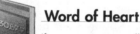
Word of Heart

If we were not all so interested in ourselves, life would be so uninteresting that none of us would be able to endure it.

—Arthur Schopenhauer (1788–1860), German philosopher

Our continuing indulgence in those desires indicates that we have not completed our evolution. But all desires can be considered altruistic or egoistic, according to the purpose with which we use them.

So the development of desire yields progress as well. As the saying goes, the problem contains the solution.

Do I Have to Have All This Food?

The discussion is not as abstract as it might seem at first glance. It's very personal.

Open your refrigerator and see what's in there. You'll find food from dozens of countries. And what those countries produce comes to them from dozens of other countries. Look at your clothes, your shoes—they come from all over the world, too.

Do you have to have it all?

The answer is twofold: we don't have to have it all if all we want is to survive. But if we want to have a life that we can call "life," the answer is most definitely "Yes." Moreover, we cannot control the evolution of our desires because they're determined by the *Reshimot*. That means that those of us who already want more than needed to merely survive cannot suppress their desires. Even if we try and succeed for a while, those desires will resurface and probably in much more unruly manner.

As a result, for most of us, having all that we have in our refrigerators, closets, and garages *is a must*, not a luxury. This will be even more true in the coming years because our desires keep growing. Actually, if you think about the purpose of creation—and remember that the final goal is to acquire the Creator's mind—then what we want right now seems quite small in comparison.

The bottom line is that our will to receive is too great today for us to settle for living in the woods and providing for ourselves. We want much more than that. We want cars and planes, we want to see the world. We want to vacation in resorts, we want to watch TV. So we don't have a choice. The only way to have great pleasures is to have great desires.

Now let's ask another question: What's wrong with wanting all that? Whom am I hurting by wanting to go to Hawaii for a luxury vacation? The answer is that the one who is hurt most by my desires is me. It's not that my desires are evil, it's that they don't give me true and lasting pleasure. The recognition of evil we first mentioned in Chapter 3 is really the recognition of *what is bad for me*. If it isn't bad for me, I will never define it as evil. After all, every one of us is born completely self-centered and therefore can define something as bad *only* if it is bad for oneself.

Word of Heart _____

Man's heart is evil from his youth.
—Genesis, 8:21

So having great desires isn't bad in and of itself. What's bad is that when we satisfy them, we don't feel happy and fulfilled.

But don't worry, for there is good reason for all our desires and wants. These desires exist within us whether we are aware of them or not. But their root is much deeper and higher than, say, the beaches of Hawaii, as beautiful as those beaches may be.

Our desires for material things are rooted in the desire to receive pleasure installed in us by the Creator back in Phase 1 (as described in Chapter 8): the pleasure of knowing the Creator, of being like Him. This desire is diminished and concealed by the chain of *Reshimot* as we climb down the spiritual worlds.

Today we are already climbing up the ladder, reexposing the *Reshimot* of our desires even if we're unaware of it. Our decline has brought us to a state of complete detachment from the Creator, and in that sense, our egoism has fulfilled its role. In a world were the Creator is not tangibly sensed, we can freely choose between spirituality and corporeality, without any temptations to choose one way or another, except our own experience.

We explained in Chapter 8 that *Reshimot* are the soul's unconscious recollections of its past states. Now that we have come to the end of our decline, they are resurfacing in us, and we are experiencing intensifying desires for both material things and for more spiritual fulfillment (hence the spirituality and New Age trends, especially in the developed countries). Because these desires are actually cravings to experience the Creator, "disguised" as desires for other things (sex, money, power, etc.), when we provide them those other things, we don't experience fulfillment.

The trick—and here's where Kabbalah comes to our aid—is to keep our minds focused on the ultimate goal: the Creator. Desires come and go. But keeping our minds focused on the Creator prevents us from feeling disillusioned when the satisfaction of a "disguised" desire fails to fulfill us.

If you work with this in mind, questions such as bad desires or good desires, luxuries and necessities, won't trouble you. Instead, you'll be bothered with much higher issues concerning your relationship with the Creator. This is why Kabbalists say that this world doesn't matter. Fulfillment exists only in spirituality, in your contact with the Creator.

In a sense, "bad" desires are actually good because they show us we haven't completed our work and where we still need to focus our attention on the Creator. When a desire first appears, you don't know that it's a desire for the Creator. You experience it as a desire for something in this world. Only when you strive to focus your attention on the Creator, despite your mundane thoughts, does the true nature of your desire (*Reshimo*) appear. At that point, you will discover that the desire was actually another facet of your desire for the Creator. This is how spiritual work happens on a day to day basis.

Kab-Trivia

It's good to keep in mind, when reading in *The Zohar*, that whenever the book writes about dogs, it is referring to reception for self, egoism. When it speaks of lions, it is speaking of bestowal, altruism.

Existing for More than Yourself

If we continue to focus on the Creator, and not on our own desires, we will eventually discover Him, by becoming like Him. When we become like Him, we discover that the whole of Nature is already like Him, existing in constant giving. Each level gives to the next, and the whole world lives in a harmonious pyramid.

The Greatest Desire, and the Highest Fulfillment

As we explained in Chapter 18, it's the law of nature that the highest degree rules over the lower degrees. Plants are higher than rocks, for instance, and you could make a case that plants help break down rocks over time for their own nourishment.

Animals rule over the plant world and, in turn, humans rule over animals. To look at it Kabbalistically, animals live at the expense of the inanimate and the vegetative, just as the vegetative lives at the expense of the inanimate. Each feeds on its lower degrees, but for a higher need than itself.

> **On Track**
>
> An animal feels life much more than a plant. It is alive, it breathes, it moves, and it has all kinds of sensitivities. It recognizes its habitat, its offspring, and its family, its pack. So the greater a creature is, the more it senses its existence, its selfness. That makes it greater and unique.

The higher orders have greater desire and, therefore, greater power over the lower degrees. Why?

A creature with a less-developed desire is like a baby. When the baby grows, it wants more things because its desire has evolved and can now detect more objects that are desirable. When it becomes an adult, the child becomes a man or a woman, goes to school, attends college, works and makes money, and has a career and family. One rises according to one's desire.

When desires push us, we become restless and progress. We don't have a choice. So desire is the motivating force for progress, for achievements.

Yet the egoistic desire drives us only to a certain point, until we despair of ever being satisfied and fulfilled this way. This is the journey we described at the beginning, in Chapters 1 and 2. This unsatisfied state forces us to change the method because we all ultimately want fulfillment. In that state, we begin to want spirituality, a uniquely human desire.

The will to receive grows even more. Gradually, as we learn about spirituality, we understand that fulfillment doesn't come only from filling ourselves directly, but from filling others. And *that* gives us the real fulfillment, just as a mother is happiest when she sees her child happy.

Here's the Kabbalah summary: the only way to have great pleasures is to have great desires. Great (unfulfilled) desires lead to emptiness. This, in turn, leads to the recognition of evil—that our desires are bad for us. Recognition of evil can lead to a desire for something entirely different, on a higher level. That something more is people's unique ability to desire and know the Creator.

A Positive Influence on Nature

How does this desire to be similar to the Creator influence the rest of nature? We never influence anything at the level of this world. In this world, we can come to some decisions only according to what is in us and what we see. Kabbalah shows that there are no actions in our world. Everything we do in our world is only to finally ask, "Am I benefiting my evolution according to the purpose of creation, or am I harming it and going in the opposite direction?"

There is an animal level in us that wants a home, a family, and everything the body wants. There is a human level in us that wants money, honor, and knowledge. And there is Adam in us, the point in the heart that has a drive to be like the Creator.

Precisely when one has a drive to be like the Creator, one changes. All other degrees can't change themselves in any way. They can't do anything. They simply exist the way they do. Everything comes to them from above. Only beings who have a point in the heart have free choice. The free choice appears in the point in the heart. When the free choice appears, if we use it correctly, we become similar to the Creator.

This is really the only choice we have: to be or not to be similar to the Creator. Because only humans have points in the heart, only humans can have free choice, and only humans can change.

Correction begins when a person realizes that his or her egoistic nature is both a source of evil and the engine of change. It is a very personal and powerful experience, but it invariably brings one to want to change, to move toward altruism and away from egoism.

To be (free) or not to be (free). We'll take a closer look at the personal nature of the choice in the next chapter.

The Least You Need to Know

◆ Globalization drives home the point that we are all interconnected.

◆ Growing desire is part of the plan, and we have to have it all.

◆ Recognition of evil means that satisfying my desires doesn't give me pleasure.

◆ Correction begins when we realize that our desires are both a source of evil and an engine of positive change.

Chapter 21

Cure Me

In This Chapter

◆ First steps to a cure

◆ How humanity is interconnected

◆ Why complete correction requires complete corruption

◆ The long and short paths to correction

It's easy to look at the world's problems and say, "There's nothing I can do …." There is something you and I can do, and it isn't to give up our way of life.

Up to this point, we have been learning the basics of Kabbalah and that the ego, or egoism, is our problem. The last two chapters focus on the way to correct our egoism. Naturally, to succeed in correcting the world, we have to first correct ourselves, which is the topic of this chapter.

Taking the First Steps

As we've said throughout this book, Kabbalah provides a method by which you see that what happens inside you is how you experience the world outside you. We have also pointed out the interconnectedness of everything in creation. Tying these two is the key to correction.

At the end of the day, the wisdom of Kabbalah is very simple: there is an infinite desire to give, which created an infinite desire to receive. Because the desire to receive is infinite, it wants to receive its own Creator. The whole "story" of creation describes our attempts to realize that this is really how things are. As long as we feel separated from others, we have to work on how to experience this unified structure of desires. But when we are corrected, we will know that we are all one creation, and then correcting ourselves and correcting society are one and the same. So let's start breaking down the correction process into pieces we can work with.

Blocking the Hole in the Boat

What you do affects the whole, and vice versa. A Kabbalah story from Rabbi Shimon Bar Yochai perfectly brings home the point. One of several people in a boat suddenly began to drill a hole in the bottom. His friend asked, "Why are you drilling?" The person drilling replied, "What business is it of yours? I am drilling under me, not under you."

Because all humankind is connected into one system, the irresponsible egoists subject themselves and all the others to suffering. It is the transformation activated by Kabbalah that makes us see the irresponsible egoists in ourselves and transform them into responsible adults, altruists in Kabbalistic terms.

Think back to Chapter 3 and remember that the Creator created only one soul, *Adam ha Rishon*. Then, in Chapter 9, we learned that he fell and his soul split into 600,000 parts. We've been trying to put them back together ever since. But for Adam to become equal to the Creator, he has to do something that will make him equal to the Creator. He must engage in giving.

Adam (you and I) is in a bind. If he gives because the Creator compels him to, it is not that *he* is giving, but that the Creator is forcing him to give. This is one reason for the double concealment discussed in Chapter 15. To bring Adam to a state where he wants to give because the quality of giving is, in itself, of the highest value, without any thought of himself, the Creator must be concealed.

We have to feel as though we live in a "Creatorless" world, without guard and government from above. We have to feel as though we alone make all the decisions and draw all the conclusions, including the conclusion that the quality of giving is the most worthy quality in reality. We are given the concealment of the Creator and the sensation that we are in contact with other people. Because the Creator (quality of giving) is hidden, we are egoistic and hate them, and they hate us. But at the same time, we are dependent on them, and they are dependent on us. This is precisely what globalization has been showing us so clearly in recent years.

So how do we reconcile our attitude toward society, where on one hand we need others and on the other we hate them and want to exploit them?

The Creator has put us between two forces, and we have a chance to see how we will choose. We can freely build ourselves as people who give to society, above our nature, and without any consideration of ourselves; or we can choose to remain as egoistic as we are today.

By choosing to give above self-interest we make ourselves similar to the Creator. To the extent that we do it, the Creator opens up to us. He doesn't have to be hidden anymore because we have become like Him.

> **Word of Heart**
>
> As we have already shown that when man is converted to loving others, he is in direct adhesion, which is equivalence of form with the Maker, and along with it man passes from his narrow world, full of pain and impediments, to an eternal world of bestowal to the Lord and to the people.
>
> —From "The Essence of Religion and Its Purpose" by Rabbi Yehuda Ashlag

A Detour Back Through Adam

By the way, this explains why Adam fell. We had to first be created as a single creature and then be separated into egoistic, distanced, and detached individuals because this is the only way for us to see our complete oppositeness from the Creator.

There are many, many others like us around. The one soul of Adam divided into a multitude of souls (or bodies) to give each of us a chance to determine his or her attitude and choose whether he or she wants to be similar to the Creator.

The original soul was very pure when the Creator created it, with very small desires. But to receive all the pleasures that the Creator wants to give, a person must have an exaggerated, infinite desire to receive. The original soul had it, but unconsciously. These desires had to be made conscious and felt.

In addition, the creature had to feel that these desires are egoistic, which required that the creature be broken or divided, for a number of reasons.

First, it is impossible to correct a powerful will to receive if there is only one person. The Creator split Adam so that each person could correct the little egoism within. Even more, Adam split to have other people with whom to work. You and I need to bond with other egoistic people just like us in order to become similar to the Creator.

Finally, in a state of depravity, we can acknowledge the pettiness, limited nature, and hopelessness of our egoistic nature. We may then develop a desire to unite, to transform our nature into the opposite, altruistic nature.

Now that you know the Kabbalistic explanation of Adam's story, what do you do? Others are treating you the way you are treating them because they are a reflection of your attitude to the world. Because we try to exploit the world and treat it badly, we think that that's the way the world is treating us. The "scenario" of reality in our brain is negative, so reality seems negative to us. This naturally makes our world seem threatening and unsafe.

> **On Track**
>
> We may have made this point less directly earlier in the book, but it's imperative to understand Kabbalah's perception of reality. Saying that we are one interconnected soul isn't a philosophical statement; it places the responsibility for correction squarely in our laps. There is no correction to the world and to ourselves—on any level—without our active participation in mind, heart, and action.

In that state, the only way to restore security and confidence is to unanimously agree to correct our egoistic desires. This is why we are discovering that simply to exist, we need each other. Moreover, we need to be treated well by everyone or we will not be able to escape the threat of destruction.

When we realize that we have no choice but to treat each other well, we will decide that we *have* to have love of our fellow beings and ask for this power from above. This power will come from the Creator, from the Upper Light, and we will reach correction. Therein lies the inherent optimism of Kabbalah.

How the Pieces Come Together

So we're all sharing life, just like cells in a body, where each cell depends on the life of the whole organism. If the other souls think about you, you will live. If they don't think about you, you will die. That Kabbalah law is the condition for spiritual life, in the souls.

Today we are considered spiritually dead; the souls we have today are called "the animate soul." The animate soul refers to our lives in this world, in a state of detachment from the Creator. Everything we feel and experience in this life, as long as we don't acquire a screen and develop the first spiritual *Kli*, is considered part of the animate soul. It exists for as long as we exist in this world, and disappears when we die. But these are far from the soul that Kabbalists refer to when they write about souls in *The Zohar* and other books. To have such a soul, we have to first decide that we want our soul, that we want eternal life, and that we want to be like the Creator.

Rabbi Yehuda Ashlag writes that all people throughout history are actually a long chain of souls, and the only difference between people is their different appearances. To see and experience this oneness of humanity, you must have an eternal soul that is connected to the eternal, to the Creator. That's the kind of soul that Kabbalists are talking about.

Now you see why your personal correction is so tightly connected to everybody else's correction. All souls are linked as one.

But here it's our own responsibility to choose. We have to decide that we want our souls, and we have to build our souls by ourselves, along with other souls.

In the language of Kabbalah, the language of souls, we say that souls are connected and integrated in a single body. For each soul to provide all the souls with what they need, all souls have to understand one another and realize that they are integrated in the others' desires. In other words, in your soul, you have to be incorporated with all the other desires, of all people, so you can provide them with what they want. Each cell in the body does just that; it feels what the body requires of it.

On a personal level, you must know what others need from you and provide what they need. In this way, you become like a complete body. You contain the desire of others within you because of your love for them, and *you* want what *they* need.

When you work with others in that way, you feel that you, personally, have grown tremendously. Then you can give them what they need, and you become one unique and unified great creature, standing opposite the Creator.

> **On Track**
>
> In Kabbalah, there is a difference between what people *want* and what they *need*. What they want is what their egos tell them they want. What they need is a desire for spirituality because this is a desire for giving, the only lasting desire that can be fulfilled endlessly. By having a desire for spirituality, you feel eternal satisfaction because you sense both the desire and its satisfaction simultaneously.

And What About Me?

When you want to give others what they need, you have become like the Creator. When you give someone else what he or she needs, in doing it, you instill part of yourself in the other person. As the other person receives, it begins to build in him or her the understanding that giving to others is good, valuable, and—most importantly—pleasurable. In time, the giver begins to feel that it is not the giving to others that is pleasurable but that giving in itself, the state of being a giver, contains something pleasurable.

If you think about it for a moment, you'll see that nothing, even in our physical world, is created without giving. How can creatures be born without their parents' giving? Newborns are born because their parents love them and want to give to them, even before they come into existence.

This brings home one point: if this world exists, it means that its Creator loves it. If we, too, want to love our world, we have to learn to see it through His eyes, beyond our self-centered egos. If you want to give people what they need, you begin to see the world through the Creator's eyes, and thus, gradually, achieve the purpose of creation: to acquire the Creator's mind.

> **Word of Heart**
>
> One attraction of Kabbalah is the pathway it provides for individual realization. Micha Odenheimer said it this way in the article "Latter-Day Luminary": "(Rabbi Yehuda) Ashlag's system gives a person tools to catch himself in any given situation and know where he is standing spiritually." That awareness itself is enough to cause great changes in the world.

When you give because giving has merit in your eyes, without any direct or indirect benefits from the giving, it's considered that your actions are of your own free will. The giving is not for yourself, but for the sake of giving.

Of course, no act goes unrewarded because, as we've just explained, the Creator *wants* to give to us. But the reward for liking to give is seemingly detached from the giving itself. It's the revelation of the giver, the Creator. In other words, the reward for acting like the Creator is discovering the Creator and why He does what He does. By that you achieve the final correction, and the purpose of your creation.

The key to the whole process is a shift in thought and awareness. You need not change *anything* in the whole world except your *own* attitude to all the other souls, all the other people. This is why the saying "Love thy friend as thyself" is enough to correct the whole world. There is no other way to influence and change the world.

> **Red Alert**
>
> Love thy friend, or neighbor, as thyself, taught by the great Kabbalist Rabbi Akiva, is a maxim that virtually all religions and teachings have adopted. But this is a very dangerous maxim if lived without its final goal—to reach the Creator. Rabbi Yehuda Ashlag writes that this is exactly what happened in Russia's communism. It was doomed to fail, and they continue to pay a heavy price because they used nature's law of altruism without its final purpose: to reach the Creator through equivalence of form with Him.

I Still Want More

A well-known maxim in Kabbalah goes like this: "he who is greater than his friend, his desire is greater than he." How does that fit with "Love thy friend as thyself"?

Here's how: in the previous chapter we said that egoism is the engine of change. The greater your desires, the more evolved you are because when you want more, you can also receive more. You can reach more and achieve more because your will to receive drives you and gives you the strength to get what you want. Such a person is stronger because of his stronger willpower.

Because desires are egoistic by nature, for yourself without any consideration of others, they are initially ill-willed. In the end, that's bad for you, too. If you care only for yourself, you become detached from others and then can't fulfill yourself. The sensation of self-fulfillment depends on the existence of others. Thus, if I'm an egoist, I can't connect to others, and if I can't connect to others, I can't enjoy. My egoism has become my own bane. This leaves me poor, deficient and suffering, because I have a big will to receive, I'm constantly chasing pleasures, and I'm constantly empty.

This is the state that, as we have said, leads to a spiritual crisis. You realize that you can't go on living like that and understand that you have to change something in your life. Your point in the heart awakens, and in that state, all the evil in you can be turned into good.

Becoming a Grown-Up

As a result, the great desire leads to a choice that is, really, no choice. If we're so dependent on others, we have to care for them and watch over them, even if we hate them.

To survive and correct, we must tend to those we hate. If we don't, if we decide to kill them, we will suffer.

So what should we do? Become true grown-ups. If we're that connected, we're also that responsible for one another. Just as grown-ups take responsibility for everything around them—their environment, their children, their employees, their friends, their neighbors, their cities and towns and countries. Everything and everyone. The Creator wouldn't want it any other way. It's His plan.

On Track

What greater pleasure is there for parents than to see their children grow up to become mature and successful adults? Similarly, the purpose for which the Creator created us is to be like Him. As a result, the goal of our lives in this world is to learn the Creator's ways of giving and, therefore, learn His thought and become like Him.

Two Ways to the Creator

According to the plan of the Creator, the entire universe must reach the state of correction, and the time allocated for correction is limited. *The Zohar* indicates that the correction must begin its final stages from the start of the twenty-first century. From this time on, humanity will be urged to correct by intensifying sufferings—read the news, and you'll see a fair case for that.

Recognizing the purpose of creation and knowing the method of correction will enable you to approach the goal consciously. This is the key, and it's faster than the suffering that will otherwise catch up with us from behind. Instead of suffering, we have the opportunity to feel fulfillment and inspiration even while still on the path of correction.

Now or Later

Remember from Chapter 8 how Kabbalah tells of a time frame for the ultimate final correction? The path to personal correction may take a while, and it will happen sooner or later. Plus, every soul must go through the process.

None of your experiences in life disappear. They are stored within your desire, and desires are eternal; they pass from one generation to another, from one incarnation to the next.

The next time you are born, as described in Chapter 12, your desire will retain the record of everything you did with regard to the Creator.

This is how the *Reshimot* play their role. Everything that you did inside your egoistical desire is stored in a "small box," which eventually gives you the "recognition of evil." And until this box is filled completely, and until you correct all of your evil, you will continue to come to this world.

Next time you show up in this world, this "box" will contain what you have gained in your current round. The small steps you make accumulate and eventually give results. Each step leads ultimately to spiritual elevation, but you get to experience the road as pleasurable and exciting or as painful and agonizing. You have a choice in the matter, and the last section in this chapter will explain how.

A Long Path and a Short Path to Correction

You can advance toward the realization that egoism is the root of evil through a long path of suffering or through a much shorter and delightful path of correction.

Moreover, the path of suffering is not a path, merely the length of time needed for the realization that you need to march on the short path.

Yet as soon as a sufficient measure of suffering has been accumulated, you realize that there is greater profit in correction than in suffering, and you work to change. Instead of treading the long path, there is a short and easy path to correction.

It's a bit similar to taking a hike with a hidden tour guide. You are walking from point A to point B, but your tour guide didn't tell you that there's a final destination to your hike. Naturally, at every point you can, you stop and want to rest. In the meantime, you try to make your hike as easy and as comfortable as you can. But your guide knows you haven't reached your destination, so whenever you stop, he urges you onward. If you "get the hint" quickly, then gentle encouragements are enough. But if you're stubborn, he has to force you to move on, and this hurts.

The short path is when you get the hint quickly, and the long path is when the guide is forced to push you. Both paths are the same, but on the short path there are no phases of suffering, only constant progress. On the long path, however, there is suffering almost every step of the way.

The wisdom of Kabbalah is the tour guide to the short path. It tells you of all the states and helps you through them easily, with gentle encouragement.

You can acquire knowledge about the structure of the world, its causality and purpose, *before* you are met with affliction. Through this knowledge, you accelerate the realization that egoism is bad and avoid the need to realize the evil in egoism under the pressure of annihilation.

Although it seems that we are free to do as we please, in truth, we follow the commandments of our genes and adhere to the influence of the social environment. Those influences and commandments determine all our values, showing us how profitable it is to be powerful and prosperous.

We work hard all of our short lives, only to win society's recognition of how successfully we keep its values. At the end of the day, we do not live for ourselves at all, but strain to find grace in the eyes of our children, our kin, our acquaintances, and society in general.

Clearly, succeeding in solving the crisis depends upon changing the values of society. That's the subject of the next chapter.

The Least You Need to Know

◆ Kabbalah provides a method for personal and social transformation.

◆ Adam had to fall to provide an opportunity for us all to reunite with the Creator.

◆ "Love thy friend as thyself" is enough to correct the whole world, provided that it is done in order to reach the Creator.

◆ There are two ways to progress to spirituality: quickly and pleasantly, using Kabbalah, or slowly and painfully, without Kabbalah.

22

Cure All

In This Chapter

- ◆ Altruism and the resolution of the crisis
- ◆ The fall of the Tower of Babel, again
- ◆ Heaven on Earth
- ◆ Society's recognition and what it really means to us

Kabbalah contains both personal and social aspects. There is no such thing as personal correction without correction of society.

As we discussed in the last chapter, we are all parts of the same collective soul. This chapter explains how the personal corrections presented in the last chapter flow through our connections to society. In the end, the individual correction we described in Chapter 21 is complete only when it contains a reciprocal connection with all of humanity.

All Together Now

Think back to Chapter 20, where we said that all the suffering in the world is a result of how we are opposite from the rest of nature. All other parts of nature—still, vegetative, and animate—follow nature's commandments instinctively and definitively. Only human behavior places us in contrast to the still, vegetative, and animate nature.

Because humanity is the height of nature's creation, all other parts of nature depend on us. Through our correction, all parts of nature, the entire universe, will rise to its initial, perfect level, in complete unity with the Creator.

Collective Responsibility

As we have said, the Creator treats all of us as a single, united, created being. We have tried to achieve our goals egoistically, but today we are discovering that our problems will be solved only collectively and altruistically.

The more conscious we become of our egoism, the more we will want to use the method of Kabbalah to change our nature to altruism. We did not do it when Kabbalah first appeared, but we can do it now because now we know we need it.

The past 5,000 years of human evolution have been a process of trying one method, examining the pleasures it provides, becoming disillusioned with it, and leaving it for another. Methods came and went, and we have grown more prosperous, but not happier.

Now that the method of Kabbalah has appeared in force, aimed to correct the highest level of egoism, we no longer have to tread the path of disillusionment. We can simply correct our worst egoism through Kabbalah, and all other corrections will follow like a domino effect. During this correction, we can feel fulfillment, inspiration, and joy.

To review a little of the history presented in Chapters 6 and 7, *The Book of Zohar* states that starting from the end of the twentieth century, humanity will reach the maximum level of egoism and, at the same time, the maximum spiritual impoverishment in it. At that point, humanity will need a new method in order to survive.

Then, according to *The Zohar*, it will be possible to disclose Kabbalah, as the method of humanity's moral ascent to similarity with the Creator. This is why Kabbalah is revealed to humankind in these times.

Humanity is not corrected by everybody at the same time. Rather, correction of humanity occurs to the extent that each person realizes his personal and general crisis, as covered in the last chapter, and to the extent that personal egoism and sensitivity to humanity's problems become connected as two faces of the same problem.

Correction starts with a human being realizing his or her egoistic nature is the source of all evil. Later, by changing the values of society, a person is subjected to society's influence.

The individual and one's social environment, the entirety of humanity, are bound by collective responsibility. In other words, humanity wanted to solve its problem egoistically and, hence, individually. Meanwhile, it found itself inevitably obliged to solve the problem collectively and, hence, altruistically.

In this respect, it is worth reflecting on Rabbi Yehuda Ashlag's four factors that comprise us, which he explains in his essay "The Freedom" and which we introduced in Chapter 3. To review and expand, the first factor is the bed, the foundation, our inherent traits, which we cannot change because we inherit them from our parents. The second is how this bed evolves, which we are also unable to change because it's determined by the bed. The third factor is the environment, which we cannot change once we are in it.

The fourth factor, however, is the changes in the environment, and *those we can and must* change by choosing the environment that is right for us. The fourth factor affects the third, which affects the second, which affects the first. By being socially aware and building the right environment for our spiritual purposes, we build a society that not only changes us toward spirituality, but also makes everybody else's way to spirituality much easier and faster. Now let's see how we can put this theory into action.

All Agree on Giving

If everyone thinks giving is good, then I, too, will think giving is good, out of my own egoistic interest. This is so because altruistic behavior is profitable for all.

Altruism rules in education, for instance. Schools teach us to be altruists. We are told to be honest, hard-working, and respectful of others; to share with others what we have; to be friendly; and to love our neighbors. All this happens because altruism is beneficial to society.

Furthermore, the biological laws of living organisms teach us that the existence of an organism depends on the cooperative work of all its parts, as recounted in Chapters 20 and 21.

> **Word of Heart**
>
> Anyone who is experienced knows that there is one issue in the world, which is the greatest of all imaginable pleasures, namely finding grace in the eyes of people, for which every effort is worthwhile.
>
> —Rabbi Yehuda Ashlag

Similarly, the perception of the benefits of altruistic behavior is present in an egoistic human society. No one in the world actively opposes altruistic acts. On the contrary, all organizations and personalities advertise their involvement in altruistic actions and pride themselves in them. No one openly objects to the dissemination of altruistic ideals in the world.

A Plan for Resolving the Crisis

The means to change our behavior from egoistic to altruistic is to change our priorities and value hierarchy. We need to be convinced that bestowal to society is much more important and worthwhile than receiving from it. In other words, each person must come to feel a much greater fulfillment from giving to society than from any egoistic acquisition.

Public opinion is the only means to facilitate this goal because the most important thing for every person is the appreciation of society. Humans are built in such a way that receiving the sympathy of society is the purpose of life.

This element is so intrinsic that people tend to deny that the purpose of every action is to acquire society's appreciation. We might claim that we are motivated by curiosity or even money, but we would not admit to the real incentive: the recognition of society.

Humans are built in such a way that the human environment determines all our predilections and values. We are entirely and involuntarily controlled by public opinion. This is why society can infuse its members with any mode of behavior and any value, even the most abstract.

Society's Purposeful Influence

It won't be easy to modify society's tasks. It will require changing the educational systems, starting from a very early age, as well as cardinal transformations in all areas of education and culture.

All media will have to appraise and evaluate events according to their benefit to society, to create an environment of education for bestowal upon society. Using every means of mass media, advertisement, persuasion, and education, the new public opinion should openly and resolutely denounce egoistic actions and extol altruistic actions as the ultimate value.

Through society's purposeful influence, everyone will aspire to receive only what is necessary for sustenance from society and spare no effort in exerting to benefit society, in order to receive society's appreciation.

At first, everyone will work to benefit society under environmental encouragement and influence. People will feel satisfied, and we will begin to see the act of bestowal upon society as the ultimate unique value, even without reward from the environment for each act of giving.

Mom, Dad, Were You Good Today?

It isn't just social institutions that need to change. So must the most prevalent and, in some ways, most "dug in" social institution: the family.

If my children at home look at me and appreciate me according to society's appreciation of me, and if my children appreciate me according to how much I give to society, then I am more likely to change.

If my kin and co-workers and generally everyone appreciate me only according to what I give to society, then I will not have a choice. I will have to contribute. I will have to become a net giver to all.

> **Red Alert**
>
> We must be very careful here. Past attempts to use society, and even kin, for altering social values, have produced the most terrible atrocities, including the Nazis and Stalin's communism. This is *not* what Kabbalah refers to when it suggests that we use society to change our values. Kabbalah merely suggests that we encourage everyone that giving is profitable and pleasurable. Then, when more people believe it, I, too, will believe it, even if at first I was coaching others to believe it without believing it myself.

All this activity will raise the level of human consciousness to the level of a new civilization.

Rabbi Ashlag was passionately committed to that far-reaching social vision, as it emerged from his understanding of the Kabbalistic tradition, writes Micha Odenheimer in "Latter-Day Luminary": "He grasped humanity as a single entity, both physically and spiritually interdependent, and believed that only an economic system that recognized this could liberate humankind and catalyze an era of collective enlightenment."

By developing a community based on love among its members and a society founded on economic justice, Odenheimer writes, Kabbalah provides a focus on individual consciousness and the mending of society and the world. Rabbi Ashlag's contribution is a "concept of social justice founded on the spiritual science of Kabbalah."

A Common Language

In ancient times, humans were not so egoistic as to be opposite to nature. They felt nature and their fellow persons, reciprocally. This was their language of communication, which, for the most part, was a silent language, similar to telepathy, on a certain spiritual level.

Increased egoism, however, detached humans from nature. Instead of correcting the oppositeness, humans dared to imagine that they would be able to attain the Creator egoistically, not through correction.

They no longer perceived nature and their fellow humans, stopped loving, and started hating one another. Through this, humans were separated from each other and, instead of being one nation, split into many.

Babel's Tower

The first level of egoistic development is marked by what we allegorically call the "building of the Tower of Babel." In the story of Babel, you may recall, people, out of increased egoism, aspired to reach the Creator, allegorically described as wanting to build a tower whose head reaches the sky.

Humans failed to direct their increased egoism toward the attainment of the governing forces because this method of attainment demanded of them to curb egoism, and they failed to restrain the increased egoism.

People's increased egoism made them stop feeling each other and the spiritual connection; the telepathy was broken. Because they knew of the Creator from their previous level of egoism, they now wanted to exploit Him as well. That's what was meant by building a tower that reaches the sky. As a result of their egoism, they stopped understanding each other, and their oppositeness from nature alienated them from it and from the Creator, and they dispersed.

We may have compensated for it well with technological development. But in doing so, we have only increased our detachment from one another and our alienation from nature (Creator). So now humanity is becoming disillusioned with fulfilling the egoism solely through social or technological development.

We are realizing that egoistic desires cannot be filled in their natural form. The very fulfillment of a desire annuls it. As a result, the desire is no longer felt, just as food reduces the sensation of hunger, and, along with it, the pleasure from eating is gradually extinguished.

Particularly today, as we acknowledge the crisis and the dead-end point of our development, it can be said that the confrontation of the egoism with the Creator is the actual destruction of the Tower of Babel.

The Tower's Destruction

Formerly, the Tower of Babel was ruined by the Upper Force. Today it is being ruined in our own consciousness.

Humanity is ready to admit that the path it chose to compensate for egoistic oppositeness from nature through technology leads to a dead end. It is no coincidence that today we are witnessing a titanic clash of civilizations that threatens the sustainability of humanity. This is one of the key factors in the global crisis.

The process that started in Babel, of separation into two groups that drew apart geographically and culturally, is culminating today. Over the past 5,000 years, each group evolved into a civilization of many different peoples. One group we call Western civilization, and the other comprises Eastern civilization, which roughly includes India, China, and the Islamic world.

We are at a similar separation point that occurred in the time of Babel, except that now we are aware of our situation. According to the wisdom of Kabbalah, this clash, the global crisis, and the surfacing of mysticism and superstition, are the beginning of the reconnection of all humanity into a new and united civilization.

It is time for the members of the single nation of humankind to reunite into one united people. Spiritual fulfillment provides a path and a perhaps unexpected truth.

Spiritual Math

One plus one means *Ein Sof* (infinity) because each of us is integrated with everybody else. With just one more person to work with, we can simulate a society, which, in turn, simulates our relationship with the Creator. The reward is huge.

Indeed, there is a special bonus to altruism. It may seem as if the only change will be putting others before ourselves, but there are actually far greater benefits. When we begin to think of others, we become integrated with them, and they with us.

Actually, each one of us is *Ein Sof*, but without a society to help you correct yourself, how will you feel it? If you remember one of Kabbalah's basic rules that the whole and the part are the same, your life will be much easier. You will be able to work on the whole (society) knowing that you are actually working on yourself, and this will make your correction much easier.

Enhanced Perception

Think of it this way: there are about 6.5 billion people in the world today. What if, instead of having two hands, two legs, and one brain to control them, you had 13 billion hands, 13 billion legs, and 6.5 billion brains to control them?

Sounds confusing? Not really, because all those brains would function as a single brain, and the hands would function as a single pair of hands. All of humanity would function as one body whose capabilities were enhanced 6.5 billion times. After all, there are much more than 6.5 billion cells in our body, and it functions as one unit. So if a single body can do it, why not the whole of humanity?

In addition to becoming superhuman, anyone who became altruistic would receive the most desirable gift of all: omniscience, or total recall and total knowledge. Because altruism is the Creator's nature, acquiring it equalizes our nature with His, and we begin to think like Him. We begin to know why everything happens, when it should happen, and what to do if we want to make it happen differently. In Kabbalah, this state is called "equivalence of form," and this is the purpose of Creation.

Eternity Now

This state of enhanced perception, of equivalence of form, is why we were created in the first place. This is why we were created united and were then broken—so we could reunite. In the process of uniting, we will learn why nature does what it does and will become as wise as the Thought that created nature.

When we unite with nature, we will feel as eternal and complete as nature. In that state, even when our bodies die, we will feel that we continue to exist in the eternal nature.

Physical life and death will no longer affect us because our previous self-centered perception will have been replaced with holistic, altruistic perception. Our own lives will have become the life of the whole of nature.

But if you've gotten this far, no matter what you might think, it's really even simpler than it sounds. You can already relate to Eternity. We're already in *Ein Sof*. We just don't feel it. We just don't recognize it. Through the journey of the wisdom of Kabbalah, we have a great guide. With great guides, we can all find our way.

The Least You Need to Know

- All of nature depends on us and our correction.

- Changing from egoistic behaviors to altruistic behaviors requires a change of social priorities and values.

- Since the ruin of the Tower of Babel, humans have relied on technology to fulfill desires and have suffered as a result.

- Society has been divided ever since the ruin of the Tower of Babel, but now we are aware of the situation and can correct it.

- When we unite with the Creator, we feel as eternal and as complete as the Creator. Right now.

Appendix A

Glossary

125 degrees   Between the Creator and creation there are five worlds, with five *Partzufim* in each world, and five *Sefirot* in each *Partzuf*. If you multiply 5 *Sefirot* × 5 *Partzufim* × 5 worlds, you get 125 degrees. See also *spiritual degree, Sefirot*.

Abraham   A man born in Babylon who discovered the wisdom of Kabbalah, taught it to all who were interested, and started the first Kabbalah group, which later became the nation of Israel. *Sefer Yetzira* (*The Book of Creation*) is ascribed to him.

Adam   See *Adam ha Rishon*.

Adam ha Rishon   The Kabbalistic name of Adam, the original soul. The breaking of Adam's soul caused the division of Adam's soul into 600,000 particular souls and individual desires.

altruism   Working for the gratification of the system of creation, regardless of one's own needs.

bestowal   The Creator's quality of giving without thinking of Himself. This is the quality the creatures (us) need to acquire in order to become like Him and discover Him.

Bina   Understanding. In Kabbalah, it generally refers to the contemplation of the ways of cause and effect and to benevolence. It also means the quality of giving, *Hassadim* (Mercy), which is the quality of the Creator.

The Book of Zohar   Written around the second century CE by Rabbi Shimon Bar-Yochai and his group. This is the seminal book of Kabbalah. It was hidden right after it was written and reappeared many years later. Probably for this reason, there are scholars who consider Rabbi Moshe De Leon to be the author, although Rabbi De Leon himself claims that he did not write the book, but Rabbi Shimon Bar-Yochai did.

correction   See *Tikkun*.

degree   See *spiritual degree*.

double concealment   The state you experience when you cannot feel the Creator. You know He exists, but you are totally unable to feel Him. See also *single concealment*.

egoism   Working for self-gratification, regardless of the needs of the system of creation.

Equivalence of Form   The form (quality) of the Creator is bestowal; the form of the creature is reception. When one can learn to receive with the intention to bestow, it is considered that one has equalized one's form with the Creator's. Both are now givers.

faith   The quality of bestowal; clear perception of the Creator.

faith above reason   When you place the quality of bestowal above (more important than) the desire to receive pleasure.

four phases of direct light   The first five stages, Root–4, by which the thought of creation created *Malchut*, the will to receive, and the Root of all creations.

free choice   A choice made without being partial toward oneself. To have free choice, one has to be above one's ego, in the spiritual world.

Haman   One of the names given to the will to receive.

intention   The direction in which a desire is used—for you or for the Creator.

Kabbalah   A science that provides a detailed method of showing you how to perceive and experience spiritual worlds—worlds that exist beyond what you can perceive with your five senses. Kabbalah means "reception" in Hebrew.

Kabbalists   People who have acquired additional senses because they have attained the ability to *lekabel* ("to receive" in Hebrew) higher knowledge. The method that enables people to transcend the boundaries of their nature is called *Kabbalah* ("reception" in Hebrew) because it enables them to know the true reality.

Kli **(vessel)**   The sixth sense; the will to receive with a *Masach* on it.

Law of Correction   States that first the easiest parts get corrected and then, with their help, the next parts are handled.

Lekabel   "To receive" in Hebrew.

Light   Pleasure, the force of bestowal that operates and fills the whole reality.

Masach (**screen**)   The ability to reject the Creator's Light if it is not used in order to give back to Him.

meta   From Greek, meaning "beside" or "after"; refers to systems, or discussions about systems. The term differentiates references to the content of a system from the structure of the system itself.

Mordechai   The will to bestow.

Moses   The next great Kabbalist after Abraham and the greatest prophet. Wrote the *Torah* (Pentateuch) and taught Kabbalah to all who listened. Moses is the point in the heart in everyone of us, the desire for spirituality.

Olam (**world**)   There are five worlds between the Creator and creation—*Adam Kadmon*, *Atzilut*, *Beria*, *Yetzira*, and *Assiya*. *Olam* comes from the word *Haalama* (concealment). The name of the *Olam* designates a specific measure of concealment of the Creator's Light from creation (us).

Partzuf (**face**)   A *Partzuf* is a complete structure of ten *Sefirot* with a *Masach* that can determine which *Sefira* receives Light and which doesn't.

person (**in this world**)   Means that the will to receive is in a state of concealment from the Creator, with no intention to receive from Him or to give to Him.

point in the heart   The last degree in the evolution of human desire, the desire for spirituality.

prayer   Any desire is a prayer. But a prayer that is answered is a desire to be corrected to becoming like the Creator. A prayer is called "the work in the heart."

purpose of creation   The reason the Creator created creation is for it to receive the ultimate pleasure: being like Him. This is the purpose of creation.

Rabbi Isaac Luria (**the Holy Ari**)   A great Kabbalist who lived in the sixteenth century in Israel. Author of *The Tree of Life*.

Rabbi Shimon Bar-Yochai (**Rashbi**)   Author of *The Book of Zohar*, the seminal text of Kabbalah. Rashbi was the student and successor of Rabbi Akiva, the great Kabbalist who taught "Love thy neighbor as thyself."

Rabbi Yehuda Ashlag   The last great Kabbalist (1884–1954). Known as Baal HaSulam (owner of the Ladder) for his *Sulam* (Ladder) commentary on *The Book of Zohar*.

reality   The part of the Creator's Simple Light that a person can perceive, depending on one's inner structure. Reality is always subjective.

reincarnation   A reincarnation is every time you make a step in spiritual growth. If you correct yourself intensely, you can experience many lifetimes in a matter of minutes.

Reshimot   The soul's unconscious recollections of its past states.

Root of the Soul   The place of the soul in the system of *Adam ha Rishon*.

sanctity   An exalted state in which you ascribe everything to the Creator. You realize that there is none else besides him and that you are equal to Him in your attributes.

screen   See *Masach*.

Sefirot   The 10 basic qualities of the spiritual world. Their names are *Keter, Hochma, Bina, Hesed, Gevura, Tifferet, Netzah, Hod, Yesod,* and *Malchut*. Sometimes they are divided into five, and then you have *Keter, Hochma, Bina,* and *Zeir Anpin*, which includes the *Hesed, Gevura, Tifferet, Netzah, Hod,* and *Yesod*; the last *Sefira* is *Malchut*.

shame   *Malchut*'s sensation of her oppositeness from the Creator. When *Malchut* realizes that she only receives and that He only gives (to her), she is so ashamed that she stops receiving, and makes the *Tzimtzum* (restriction).

single concealment   The state you experience when you feel the Creator's existence, but feel what's coming from Him as bad. See also *double concealment*.

soul   A desire to receive with a *Masach* and the intention to bestow is called "a soul." Also, *Adam ha Rishon* is considered the common soul from which we all came. Adam represents the first person to have a *Masach*, and we are all his "spiritual" children. See also *Adam ha Rishon*.

spiritual degree   An ability to receive a certain amount (and kind) of pleasure with the intention to bestow upon the Creator.

Surrounding Light   The Light that wishes to fill creation, as well as the Light that is destined to transform egoistic desire into altruistic desire.

tetragrammaton   In Greek, literally "four-letter word." Designates the sacred name of God. In Hebrew, it is the *HaVaYaH* (*Yod, Hey, Vav, Hey*), or the four phases of direct light.

Three Lines   The right line is the Creator's giving; the left line is man's will to receive; the middle line is Man's intention to work with the will to receive for the purpose of giving back to the Creator.

Tikkun (**correction**)   Kabbalists refer to correction to mean turning the intention with which we use a desire from "for me" to "for the Creator." No one will tell you that you are correct or incorrect. But if you've used a desire to make you more Creator-like, you've done the correct thing.

Torah   The Five Books of Moses. Torah means "light" as well as "instruction." The text of the Torah holds within it the instructions to receive all the light of the Creator, if you know how to read it right. Today, we need to study Kabbalah to be able to understand it correctly.

transgression   When you realize that the act, or desire you tried to work with in order to give to the Creator, was actually for yourself, you define your action as a "transgression."

The Tree of Life   The Ari's (Rabbi Isaac Luria) principal text. This text is still the center of contemporary Kabbalah. Because of the importance of the Ari's book, the term *Tree of Life* has become a synonym of the term *The Wisdom of Kabbalah*.

Tzimtzum (**restriction**)   Not receiving Light despite wanting it. When *Malchut* discovers that she is opposite from the Creator, her shame makes her stop receiving His Light although she has a great desire for it.

Yam Suf   The Red Sea. *The Book of Zohar* calls the Red Sea the "Sea of the End," representing the ego's final frontier. Beyond *Yam Suf* begins the spiritual world.

Resources

On the Internet

General Material (in English)

www.kabbalah.info

www.kabbalahmedia.info

www.kabbalahstudy.org

www.arionline.info

www.kabtoday.com

Articles Mentioned in the Book

"Peace in the World": www.kabbalah.info/engkab/articles/peace_in_world_complete.htm

"The Essence of the Wisdom of Kabbalah": www.kabbalah.info/engkab/matan_torah/essence_of_kabbalah.htm

"The Freedom": www.kabbalah.info/engkab/matan_torah/freedom.htm

"The Peace": www.kabbalah.info/engkab/matan_torah/peace.htm

Hebrew Resources

www.kab.co.il

www.ashlag.info

www.kabbalah.info/hebkab/index.php

Books

In English

Kellogg, Michael R. *Wondrous Wisdom*. Upper Light Publishing, 2006.

Laitman, Michael. *Attaining the Worlds Beyond*. Laitman Kabbalah Publishers, 2002.

———. *Awakening to Kabbalah*. Jewish Lights Publications, 2005.

———. *The Kabbalah Experience*. Laitman Kabbalah Publishers, 2005.

———. *The Path of Kabbalah*. Laitman Kabbalah Publishers, 2005.

———. *Basic Concepts in Kabbalah*. Laitman Kabbalah Publishers, 2006.

———. *Kabbalah, Science and the Meaning of Life*. Laitman Kabbalah Publishers, 2006.

———. From Chaos to Harmony. Laitman Kabbalah Publishers, 2007.

In Hebrew

Ashlag, Baruch. *Shamati*. Michael Laitman, 1991.

———. *Shlavei HaSulam*. Bnei Baruch, 2000.

Ashlag, Yehuda. *Talmud Eser Sefirot*, 1st edition. M. Klar, 1937.

———. *Pri Hacham, Igrot Kodesh*. Abraham Yehezkel, 1985.

———. *Pri Hacham, Maamarim*. Abraham Yehezkel, 1985.

———. *Matan Torah*. Ohr HaGanuz Publishing, 1995.

———. *Beit Shaar HaKavanot*. Ohr HaGanuz Publishing, 1996. Laitman, Michael. *HaDor HaAharon*. Laitman Kabbalah Publishers, 2006.

Luria, Rabbi Issac (the Ari). *Etz Chaim*. Printed in Warsaw, 1891. (Available for free download at www.kabbalahgroup.info/eng/library.php?lang=eng&cid=22.)

Raziel HaMalaach (Hebrew and English versions available on Amazon.com.)

Sefer Yetzirah (Hebrew and English versions available on Amazon.com.)

The Zohar (with Yehuda Ashlag's *Sulam* commentary), 1st edition. M. Klar, 1953.

Organizations and Associations

ARI Films
Contact person: Avraham Cohen
P.O. 1552
Ramat Gan 52115, Israel
Telephone: +972-3-9226723
Fax: +972-3-9226741
E-mail: acohen@arifilms.tv
Website: www.arifilms.tv

ARI Online Kabbalah Education Center
Website: www.arionline.info

Bnei Baruch (Kabbalah, Education & Research Institute)

In Israel

Contact person: Leah Goldberg
P.O. 1552
Ramat Gan 52115, Israel
Telephone: +972-3-9226723
Fax: +972-3-9226741
E-mail: english@kabbalah.info
Website: www.kabbalah.info

In London, England

Telephone: 0044 7951 98 28 11 or 0044 1883 343 844
E-mail: orlondon10@yahoo.com

In Sydney, Australia

Level 1, 504 Dover lane
Rose Bay NSW, 2029
Telephone: +61 2 93713382
E-mail: info@kabbalah.net.au

In Toronto, Canada

3701 Chesswood Drive #216
Toronto, Ontario
M3J 2P6
Telephone: 1-877-STUDY06 (1-877-788-3906) or 416-840-5487
E-mail: info@bbtoronto.info
Website: www.bbtoronto.info

In the United States

Boston, MA

The Kabbalah Institute of Massachusetts
Phone: 1-877-850-0468
E-mail: info@masskabbalah.info
Website: www.masskabbalah.info

Chicago:

251 East Dundee Road #10
Wheeling, IL 60090
Telephone: 847-960-3732 or 847-372-2223
E-mail: chicago@kabbalah-study.com

Dallas:

7900 Northaven Road
Dallas, TX 75230
Telephone: 972-578-2817
E-mail: bbdallas@gmail.com

Los Angeles:

Telephone: 818-772-7177
E-mail: los_angeles@kbb1.com

New York:

194 Quentin Road
2nd Floor
Brooklyn, NY 11223
Phone: 646-435-0121 or 1-800-540-3234
newyork@kabbalah.info

San Francisco:

American West Learning Center
22 Monterey Blvd.
San Francisco, CA 94131
Telephone: 415-469-9394
E-mail: sfkabbalah@yahoo.com

St. Louis, Missouri:

6417 Forsyth
Clayton, MO 63105
Telephone: 636-391-1400, 314-849-5961, or 314-540-2093
E-mail: kabl-stl@sbcglobal.net

Index